Lionel Esher

A Broken Wave

The Rebuilding of England 1940–1980

Allen Lane

ALLEN LANE
Penguin Books Ltd
536 King's Road
London SW10 0UH

First published 1981

Copyright © Lionel Esher, 1981

The Acknowledgements on page 320
constitute an extension of this copyright page

ISBN 0 7139 1199 9

Set in Monophoto Photina
Composition by Filmtype Services Limited, Scarborough, England
Printed in Great Britain by
William Clowes (Beccles) Ltd
Beccles and London
Designed by Gerald Cinamon

Contents

'When a moral philosopher has placed a course of action in its moral context ... related its character, motive, goals to the constellation of values to which it belongs ... then he has done his job as a philosophical adviser. It is not his business to preach or exhort or praise or condemn, only to illuminate.'

Isaiah Berlin, 1978

Preface

This is a book about the rebuilding of England which began during the blitz years of the 1940s and had been completed by 1980, as far as such an operation can ever be completed. It was not the first such rebuild. The City of London had to be almost totally rebuilt in the seventeenth century, and nearly all of our cities received new faces in the eighteenth. Then in the industrial cities the explosive forces of the nineteenth century caused it all to be done again.

Urban history can be written in exclusively socio-economic or architectural terms, but this book starts from the proposition that specialization of this kind is one of the causes of failure in understanding and then of failure in action. I have tried to treat the two aspects as inseparable.

This is a piece of English, not Scottish or Welsh, history because I was weaned on English history and on its continuing relevance to the world. On the same principle, it does not attempt to tell a little about a lot of cities, but to give as much detail as the general reader will want about a few. The five case studies have been chosen not for their glamour or their horror but because they are places for which I feel affection and admiration, and because they were challenges that attracted the brightest talents of two generations. There seemed no point in looking into places that either did not aim so high, or had it comparatively easy. The five could perhaps have been doubled to ten within these criteria, and there are places as large as Leeds and as small as Swindon I would like to have included, but this would have meant covering similar ground too many times. The five cover between them the spectrum between triumph and disaster.

My whole working life has been grist to the mill of this book, and many of the protagonists were my friends. Several have sadly not lived to be consulted, but among the many people who have been especially helpful or have read parts of the typescript I must mention David Alton, Walter Bor, Lord Campbell of Eskan, E. G. Chandler, Oliver Cox, Professor R. Gardner-Medwin, Denis Harrison, Sir Stanley Holmes, the late Professor J. R. James, Brian Jefferson, Sir Stirrat Johnson-Marshall, Sir James Jones, Sir Denys Lasdun, R. Whitfield Lewis, Sir Leslie Martin, Frederick Pooley, Sir James Richards, Diana Rowntree,

Lord Sefton of Garston, Graeme Shankland, Nicholas Taylor, Sir Roger Walters, Margaret Willis, Lewis Womersley and Peter Yates.

In the text, I have not generally attached to people's names the 'handles' many of them later received, and in the case of firms of architects, which are apt confusingly to alter, I have sometimes for clarity used only the name of the senior partner.

I must particularly, if anonymously, thank councillors, city planners, architects and administrators in the five cities I have worked in, without whose help and advice the work would not have been worth doing. The same can be said of the ever helpful staff of the British Architectural Library.

I am grateful to Martyn Beckett, Anthony Gascoigne and Quentin Hughes for specially taken photographs and to the photo-librarians of the GLC, Lambeth, Newcastle, Sheffield, Liverpool and Milton Keynes, the Civic Trust and the Architectural Press, who were quite surprised to meet a borrower who was not looking for knocking copy. But wherever possible I have photographed scenes as they are now and resisted the glamorous versions of earlier photographers.

Finally I congratulate my secretary Heather Crowe on her intuitive grasp of my handwriting.

As to books, my primary documents have been the innumerable reports on planning and housing which, facilitated by new reprographic processes, have poured out of central and local government since the war in an ever-increasing flood. The bibliography of modern architecture, planning and housing in England, necessary background knowledge for any writer on these subjects, is again too vast to be set out here. However, to supplement the references in the text and notes to individual books, here are a few more which the general reader might not otherwise come across. C. L. Mowatt's *Britain between the Wars* (1955) has a good bibliography covering the historic roots of our period, and the catalogue of the Arts Council's *Thirties* exhibition (1979) gives a useful visual conspectus. Thomas Sharp's *Town and Countryside* (1932) is a canonical statement of 'enlightened' pre-war opinion. Similarly, Percy Johnson-Marshall's *Rebuilding Cities* (1966) encapsulates post-war attitudes. Trevor Dannatt's *Modern Architecture in Britain* (1959) and Robert Maxwell's *New British Architecture* (1972) are now supplemented by Charles Jencks's *Late Modern Architecture* (1980). Cullingworth's *Town and Country Planning in Britain* (1977) is an excellent general reference book. Political influences are described in A. Jackson's *The Politics of Architecture* and in *Politics and Land-Use Planning – the London Ex-*

perience by Stephen Elkin (1974). J. M. Simmie's *Citizens in Conflict* (1974) gives a Marxist viewpoint, Peter F. Smith's *Dynamics of Urbanism* (1974) a psychological one and Hugh Stretton's *Urban Planning in Rich and Poor Countries* (1978) an internationalist one. The last six are all in paperback. In the field of housing Cleeve Barr's *Public Authority Housing* conveys the urgency of 1958, and other useful textbooks are John Burnett's *A Social History of Housing 1815–1970* (1980), Murie, Niner and Watson's *Housing Policy and the Housing System* (1976) and Duclaud-Williams's *The Politics of Housing in Britain and France* (1980). Susan Beattie's *A Revolution in London Housing* (1980) tells the story of the LCC and the GLC.

A Broken Wave

The Rebuilding of England 1940–1980

CHAPTER 1

Consensus

When the German army reached Paris, one knew that the thirties were over at last. In the familiar style of that decade, the war had started out another phony; it had run out of steam; it had threatened to shunt us back into a period we thought we had left for ever. But after the scarcely credible events of the summer of 1940 it was plain that Europe could never be the same again: one entered the unimaginable new decade not with hope, for there could be none, but with relief. For while the feeling that the older generation of politicians has made a hash of things is common in all ages, it was more firmly based than usual in the young of 1940. These young had been brought up by shell-shocked or bereaved or mutilated people in the confidence that nothing so horrible as the War could ever happen again. Then, as students, they had seen a succession of British and French leaders of outstanding mediocrity and pusillanimity lose every trick, give in at every confrontation, fork out to every tongue-in-cheek demand for blackmail. The best, lacking all conviction, had ceased to be so, and the worst's passionate intensity had flowered into the highly publicized jollity of *Giovinezza* and *Kraft durch Freude*. Unemployment had been disposed of in Italy and Germany long before rearmament presented the 'pluto-democracies' with a solution of sorts. Emotional release through mass protest was not yet highly developed. One minority joined the Communist Party and fought in Spain. Another joined the Peace Pledge or Federal Union. Neither could stem the tide.

History nevertheless shows that political disasters do not tarnish a period's cultural image. In admittedly accident-prone France, it even shows that the reverse is the case. We think no less of the age of Ronsard and Philibert de l'Orme because it disintegrated into the Wars of Religion; or of the Enlightenment, because failing to deliver elementary social justice it was engulfed by the Revolution; or of the *Belle Époque*, because out of sight of its artists it indulged in an arms race which brought about a catastrophe from which European civilization has never recovered. The same can only in a lesser degree be said of the thirties in Paris, still the undisputed cultural capital of the world – the years of Art Deco on the one hand and of Le Corbusier's classic buildings and projects on the other, the years of Léon Blum's short-lived Popular Front, the only intellectually respectable response to the terror ahead. Writing in 1938, R. H. Wilenski recorded the ages of the leading figures in the *École de Paris*: 'Bonnard and Vuillard are seventy-one, Matisse is sixty-nine, Rouault is sixty-seven, Vlaminck is sixty-three, Dufy, Picabia and Friesz are fifty-nine, Derain is fifty-eight, Picasso and Léger are fifty-seven, Braque is fifty-six, Utrillo, Metzinger and Severini are fifty-five, Segonzac is fifty-four, Ozenfant is fifty-two, Chagall is fifty-one, Chirico is fifty, Ernst is forty-seven, Lurçat is forty-six, Miró is forty-five, Masson is forty-three, Tchelitchew is forty and Dali is thirty-four.' Such a constellation would not be seen again in our time. But the artists and philosophers, the designers and decorators, the whole 'intellectual' resistance to fascism, turned out to have no roots in French society, which was deeply cynical and defeatist. The *Ville Lumière* of the thirties was as shallow a show as the Swinging London of the sixties.

England was in the opposite case: the roots were reasonably sound, but the tree bore no fruit or flowers. In its upper reaches English Society, whose philistine tradition now had a respectable pedigree going back a century or so, was in the grip of cultural as well as political paralysis. Compared with Apollinaire, Sartre and Aragon we had only youthful MacSpaunday,[1] glumly resigned to the inevitable:

> Who live under the shadow of a war,
> What can we do that matters?

Yet this Devil's Decade, the decade when nothing could go right for 'men of good will', as they had characteristically called themselves, had not been as hellish to live through as it seemed in the retrospect of 1940. Only a minority had felt in their imagination the onset of the catastrophe that was to have enveloped whole cities in mustard gas. Another minority, though a larger one, endured for a few years more the privations that were later to become the life-style of countless millions of the human race. But for most people all sorts of escape routes had been thrown open. Great numbers had been able to buy a sunny gabled home for a few hundred pounds, and a car for under a hundred. Stupendous super-cinemas had opened up in every town, naughty road-houses with swimming pools on every by-pass and Billy Butlin's holiday camps at Skegness and Clacton. Sir Malcolm Campbell had driven his Bluebird faster than Sir Henry Segrave's Golden Arrow, Squadron Leader Orlebar had won the Schneider Trophy in his Supermarine S.6. seaplane, and Britain had 'wrested' the world speed records on land and water from the Americans in David and Goliath contests in which elegant design satisfyingly humiliated brute horsepower. The English countryside was at its most bosomy, lawn tennis was still played on striped lawns, fields were still stooked with corn, yellow A A signs marked the secret entry into pleasingly decayed villages with yokel pubs and teashops run by ladies in reduced circumstances. Italy was unbelievably cheap, Germany welcoming and full of flowers, and you only needed a Morgan three-wheeler or an M G Midget to swish down the straight roads of France to the empty beaches of the Riviera.

It has become customary to look at the thirties through this mist of nostalgia not only because in its loss of confidence the culture of the seventies looks back at the whole of the past this way, but more specifically because one can now see that this was the last decade before the World War II technological explosion, symbolized by the atomic bomb, put at risk the whole eco-system in which the English found so much consolation. Knowing the outcome, the cheery and docile fatalism of the workers, the rousing style of the newsreel commentators, the lush escapist movies themselves, the adulation of the monarchy and the aristocracy, the insularity and the complacency of politicians – all can be seen as a kind of prelapsarian innocence.

A strong component of this innocence, of this schizophrenia, of this escapism, was the conventional image of rural England. The iconography had survived intact since the Edwardian summer in which artists like C. P. Wade had illustrated Unwin's *Town Planning in Practice* and Sydney R. Jones had illustrated Ditchfield's *The Charm of the English Village* – both in 1908. Wavy road verges, hollyhocks and topiary, tea-cosy cottages, black cumuli of elm, white cumuli of cloud – George Clausen and John Nash, Arnesby Brown and Rowland Hilder fixed the stereotype at every Summer Exhibition, and there were still enough thatched haystacks and stooks and shire horses for the *Times* photographers to reinforce it.

> The cows are almost cooing
> And the turtle-doves are mooing
> Which is why a Pooh is poohing
> In the sun
>
> *A. A. Milne*

Fauves and Vorticists[2] had come and gone, leaving scarcely a trace. The pipe-smoking vicar at the village cricket match advertising Three Nuns, the pipe-smoking Prime Minister, the inexhaustible Batsford

1. Stereotype of the English village, from Unwin's *Town Planning in Practice*, 1908

books and the implausible railway posters were all good for a laugh in left-wing circles, within which it was plain that the Empire and the landscape that had been created simultaneously in the eighteenth century were going to disintegrate simultaneously in the twentieth. But whereas the concept of an emergent Commonwealth of free nations made it possible to see the first creatively, no equivalent concept existed for the second, and it would be forty years before it did.

Meanwhile, in 1930, the problem was not seen as one of absorption, but of resistance. Enemies could be particularized: advertising hoardings, concrete kerbs, conifers, filling stations, power lines, ribbon development, alien building materials, flat roofs; and the only thing was to go for them one by one, first by a letter to *The Times*, and then if possible by legislation. Piecemeal regulation, legislation that was reactive rather than prescriptive, was very much in the Victorian tradition. Since the building by-laws of the local district councils had more or less stopped people building slums, it was hoped that the 'town planning schemes' of the same authorities would stop people gobbling up the countryside. But the hope was vain. Local authorities anywhere within hailing distance of new development faced two powerful disincentives to resistance – loss of rateable value and heavy compensation; so they collectively zoned enough housing land for 350 million people. This was about as useful as no zoning at all. Moreover, it took so long for a planning scheme, where such existed at all, to become statutory that developers had the easy choice of either applying for 'interim' approval which was generally given, or not risking a refusal and chancing their arm in the confident hope that, if a scheme did eventually materialize, *faits accomplis* would be taken on board. So the 3,200,000 new homes of the thirties went up where the market was – in the Home Counties; the north was left out in the cold.

Only a handful of high-minded or hack architects had much at all to do with planning or housing. The 'private sector' dominated so easily that the phrase had not yet had to be invented. These men were individualists, non-joiners. The successful architect of the thirties would have been a mildly artistic boy from one of the 'minor' public schools – snobbishly so called by the elite of Eton, Winchester and Harrow. With his gift for drawing, he would have been steered by his parents, themselves probably professional people, into this gentleman's profession in which mediocrity would matter less than in Art. On concluding his articles and passing the RIBA examinations, he would have got a start 'doing up a cottage for his aunt' and thence through other family or school connections. James Spinlove, the sensitive and conscientious hero of H. B. Cresswell's *The Honeywood File*, was just such a person, and the book perfectly reflects the social ambience of the late twenties, with *nouveau riche* client, sound and workmanlike country builder, sharks promoting shady new materials and corrupt council official. Spinlove learns through rough experience, like the young subaltern from his fatherly but ever tactful CSM, and the moral is that there is no better school.

Historicist concentration on the origins of the modern movement in England has until lately diverted attention from almost the whole of the architecture of the thirties, of which only a minute fraction was part of that development. Was it as worthless as the modernists made out, or as absurd as Osbert Lancaster affectionately but devastatingly drew it?

The story is complicated, as it had not ceased to be in England since the Gothic Revival. There was, for a start, a broad mainstream. Sir Guy Dawber, writing shortly before he died in 1939, describes it:

Looking back to the close of the last century, when great country houses were being built by Philip Webb, Eden Nesfield, Norman Shaw, Ernest George and many others, and comparing them with those now being built, the gulf between the outlook of that time and now seems very wide, for there is no question that we have greatly simplified the problem of living today, and have learnt much in the hard school of necessity. At the same time the debt which is due to these men, Norman Shaw especially, is never fully recognized, for to him more than any other in the last century we owe the revival of English domestic architecture.

The idea then was to get as much picturesque irregularity as possible, and very charming houses were built in this way, surrounded by trees and gardens, and away from the noise of traffic; but with the revival of classic forms, a greater regularity and symmetry of treatment was demanded, with carefully balanced façades, the romantic gradually giving place to the scholarly, until it merged into the restrained and quiet dignity of the eighteenth century, which pervaded not only the inside of the houses but even the gardens.

Both in brick and stone, this thoroughly English style always takes its rightful place, either in town or country, and it is regrettable that we did not carry on this delightful phase of architecture, adapting it to our changing needs and ideas.

2. Survival of neo-Georgian - a 1980 house in Gloucestershire by Erith and Terry.

Well, we did and we do. Dawber's own last country houses, and those of Edward Maufe, Oswald Milne, Hubert Worthington, Darcy Braddell, S. D. Adshead, Clough Williams-Ellis, A. S. G. Butler, C. H. James, Louis de Soissons and a great many camp-followers continued to be built right up to the war. The pride of these architects was that they spoke the language of their craftsmen, were deep in the tricks of the trades, had their own way of resolving the little problems of domestic architecture, so that their details not only looked right but weathered right. Labour troubles were unknown, and site visits were pure pleasure – the best day of the week. There was no lack of proof that neo-Georgian still worked in a decent, dull way, at any rate at the domestic scale. Nor was it surprising that of these men, several of them his pupils, only Lutyens himself was still able to breathe life into it. Even in its great age, only a few had had the genius to transform the classical language.

What finally routed the neo-Georgians was the attempt to scale up the style to that of the big city, long since so masterfully managed by the Victorians. This was mainly demonstrated in the London region, where the population explosion gave rise to unprecedented needs, but also to a lesser extent in those provincial cities such as Leeds and Bristol and Nottingham that were not dependent on the decaying heavy industries and could therefore participate in the consumer boom. The rapid expansion of London into the Home Counties spawned swollen or brand-new suburban boroughs, many of which needed town halls, and led to the competitive building of high-street banks by the Big Five, which in turn created the need for big new head offices in the City of London. These, splendid though some of them were, proved that the Victorian tradition of dressing up town halls and clubs and banks as palaces only worked before these institutions developed a need for large areas of ordinary office space. The tail then began to wag the dog. It was probably Howitt's expensive and soulless Council House at Nottingham that finished off the *genre*. In the series of competitions for new town halls that now occupied the energies of the conservative core of the profession, 'something simpler' was called for.

As was customary, one took a trip on the Continent, and first to Stockholm, where since 1923 Ostberg's romantic Town Hall had established itself as the realization of all that the Arts and Crafts movement had struggled to achieve in England. But it proved to be inimitable. Only the grand and subtle tower introduced a fashion for civic towers in England, scaled down as always. What did strike the

3. Swedish neo-classic at Norwich, 1938

English as usable was the attenuated neo-classic of Tengbom's Concert Hall. C. H. James and Rowland Pierce proceeded to win the
competition for Norwich City Hall by combining the tower with the
attenuated portico. Soon Bristol, Southampton, Dagenham, Watford,
Hornsey and other places in the expanding south-east had followed
suit, and the seal was set on the new deflowered classic by Wornum's
RIBA building, opened by the King in 1934.

Then there was Holland. Here were two usable models, the curvy,
horizontally banded brickwork of the Amsterdam School of the early
twenties (deriving from Berlage) and the more recent hard-edged

cubist brickwork of Dudok in Hilversum (deriving from Rietveld and Wright). Both found a ready market in England, particularly the Hilversum style, in which the Glasgow firm of Burnet, Tait and Lorne made a special corner. The bricky nature of these styles seemed to English eyes to hold them at a safe distance from modernism, and it produced the nearest approach to a People's Architecture of the thirties in the London underground stations of Charles Holden commissioned by the austere and high-minded Frank Pick, though Holden was neo-classic by instinct and later relapsed.

4. People's Architecture of a London underground station by Holden and Pearson, 1935

More complex and far more chic were the imports from France. Only architects went to Hilversum; but everybody went to Paris, the wives of company directors to 'get ideas', and the ideas they got were largely those of the *Exposition des Arts Décoratifs* of 1925. Unacceptable to the art elite, unspeakable to purist architects, unknown to the Chippendale establishment, Art Deco offered the business world its shot of vulgarity. The description has come to be applied loosely to almost any 'novelty' produced in the twenties and thirties. It would be clearer to confine it, as people did when the word was first used in 1935, to the elegant, prettily crafted style of the *Exposition* itself, much influenced by dress designers like Lanvin and Vionnet, and nicely represented in England by Curtis Green's Dorchester Hotel, by Goodhart-Rendel's offices in Brighton, and by the Shakespeare Memorial Theatre at Stratford-on-Avon designed by the youthful

5. English Art Deco: the Shakespeare Memorial Theatre, Stratford-on-Avon, 1932

Elizabeth Scott after an open competition – though none of the three would have acknowledged or liked the attribution. All through the thirties the highly mannered figurative sculpture and metalwork of Art Deco was almost obligatory on institutional and municipal architecture.

But all sorts of other influences were beginning to fuse with it. There was the jazz style, with its cubist and Russian Ballet associations, which exploded into London in 1930 with Oliver Bernard's foyer of the Strand Palace Hotel (now in the Victoria and Albert Museum), and whose best-known surviving example is Wallis Gilbert's Hoover factory of 1932. Motifs from both sources were freely drawn upon for Odeon cinemas up and down the country all through the thirties, and were capable of almost infinite vulgarization. Consequently by 1930 it had become essential for 'smart' designers to dissociate themselves, and we find in the Savoy Theatre of Basil Ionides and in the domestic interiors of Oliver Hill and Gerald Wellesley a classicizing simplicity enriched by silver and gold leaf and carefully chosen antiques, generally Empire or Regency. By 1935 the new breed of self-taught dilettante decorators had come on the scene; the fawns and sea-horses, the shagreen and vitrolite, the cascade lighting and the peach mirrors of the jazz age had vanished into suburbia, and the all-white drawing-rooms of Syrie Maugham and Sibyl Colefax, Curtis Moffat and Oliver Messel, with their great white settees by Arundell Clarke, would be enlivened by T'ang horses, west African masks, and contemporary works by Brancusi, Dufy and Marie Laurencin. The rest of the furniture would be stripped-down French provincial, invariably painted and perhaps further decorated by Duncan Grant or Vanessa Bell. The only gesture towards the abstract would be a big rug by Marion Dorn or Francis Bacon.

The influence of Paris was still strong right up to the outbreak of the war, for the French rich, rootless and Paris-based ever since the time of Louis XIV, were patrons of the new in a way that the English landed gentry neither needed nor wished to be. No conflict existed in Paris between 'period' and 'modern'; for the latter had none of the 'foreign' connotation that dogged it in England. Charles de Beistigui's surrealist transformation of a Le Corbusier penthouse in 1935 was an eye-opener, and indeed surrealism sanctioned and gave a new *frisson* to any conceivable juxtaposition. Even in London a cult of Dali emerged after Roland Penrose put on the Surrealist Exhibition in the New Burlington Galleries in 1936. So by the late thirties Mayfair had taken on board plate-glass tables supported by pale hands, lighting brackets borne by waving arms, and life-size blackamoors at the foot of stairs. 'Curzon Street Baroque' was already on its way down the social scale to the nightclubs and the hairdressers. This *ancien régime*, which would be extinguished by the war, was already sobered up by the slump. By the late thirties the smart thing was to be 'poor', and the cheapest way for young couples with 'more taste than money' (*Vogue*) to furnish their first flatlet or tiny town-house was by raiding the Caledonian Market for Victoriana. The alternative was to go to Peter Jones in Sloane Square, where an eclectic selection of pickled pine pseudo-Spanish furniture, wrought iron screens, tiny Venetian glass chandeliers, curvaceous padded bed-heads and kidney-shaped dressing-tables with chintz skirts was on offer at remarkably low prices. For the more high-minded there were more purist department stores, but they are part of another story.

Few if any of the people who bought these objects were aware that alongside the Rule of Taste there was another universe with equally strong roots in England – the Rule of Conscience. The public sector plugged away in almost total obscurity in the thirties, its central preoccupation the Housing Problem. The architects who worked in it were plain men, grammar school rather than public school; few of them aspired to membership of the RIBA Council, which was still a club for private practitioners; none had yet achieved the presidency. The generation that was to see its destiny in their field was still in the schools.

When the National Government took office in 1931, a census had revealed a shortage of a million dwellings and a good deal of overcrowding in many of the dwellings there were, with 4·5 million in England and Wales living two or more to a room. This was a fearful disappointment for a country which since the Great War had poured more money into subsidized housing than any other in Europe. The Government's solution was to turn the problem over to the speculative builders: it was they, after all, who had done it all in the nineteenth century. In 1932 the Minister of Health, after consulting the National Federation of House Builders, abolished all subsidies except for direct slum clearance, and with low prices and low interest rates the builders were given their head. Numerically, it worked. Over England and Wales, compared with 196,500 dwellings in 1931, 369,903 were built in 1937. But we know what they were: the familiar by-pass 'semis' – four times as many of them as of council dwellings, and whereas it had been hoped that, as in the nineteenth century, most of them would be for letting at rents working people could afford, in the event most of them were for sale at prices they could not. And the target of slum clearance established what was to be its familiar character of perpetual recession. By 1939 half the so-called slums of 1931 had been cleared, but many more were to be added to the other half before the programme could be reactivated.

This was a period in which quantity took absolute precedence over quality. Practically none of the interminable square-miles of speculative housing was planned by architects or with any pretence of consumer consultation, and most of the council housing was little better. It was plainer and, since it was plain, the builders made their houses as fancy as they could afford so that there could be no possibility of confusion. The waste of land was appalling: between the wars the built-up area of London was doubled, for a one-fifth gain in population.

Yet the stock of knowledge and experience in England was by no means contemptible. Raymond Unwin's *Town Planning in Practice*, in which the wisdom acquired in the building of Hampstead Garden Suburb was distilled in minute detail, had been published as long ago as 1909 and repeatedly reprinted. Adshead and Ramsey had laid out the Duchy of Cornwall estate in Kennington, Louis de Soissons had planned Welwyn Garden City and Lutyens New Delhi on identical principles. As far back as 1912 the London County Council had developed delightful housing groups that were already mature and

6. London County Council cottages of 1913

have never been bettered. Of course you could fault the Unwin prototype. It was excessively prim and symmetrical, rather French in character with its pleached limes; and this was remarkable since

nearly all the book's illustrations were of gingerbread medieval German towns, of the picturesque theories of Camillo Sitte and of the
huddled roofs of English villages. Only Clough Williams-Ellis at Port-
meirion, in very special circumstances, had carried on where Unwin
had left off. Still, most people would have settled for the early Hampstead model, but in the thirties it ceased to be built. For one thing, the
motor car had to be got in, with its sight lines and set-backs for
parking; for another, Fletton bricks and Crittall windows and
machine-made tiles at lower pitches ruined the imagery. Finally the
council engineers reasserted themselves with updated by-laws and
the architects moved away to lusher pastures.

Those few pundits who interested themselves in the problem could
see that a return to the terrace house was the only answer. 'Urbanity'
and 'good manners' were the cry, in increasingly distraught tones,
though both expressions (characteristically Georgian in connotation)
were irremediably middle-class and meant nothing to the people concerned. Thomas Sharp, correctly pointing to Kennington as his
urbane exemplar, spoiled his case by naughtily picking on Welwyn as
his suburban bestiary: those ill-starred words 'Garden City' were to
raise the hackles of generations of metropolitan critics. Trystan
Edwards, in the deeply felt campaign for A Hundred New Towns
which he initiated under the alias of 'Ex-serviceman J47485', laid it
on the line:

> It would be fully established to the satisfaction of the average man that in
> formations of continuous architecture, whether of streets or quadrangles, not
> only can he have housing accommodation exemplifying comfort and
> hygiene, but he may also be privileged to dwell in buildings more expressive
> of human dignity than are the vulgarly designed little villas against which the
> Council for the Preservation of Rural England and other cultural agencies
> have for so long been protesting.

Probably the most level-headed of the housing experts of the thirties
was Elizabeth Denby, who put a Leverhulme grant to admirably constructive use by visits to continental capitals in the summer of 1933.
In *Europe Re-housed* she maintained that there was ample space to
replace and rebuild within existing city boundaries. 'For example,
Vienna with 1,800,000 citizens has 14 square miles of built-up area
and 93 square miles of woodland, while Manchester with only
759,000 inhabitants covers 43 square miles, under 4 square miles of
which is open space. How absurd', she goes on, 'for questions of
existing city density to be disregarded. How lazy to advocate

decentralization and the creation of new satellite towns! Is there not a good case before redevelopment begins for examining the structure of each town and relating the new areas to the best traditions of the past instead of indulging in the extremes of beehive building in the centre and chicken-coop building on the outskirts of town; of new estates spread over agricultural land, and of densely developed tenements for working men and their families in central city areas?'

The trouble was that the repetitive narrow-fronted terrace houses they both advocated sounded no better than an updated version of the Victorian slum terraces that had housed so much misery. So Unwin's cottage imagery held undisputed sway where there was space to build it, as in the huge council estates on the fringes of London, Glasgow, Birmingham and the northern cities. In the small patches of rebuilding in the inner cities, where space was at a premium and the maximum numbers craved for housing near their work, the problem was seen as the simple one of giving the walk-up tenement a new look, with red brick, tiled roof and sash windows. One thing you could say

7. London County Council flats of 1929

for this moribund architecture: it was the last generation of multi-storey housing to weather well.

That it *was* moribund is a historic fact. Need it have been? It had a good deal going for it – its materials for one thing. Craftsmanship, though much misapplied in fancy veneers and pseudo-Gibbons carving, still existed and was widely enjoyed. Portland stone or hand-made brickwork redeemed countless conventional façades and gives increasing pleasure with the lapse of time. For those building in Oxford or in the Cotswolds, local stone could still be afforded and was invariably used. Roofs, traditionally constructed, did not leak. Doors and windows, ditto, did not warp. And of course there was the added bonus that vandalism had not been invented.

Yet this whole world, with all its assets so soon to vanish, seemed to the students of the thirties either frightfully bogus or utterly dim (their phraseology). For the modern movement had landed in England – emphatically *not* a style, more a way of life, to which they were as earnestly dedicated as any Oxford undergraduate of the 1840s to Pugin's Christian Architecture. Two great writers dominated the imaginations of this generation – Le Corbusier and Lewis Mumford. *La Ville Radieuse* had appeared in Etchells's English translation in 1929, *Vers une Architecture* in 1931 and Mumford's seminal *Technics and Civilization* in 1934. Ostensibly the first was an essay on urbanism, the second an account of the principles of architectural composition, the third a history of technology strongly influenced by the Scottish biologist Patrick Geddes. In fact all three were poetry and their effects were visionary. Vulgarized as it has been as a vision of glass towers in clover-leaf intersections, we have to make a conscious effort now to recapture the pristinity of this vision. Properly, it starts with Mumford's amplified and far more compellingly documented version of Geddes's three periods of human history: first the eotechnic, when Man lived off the planet's energy income – the winds, the rivers, the tides, the prodigality of fauna and flora, leaving the capital resources untapped and putting no pressure on his environment; then, for the last century or so, the palaeotechnic, the age of coal and steam, with its brutal exploitation of the biosphere, its pollution of air and water and its population explosion; and, now dawning, the neo-technic, with its return to the inexhaustible sources of energy for the creation of the beautifully clean, invisible, magical power of electricity, spun through the air and taking the squalor out of every aspect of life.

When Le Corbusier in his grandly evocative French spoke of *la splendeur de l'espace* he echoed Mumford's vision. His affection for those life-expanding words *clarté, radieuse, rayonnant, éclatant*, his townsman's romantic belief in the therapeutic qualities of sunlight and verdure (even in translation how touching is his reference to the tree – 'a kind of caress in the midst of our severe creations'), all this found an echo in the equivalent English romantic tradition. Le Corbusier seemed to seize on the Garden City ideal with its rather prim and middle-class associations and lift it to the scale of the great city, of the region, of the planet itself. 'Men can be paltry; but the thing we call Man is great.' Unlike earlier utopias the thing could be done: we had the technology. 'What gives our dreams their daring is that they can be realized.' In such a context, who, aged say twenty-two, could rest content with the available English concepts – Good Manners, Urbanity, Civic Design?

Much of Le Corbusier's writing is in the grand manifesto language of the historic *avant-garde*, introduced by Jean-Jacques Rousseau and thereafter the familiar currency of the Romantics, first in France and later in Germany, Italy and Russia. 'Man was born free, and everywhere he is in chains.' So powerful has the protest been that despite innumerable disappointments it survives in what Lionel Trilling has called the Adversary Culture of the present day. To dislike our world has been so much easier than to mend it that we have lived by the dislike alone. The great asset of this wing of the *avant-garde* was that it was constructive: you could hate and love at the same time. In joining it, one demonstrated not only one's aesthetic sensibility but one's social conscience. What none of its liberal converts seemed to notice was its totalitarianism. 'There have been golden moments', they read, 'when the power of the mind dominated the rabble . . . such are the Place des Vosges, under Louis XIII; Versailles and the Ile St Louis, under Louis XIV; the Champ de Mars, under Louis XV; l'Étoile and the main roads leading to Paris, under Napoleon; and finally, that magnificent legacy left by a monarch to his people: the work of Haussmann under Napoleon III.' And later, he prefigures the post-war world. 'It is useless to say that everything is possible to an absolute monarch; the same thing might be said of Ministers and their Departments, for they are potentially at least absolute monarchs.' In place of the multiplicity of individual dwellings adding up to monotony, the aim was to standardize and mass-produce the individual cell and thereby to achieve great compositions – cities which one would be proud to live in. 'No one is going to make a

politician of me,' Le Corbusier proclaimed, and rightly, because he
seems to have been happily unaware that his plans went straight to
the heart of twentieth-century politics.

If the authoritarian character of the modern movement was typically French, its idealistic character was typically German. For Total
Architecture, Gropius (who invented the expression)[3] looked to the
'composite mind' of the team of designers – the prototype of the 'whole
man', which would have the capacity to grapple with the totality. 'We
still meet too often a deep-rooted inclination to dodge a large-scale
conception ... and to add up instead piecemeal improvements.' Like
Le Corbusier, he had no use for the city as it stood. 'Nothing less than
a complete overhaul of their sclerotic bodies can turn them into
healthy organisms again.' For housing he demonstrated simplistically
that, given a certain sun angle, the taller the slab the greater the gain
of cleared ground, and he was quite content with the parallel rows of
correctly oriented slabs (*Zeilenbau*) that inevitably emerged. This inspired impresario of imaginative artists and designers could be very
dull in his own field. His importance was his grasp of what Lilienthal
called the 'seamless web' of total design stretching from the wrist-
watch to the region.

The fresher winds blowing from Europe were not only literary and
ideological. There was a lot to look at on the ground. In 1927, by way
of response to the trivialities of Paris 1925, the miles-ahead Germans
put on a 'live' exhibition of pristine modern movement housing at
Weissenhof, Stuttgart, in which all the continental stars participated.
In 1930 the Stockholm Exhibition had the best of both worlds. Here
was Asplund, the rather solemn neo-classic Swede to whom the older
generation looked for inspiration for their latest town hall, throwing
it all overboard for the most tenuous and light-hearted version of
German modernism (helped a lot by a fine summer and the blue and
yellow Swedish flag). It could no longer be said, as was shamelessly
said by Sir Reginald Blomfield, that *modernismus* was an invention of
Germans and Jews. Stockholm was the predecessor of the new-series
international exhibitions which turned out to be competitions in
architecture as well as chauvinism. Here nations mirrored themselves, embarrassingly or otherwise – the fascist or communist dic-
tatorships indistinguishably vulgar, the British decent but dull, the
Americans and French structurally heroic in a rather jazzy way.
Lesser breeds fell back on folk art. But repeatedly the star performers
were the small European democracies, Swiss, Dutch or Scandinavian.
Against a Finmar plywood chair, the British could set nothing better

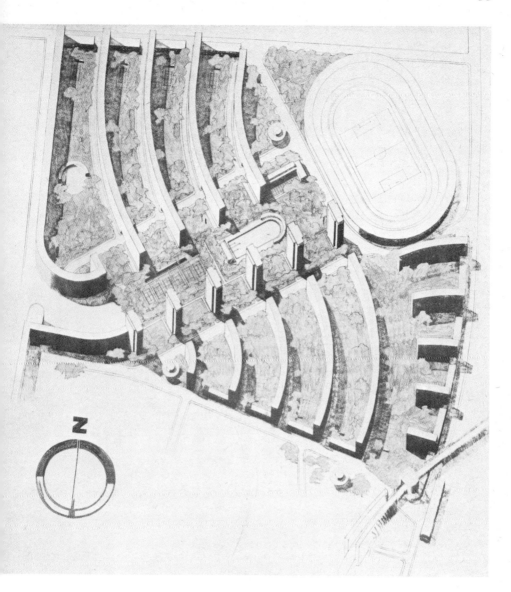

8. *Zeilenbau.* The *Architectural Review*'s 1936 caption reads: 'The application of scientific principles as regards the incidence of sunlight will influence the siting of streets and buildings in both their orientation and the relation between space and height. This and many other considerations which have been ignored or unrecognized in the past will do much to determine the appearance of the towns and cities of the future. This perspective shows a design for a housing scheme on the White City site; eight-floor family flats to the north, with shops and three-floor flats at the end; central playground and garages; one- and two-room flats in the towers. Mendelsohn and Chermayeff, architects.'

9. The Stockholm Exhibition, 1930

than a pair of riding boots. This was certainly not for lack of high-minded effort extending right back to the 1840s. 'Design for Industry' had been on the agenda of English higher education long before the modern movement was ever heard of. We need to be clear about this curious feature of the young architect's environment.

The British have never straightened out the relationship between architecture, art, design, craft and manufacture. First in the field in mass production, they (or more specifically the Prince Consort) soon saw that both their cultural image and their export trade required the application of Art to Industry. A National College of Design was set up in London in 1837 (later to become the Royal College of Art) and proliferated into a remarkable network of local art schools controlled (in curiously Gallic fashion) by a national examination system. But what emerged were artists capable of decorating industrial products a little less hideously than in the past, and what signally failed to emerge were designers capable of influencing or even understanding the industrial process. The arrival on this scene of William Morris and company was a disaster. By branding the machine itself as the enemy and hiding from it in a never-never-land of pseudo-medieval guild socialism, Morris and his followers reinforced the aesthetic escapism that was already rife among the mid-Victorian rich, while at the same time diverting the energies and the imagination of creative minds away from the real world of steel and glass to the handicrafts. By the early 1900s it was already clear in official circles that the Germans, with their *Werkbund* campaign aimed at the education of designers in industry and of industry in design, had the answer: but the Great War intervened. The Design in Industry Association (DIA), courageously set up in the midst of it on the German model under the inspiration of Lethaby, had by 1930 still achieved nothing of significance.

Lethaby was the heaven-sent antidote to Morris. Brought up in the tough but humane atmosphere of Norman Shaw's big office, he was instinctively anti-elitist and was able to speak of a new architecture more attractively, and more in the language of a later generation, than any other Englishman, even though he had never emerged from his ninety-ish visual habits into building it. But by 1930 he was already seventy-one, and he died in the following year. None of the younger men in the DIA, whether they were craftsmen, designers, retailers or manufacturers, possessed the power of leadership that enabled Gropius to transform the Bauhaus. By the time Gropius himself arrived in England, even Frank Pick, who had written the introduction to the English edition of his book and was by then Chairman of the Government's new Council for Art and Industry, failed to use his influence to have him appointed to the Royal College of Art or the Central School, thus playing true to the form of this decade of missed chances. Gropius gave a lecture or two and got a few minor building commissions through the dedicated determination of his young collaborators Jack Pritchard and Maxwell Fry, then left for America.

Thus, to the young architect of the thirties the industrial design scene in England was by continental standards depressingly staid.

The Heals and the Russells had decent craftsmanship in fine woods on offer, but it did not exactly lift the spirits alongside the work of Aalto, Breuer and Mies. A. B. Read's functional light fittings did duty, but were a world away from Moholy-Nagy and Charles Eames. And all of them, including enlightened industrialists like the Crittalls and the Hopes, advertised their products in Georgian Baskerville type. Only London Transport through the initiative of Frank Pick and Jack Beddington had the wit to use brilliant graphic artists like Paul Nash and McKnight Kauffer. Perhaps the most useful result of the major exhibition of British-designed products and interiors at Dorland Hall in 1933 was the emergence of a few retailers like Dunn of Bromley and Bowman of Camden Town to challenge the Heal monopoly and show the best from abroad as well as the UK. But the Arts and Crafts mentality was still going strong when the war came, and only then lay low to await revival in a totally changed environment. Meanwhile the brighter architects took a fairly snobbish view of the low I.Q. output of the art schools, an attitude that was to be repaid with interest later on.

They themselves had mostly been to schools of architecture, which between the wars progressively replaced the old pupillage system. Of these, three were outstanding, and all three had really got off the ground in the early years of the century, though the Architectural Association (AA) in London had been founded as long ago as. 1847 as an evening venue and mutual aid society for what Summerson called the Chuzzlewits of architecture – the articled pupils of early Victorian practitioners. The first full-time course had been set up in Liverpool University in 1894, but the School of Architecture was the creation of one man, Charles Reilly, a figure of boundless energy and enthusiasm, who expanded it from a mere dozen pupils (1904) to a couple of hundred and in 1909 persuaded William Lever to endow the country's first Chair of Town Planning in the University. Reilly's predilections and the tone of the School were neo-classic in the Swedish manner, but he was not unsympathetic to modernism. A. E. Richardson, on the other hand, head of the Bartlett School in University College, London, through the whole of the inter-war period, who was reputed to dine in periwig and knee-breeches in his Georgian house in Ampthill, was violently so, as was his deputy Corfiato, who had trained at the *École des Beaux Arts* in Paris. The corresponding figure at the AA, the Canadian-born Howard Robertson (1920–35), was also a *Beaux Arts* man, who saw it as his role to absorb his own eclectic version of the new architecture into the Principles of Architectural Composition he had learnt there. But the essence of modernism was that all such principles were abrogated. Thus in all three schools the new generation found a necessary amount of resistance to push off against.

The Jesuits of the new faith were the celebrities who had come together in 1928 at the invitation of the Swiss *animateur* Siegfried Giedion to form the committee of CIAM (*Congrès Internationaux d'Architecture Moderne*). Its English offshoot, the MARS Group, set up by Wells Coates and Morton Shand in February 1933 (also at the invitation of Giedion), was predictably more relaxed dogmatically, though Coates, with his passion for precision and his nervous energy, had hoped to keep noses to the grindstone with a programme of Research, soon to be a word of some magic in the movement. He never succeeded, until the war created enforced leisure and a pool of distinguished refugee talent. But even MARS felt it necessary to be reasonably exclusive, and was not prepared to admit eclectics like Howard Robertson, Grey Wornum or Oliver Hill to membership (if they applied).[4] What the Group really could encompass was talk. Five leading members joined the famous Aegean Cruise of 1933 – a hedonistic think-tank which was to re-emerge in the sixties at the invitation of Doxiadis – and these wrote the movement's obligatory manifesto, known as the Athens Charter. This, in rather Chinese style, set out the Four Functions of the city as Work, Residence, Recreation, Circulation. Human need and new technology were correctly seen as the two poles of the movement. Bringing them together was to be the theme, the test and finally the bitter fruit of the next age. Meanwhile some euphoric propaganda for the new architecture was in order, and this was brilliantly accomplished in the MARS exhibition at the New Burlington Galleries in the winter before Munich. 'On 19 January,' wrote Le Corbusier in the *Architectural Review*, 'I dropped out of an aeroplane into the midst of a charming demonstration of youth, which revealed the architecture of tomorrow to be as smiling as it is self-reliant.' His introduction concludes on the high note expected of him:

The benefits of the New Architecture must not be confined to the homes of the few who enjoy the privilege of taste or money. They must be widely diffused so as to brighten the homes, and thus the lives, of millions upon millions of workers. That is why our generosity impels us to pursue this aim and assure its triumph. It necessarily postulates the most crucial issue of our age: a great campaign for the rational re-equipment of whole countries regarded as indivisible units. Granted a due aesthetic sensibility to form, that campaign will enable us to carry out vast undertakings, like the rebuilding of our towns, in a spirit of grandeur, nobility and dignity.

For the time being, 'homes for the few' were almost the only commissions available to our first generation of modernists, and they made the most of them. The Modern House became the emblem of the movement. Clients were mostly from the *haute bourgeoisie*, though for one of his most glamorous houses Maxwell Fry was able to ensnare a much less sophisticated patron.[5] The highest common factor of these houses was their abstract beauty in sunlight before their first

10. The Modern House, emblem of the movement; this one by Maxwell Fry at Kingston on Thames, 1937

winter's staining; their lowest common denominator the bleak dullness of their interiors, which drew an early protest from Raymond Mortimer, with his Bloomsbury affiliations, at modern English architects' blinkered ignorance of modern art.[6] Of course there was a spectrum stretching from 'primitives' like Amyas Connell, George Checkley or F.R.S. Yorke at one end to cosmopolitans like Coates and Chermayeff at the other, but over the general run of it the refusal to make any use of centuries of visual sensibility and building skills was deliberate and damaging. The ideological use of poorly designed factory-made components, ignoring the Bauhaus doctrine that they must be perfected first, made matters worse. Some sooner, some later, these houses succumbed to the weather, to necessary modification or to ideological mutilation. Yet as gestures of defiance of the cosy and conformist thirties, their images in Dell and Wainwright's heavily filtered photographs in the *Architectural Review* are still moving historical documents, breathing the heady air of a spring in which anything seemed possible.

The *Architectural Review*, the property of the Hastings family, had turned from Georgian-Swedish to DIA influences on the arrival of Christian Barman in 1933, but its great days started in 1935 when H. de C. Hastings became its editor and J. M. Richards succeeded John Betjeman as deputy. Unique among architectural magazines in its visual catholicity, the *Review* also had the literary intelligence to engage Osbert Sitwell and Ozenfant, Clive Bell and Cyril Connolly, Wyndham Lewis and D. H. Lawrence. Two particular strokes of editorial genius were the appointment of the unknown and brilliant Morton Shand (the father-in-law of James Stirling) to cover engineering technology and continental developments, and the lifeline thrown to Nikolaus Pevsner when he landed in 1935. Hastings and Richards set themselves to enlarge the consciousness of designers, to cultivate 'the exploring eye' and to enrich England's impoverished visual culture. But they denied the modernists the gift they needed most – criticism. This was deliberate: there were too many enemies for it to be safe to attack one's friends. So it was, in this sense, a conspiracy: like all embattled progressive movements, this one saw enemies on every side. And again as in all such situations, it was not so much the straight Right that preoccupied it – the old neo-Georgians and the pseudo-Swedes – as the heretics of the Left. It was mortifying and maddening that some laymen could not see the differences between modern and modernistic, the word progressives used for all the cubist-jazz-streamline derivatives of Art Deco, the Pop Art of the day.[7] They little imagined that forty years later it would be this, and not their hard-won architecture, for which the period would be affectionately remembered.

The liaison with the continental *avant-garde* for which the MARS Group officially existed was soon accomplished by the arrival of half of it in England. Gropius, Mendelsohn, Breuer, Korn and Lubetkin were a formidable accession of strength. There was an immediate gain in sophistication, for which the radical intellectual Lubetkin, with his Parisian experience, was chiefly responsible. His first little job, the Penguin Pool at the London Zoo (achieved through Godfrey Samuel and Solly Zuckerman), marked the entry into architecture of Ove Arup, the brilliant British-born Danish engineer who turned out a born architect, as well as a loyal if critical ally of the *avant-garde*. The Lubetkin/Arup link-up went on to produce the first, and to purists the only, canonical masterwork of the thirties in England – the Highpoint One flats in Highgate, London, of 1935. But

11. Highpoint One, Highgate, London, by Lubetkin and Tecton,
England's first major building in the new style

it turned out a false dawn. Lubetkin was not only a perfectionist and an autocrat, which made life hard for his young partners, and eventually for himself, in English practice; he was also a 'formalist', deeply classical by temperament and training. Thus the young Corbusian Denys Lasdun, who came to him from Wells Coates and brought into the office its first major housing project in Paddington, could not live with him for long. In the last years before the war, with projects of any size vanishing over the horizon, it became apparent that the movement was in danger of contracting into a cult – the very fate that both Gropius and Le Corbusier had warned against.

For a new generation that thought in these terms was already emerging from the schools of architecture, and in particular from the AA. To these students, already unionized and militant, the enemy was no longer the 'old guard', but aestheticism as such; whether classical or modern was irrelevant. 'Beauty' to them was like the barrow of the labourer, who when asked why he pulled instead of pushing it replied, 'Because I'm sick of the sight of the bloody thing.' Writing in their magazine *Focus*, Le Corbusier had advised: 'Look at the backs of buildings if you want to learn about them.' The manifesto of this generation, the *Yellow Book* of 1937, blames their public school background for its indifference to social and cultural history, cool contempt for 'enthusiasm' and philistine division between 'work' and 'games'. The appointment of Goodhart-Rendel, witty, cultivated, musical and archetypally 'elitist', to the directorship of the School led straight into confrontation. Against the cult of the brilliant Concept, the students proposed Research; against competition, group-working; against teaching, 'facilities'. 'Nothing should be taught; only information should be available.' In the awesome July of 1938, 'at a meeting of almost unbelievable tension and solidarity', the students voted for 'strike action' if their demands were not met – then dispersed for the summer holidays. They returned to find that Goodhart-Rendel had resigned and was shortly to join the Grenadier Guards.

Writing on the eve of war, with all passion spent, Anthony Cox, the most articulate of the rebels,[8] quoted the rival schools of thought. To Goodhart-Rendel, 'art is a hold on the eternal and must be independent of social forces'. To Herbert Read, 'art is an expression of society; the conditions for great art do not exist today'. What mattered was social consciousness and commitment. 'Our rejection of the aesthetic ideal has been forced upon us by events.' How shocking that 'at Taliesin [Frank Lloyd Wright's community] they are said not to read any newspapers'. For 'if we want to find for architects a better, more vital place in society, we can find it only in the environment of a new society'.[9] 'Freedom,' Cox finally quotes the fateful phrase, 'lies in the knowledge of necessity.'

This was the sombre note of the forties, the natural accompaniment of total war, though for the fortunate British 'the knowledge of necessity' was only 'for the duration'. Taking freedom as the norm, they undervalued it. When eventually the high-sounding British

Liberation Army landed in Normandy, liberating was the word the troops used for looting, which they pursued enthusiastically. For the more serious, Day Lewis expressed the mood of 1940:

> They who in folly or mere greed
> Enslaved religion, markets, laws,
> Borrow our language now, and bid
> Us to speak up in freedom's cause.
>
> It is the logic of our times,
> No subject for immortal verse,
> That we who lived by honest dreams
> Defend the bad against the worse.

The strange word 'honest' is used here no doubt in the Shakespearian sense ('honest Bardolph'). It implied the rejection of all the complacencies, hypocrisies, snobberies and injustices of the escapist thirties. But how honest were the dreams of architects? They were seen, to begin with, as an expression of 'social justice'. This was the bedrock on which our new society would be built. Britain's wartime economy, less corrupted by black markets than those of most other countries, showed we could do it. It would be tame, unexciting, even threadbare, but this the wartime generation, yearning for fireside pleasures, could accept. And it would be achieved by Planning – in the forties always awarded a capital letter. 'We are all socialists now.'

When the excitements of 1940 were over, when the measure of the German Air Force had been taken and the war had settled into its long middle period of delays and disappointments, there was time to think at all levels, from Royal Commissions to rankers drafted to ABCA lectures, to sapper officers improvising techniques of prefabrication elementary enough to be used under stress, to administrators blue-printing new social systems.[10] The life-style, the thought-style, were austere, egalitarian, rational, positivist and sceptical. Above all, it tried to think systematically: first things first. First must come a humane society, to be codified in Social Security and the National Health Service, the twin triumphs of post-war Britain. Next, the ship must be properly trimmed: the lurch of the population away from the old heavy industries of the north and west into the south-east, reversed by the war, must not be allowed to start up again. The report of the Barlow Commission, which had been set up to look again[11] at the problem just before the war, no longer seemed to match up to the potentialities opened up by wartime controls over the location of industry. Abercrombie was encouraged to assume that new machinery would succeed in holding the population of the London region down to its present figure and to plan accordingly.

The 1944 White Paper *Control of Land Use* clearly and correctly identified this as the pivotal point of the new machinery. 'Provision for the right use of land, in accordance with a considered policy, is an essential requirement of the Government's programme of post-war reconstruction. New houses, whether of permanent or emergency construction; the new layout of areas devastated by enemy action or blighted by reason of age or bad living conditions; the new schools which will be required under the Education Bill now before Parliament; the balanced distribution of industry which the Government's recently published proposals for maintaining active employment envisage; the requirements of sound nutrition and of a healthy and well-balanced agriculture; the preservation of land for National Parks and forests, and the assurance to the people of enjoyment of sea and countryside in times of leisure; a new and safer highway system better adapted to modern industrial and other needs; the proper provision of airfields – all these related parts of a single reconstruction programme involve the use of land, and it is essential that their various claims on land should be so harmonized as to ensure for the people of this country the greatest possible measure of individual well-being and national prosperity.'

There is no need to describe here the great package of legislation through which this was achieved. It became world-famous and widely admired, though little imitated. Helped by static population forecasts, buttressed by the Board of Trade's negative controls and positive incentives for the location of industry, the new county and city planning authorities now had the context, though few had the technical capacity, to produce definitive and rational development plans. The general theory, deriving originally from Ebenezer Howard, was by now uncontroversial – hold the great city at its present limits by a wide green moat, and move out beyond it the constricted industries and their slum-housed workers into self-contained industrial towns, either on virgin sites or by major additions to existing towns. Thus, and thus only, would elbow room be gained for the civilized renewal of the inner city, now moth-eaten but, with famous exceptions like Plymouth and Coventry, inadequately cleared by the blitz. Patchwork and not a new garment was going to be the general pattern.

Popular writers of a later generation give the impression that the planners' dreams for the inner cities were slavishly Corbusian. This was far from the case. In 1941, a year in which all the relevant institutions from the Royal Academy downwards organized any of their members who were still in town – pensioners, pacifists, refugees – into 'reconstruction committees', the tone had been properly demotic. 'Planning is for People.' There were two inevitable obsessions: what to do about traffic, and what to do about densities. An enlightened policeman, Alker Tripp, published a slim volume full of common sense about vehicular movement and introducing the idea of the traffic-free precinct; and the principle of segregation was further developed in a project published by William and Aileen Tatton Brown in the *Architectural Review* in that same year of hard thinking. Here the pedestrian deck, 'a completely new ground level for pedestrians', makes its appearance in the form which was to sweep all before it in the sixties. But on high buildings a strictly utilitarian view is taken. 'Congestion results from the employment of building units that are too small. It is immaterial whether the increase of scale is vertical or horizontal so long as it is one or the other.' The model in fact shows both, with the 'Levels', wide top-lit podia embracing green squares, and slim slabs of offices bridging the heavy traffic routes – a forerunner of what Colin Buchanan was later to call 'traffic architecture'. But there is a very English concern for the familiar. 'Aesthetically, the main problem in joining old with new is the question of scale. The old is so often dwarfed by the mere bulk of the new. But in this case the Levels, which are the buildings adjacent to those already existing, are only two to three storeys in height. They would, therefore, be lower than the majority of the old town, which would gain rather than suffer by comparison ... The man in the street is, in practice, two people, the man-in-the-motor-car and the man-on-the-pavement. From the motorist's point of view, the advantages of a town free from congestion, traffic cops, parking restrictions and pedestrians needs no further comment. The man-on-the-pavement's wants are more complex. He longs for the lights, the movement and bustle of urban life. He wants the familiar landmarks, the pub-on-the-corner. He wants room to stand and gaze into the shop windows without being pushed off the pavement, and at the same time he wants to be made aware that every inch of the town is throbbing with life and activity ... The new town would present, first of all, the impression of a big exhibition, a vast area of display free from the perils of the motor car. The novelty of the promenades and bridges would

12. A 1942 project published in the *Architectural Review* shows a bombed London district rebuilt with a traffic artery spanned by a slab of offices and low-rise buildings wrapped round surviving monuments.

excite his curiosity and stimulate his desire to explore: not only the main routes, but small courts off the beaten track, raised terraces, cloisters and colonnades, places where he could sit and rest and watch the world go by. There would be room for him to come into contact with architecture on a more human and intimate scale than has ever been possible before in the centre of any great city.'

It is fair to add that even the preservationists of the forties saw the great mass of our Victorian 'twilight areas' as expendable. Six years of war had reduced these parts of London and the great provincial cities to a sinister squalor that recalled the darkest passages of *Bleak House*. Where the dingy terraces still stood, rotting sandbags oozed on to the pavements, rats infested the cellars, summers of uncut grass choked the back gardens, and black tape or dirty plastic blinded the windows. Britain could take it, but on the clear understanding that all this mess would be swept away.

While the politicians gave their pledges and the architects made their models, officials in Reith's new department set about rewriting the rules. A planning technique group under W. G. Holford and later Gordon Stephenson prepared a textbook, *The Redevelopment of Central Areas*, to go out to the new planning authorities set up under the 1947 Act, which contained the kit of tools – use-classes, plot ratios, daylight factors, sight lines, parking standards and so on – by means of which city engineers could set about their work, sometimes in uneasy double-harness with consultant planners. They proceeded in a conscientious manner that was typical of the time to reproduce in their several cities almost exact copies of the aesthetically null, if purely imaginary, model projects in the handbook. The monuments of that era, Plymouth and Exeter, Bristol and Hull, with their shopping boulevards and bowls of flowers and shrubby roundabouts and patterned paving and utility brick or Portland stone façades, dated very rapidly, both functionally and aesthetically, and were consequently in the late seventies just beginning to come back into fashion; their domestic scale redeemed them.

Densities for new housing, which could have huge cumulative effects on the shape and size of cities, were now painstakingly reviewed. The 1944 Housing Manual, the first of a series which paternalist Ministers were to put out after the war, started from the neighbourhood of 5–10,000 people as the social unit out of which the new Britain was to be composed, and envisaged it in three forms: 'open development' at 30–40 persons per acre on lines that had become monotonously stereotyped before the war; 'inner ring' housing at 70 p.p.a., achieved by narrower frontages and longer terraces with an occasional block of 3-storey flats; and 'central area' housing at 100–120 p.p.a., which would be predominantly in walk-up flats. The main thrust, deriving from the pre-war propaganda of Edwards, Sharp and Denby, was to persuade the English of the merits of the terrace house, but the terraces were still seen as lining a commonplace suburban road, and even in 1952, when a detailed Manual on densities was published in an attempt to tighten them up, the absurd convention of 70 feet between frontages was endorsed as 'generally agreed'. It was also cautiously (and incorrectly) pointed out that any density higher than 70 p.p.a. would produce a higher proportion of flats than 'demography' required. A happy mean was all that was required at this stage.

Indeed, by the late forties a serviceable brick-and-tile vernacular had evolved in the Nordic democracies and in Holland which was to become the hallmark of the first-generation New Towns. It was not Georgian; it was not Modern: given the standard components and the standard layouts without which cost targets could not be hit, it designed itself. Movement was by bus and bike: only ten per cent of houses were allowed a garage. Only an occasional group of walk-up flats broke the horizontal lines of 2-storey terraces, which had to be brick with concrete roof tiles because no amount of rationality would persuade contractors to price dry prefabricated systems, such as the schools were using, as low. When the target was the £1,000 house, every pound counted. Trees were preserved and liberally planted and

13. Housing at Hatfield in the New Town style of 1950

would soon, as at Welwyn, blot out the architecture. A tiny minority of the 1,434 housing authorities in England and Wales handled this vernacular with sensibility, among them the little rural district of Loddon in Norfolk, whose cottages by Tayler and Green were among the best and most characteristic products of the forties. For those few one-off institutional buildings for which licences could be obtained a prettier version, with a few feminine accessories, the architectural equivalent of the New Look, was available from the same source, and was given the *cachet* of capital letters in the *Architectural Review* (May 1947) – the New Empiricism. Impeccable modernist personalities of the thirties, like Oud and Dudok in Holland, Markelius and Lindström in Sweden, Fry, Spence and Gibberd in England, had switched to it, for the psychological need was manifest. After the rigours of warfare in foreign parts, people had had enough concrete to be going on with. As Eric de Maré succinctly put it in his review of the Swedish scene: 'Cosiness is coming back.'

This was a far cry from the *Ville Radieuse*, and equally far from 'the logic of our times' so clearly perceived by the heroes of 1938. For, given the immense burden of urgent repairs, there were neither the bricks nor the timber nor the skilled men to get roofs over heads in this traditional way. The obvious answer was to switch redundant aircraft assembly lines to the mass production of prefabricated metal dwellings, and over 150,000 'temporary' Portal bungalows were run off in double-quick time. Governments love hutments and in wartime people had grown used to living, learning, working and dying in them. But fortunately when in 1945 hutments were, as usual, proposed for the new primary schools, two young architects called Stirrat Johnson-Marshall and David Medd set themselves to move matters in another direction. In the army they had worked together on deception structures on the Channel coast, and had experienced the speed in action of briefing and prototype design, manufacture, testing and personnel training all being controlled by one group. This was the teamwork the AA students had predicated, with the architect stepping down from his Renaissance pedestal and becoming an anonymous part of the process modestly described as Development. For the old prestige the designer traded the new power he would gain by having 'the order book in his pocket'. Marshall and Medd saw that if there was to be any human variety in post-war architecture the vital thing was to prefabricate the components, not the buildings, and to find manufacturers who were prepared to shoulder the risks of development. By 1947 through the courage of a single county architect, C. H. Aslin, the first of the post-war schools, with their 'light and dry' meccano structures and relaxed planning and airy internal spaces, were spreading themselves in the elmy fields of Hertfordshire.

It was remarkable in retrospect that the post-war consensus should have lasted for twenty years. There were two reasons for this. First, it was bipartisan. Wartime unity of purpose in the country at large took time to dissolve and, when it did, Butskellite loyalty to the fundamental aims of the Welfare State overrode what still seemed minor differences of emphasis. Second, it was flexible. Far more dependent on officials than pre-war society had been, it benefited from their trained capacity to serve new masters. And, as we shall see, it needed to. Those twenty years from 1945 divide approximately into two decades of sharply contrasted character. The first was the Age of Austerity. The Attlee Government took office in a mood of exhilaration and dedication, 'walking with destiny' in the words of Hugh Dalton. 'Plan boldly', advised the new Minister of Town and Country Planning, Lewis Silkin, as though the bitter fruit of earlier wars had not been part of our national experience. Within a year, it had to be tasted again. Rescued by the Marshall Plan from virtual bankruptcy in 1947, the country still lived under a bleak war economy. 'First,' decreed Stafford Cripps, 'are exports ... second is capital investment in industry; and last are the needs, comforts and amenities of the family.' 'The Kingdom,' recalled Evelyn Waugh, 'seemed to be under enemy occupation.'

We were let out of school in the wet summer of 1951 for the Festival of Britain, sold to the new Government soon after the war by the editor of the *News Chronicle*, Gerald Barry, as 'a great Trade and Cultural Exhibition' in the tradition of 1851 and so subsumed by the first of Cripps's priorities, but in fact primarily a tonic for the home front. This it brilliantly was. For the first time, in the misty sunlight of that fine May, it was possible to feel that 'we witness here the long-awaited opening of the flower of modern architecture'.[11] But it was a false spring: the flower lacked the hardiness to survive the blasts ahead. The excess of charm and whimsy, the parade of long-vanished British eccentricity (Victorian balloons, penny-farthings, Emmett trains) represented, as Michael Frayn was later to point out, 'the Britain of the radical middle-classes, of the do-gooders ... the posthumous work of the BBC news, the Crown Film Unit, the sweet ration, Ealing comedies, Uncle Mac and Sylvia Peters'. Gerald Barry's claim that this was 'the people's show, not organized arbitrarily for them to enjoy but put on by them, by us all, as an expression of the way of life in which we believe' was ex-wartime euphoria and would be blown sky-high before the decade was out by Elvis Presley, the Teds and the Rockers and the New Brutalism. It just saw us through the Coronation in 1953, but that was its swan song.

The prototype and test-bed of the fifties was Coventry. This prosperous small city, with its hopeless medieval street plan and high-minded social-democrat Council, had seen the light as long ago as 1938, when it had decided to take architecture and planning away from the City Engineer and appointed 30-year-old Donald Gibson to

14. The first shopping mall, Coventry, 1955

set up its first Architect's Department. Before much had been done, the city centre and its Cathedral were burnt to the ground in the raid of 14 November 1940. Gibson, like Holford, had been trained in the axial *Beaux Arts* tradition, and though his scheme for a parkway-girdled civic and commercial centre went through many variations in the long years before it could be built, one feature never varied – the axial shopping mall aligned on all that was expected to survive of the Cathedral – its spire. This was an architectural solecism, since Gothic churches should not close symmetrical vistas, but it was a good mall and the first of its kind, and it exploited its slope to provide two levels of shops inspired by the Rows of Chester. More embarrassing as time passed was the formal traffic island featuring Lady Godiva, and featuring also a shoddy row of temporary wartime shops which the Council unaccountably failed for many years to remove from the central vista. Coventry in fact was no paragon, yet its myth secured it in the affection of visitors, and when Basil Spence's equally imperfect but popular Cathedral opened its glass doors in 1962, the city centre was firmly embraced among the tourist attractions of England. Sadly, the two spires that had for long marked it from afar were not protected against the craze for tower blocks that reached the city in the sixties, Gibson's successor himself building one for Lanchester Polytechnic only a few yards from the Cathedral. Coventry, it could be said, remained at the centre of the Consensus right through, and Gibson's office was the nursery of those who formed it.

Meanwhile, between 1952 and 1955, there occurred a transformation in the political and economic climate, as the country moved out of the Cripps era into the Macmillan one. In putting this wily and relaxed politician in charge of planning and housing, Churchill made an uncommonly sensible choice. In the golden glow of the New Elizabethan Age, and of the 1953 'bonfire of controls', Macmillan's 'crusade' to get 300,000 houses built in a year was comfortably achieved, builders not yet having caught the scent of the rich pastures of urban renewal. They were smaller houses than the Labour Government had sanctioned in Bevan's time, but they were there – most of them out on the edges of the conurbations, nudging such green belts as existed, or else out beyond them in the New Towns. This centrifugal swing was of course deliberate, relieving the pressure on the inner cities, so that the rebuilding of the slums could at last begin.

By the late fifties the change of atmosphere was tangible. It had two aspects: a 'baby boom' soon to be dramatically registered in the 1961 census, and an economic boom, registered in 1959 by 'Supermac's' deathless 'You never had it so good'. This was true but was not, to the surprise of the simple, received with applause. Professor Shils[13] points out that 'the intellectuals' tradition of hostility and disparagement of their own society is a long and honourable one' and that the 'widespread reconciliation which followed the Second World War' was altogether exceptional. He sees 1956, the year of Suez and Hungary, as the start of the break-up of the post-war social honeymoon. In that year two liberal images collapsed simultaneously – the decent image of post-war Britain and the heroic image of Soviet Russia. British socialism, traditionally puritanical and suspicious of bourgeois hedonism, found itself overtaken by a New Left, sexually liberated, contemptuous of the paternalist 'mixed economy', but itself schizo-phrenic because unable to reconcile its distrust of authority with its insistence on governmental protection, provision, regulation and initiative. With the Tory government of 1959 cynicism, the shared mood of Right and Left, took over and carried us through the boom years. The satire industry, amply supplied by the spy scandals of the early sixties, came into its inheritance.

Underlying and underlining the change were the population projections that emerged from the 1961 census. The forecast for England and Wales at the turn of the century, which had been 46 million in 1955, was now 66 million. Obviously all the assumptions on which the regional distribution of industry and population had been based were obsolete.

The most conspicuous symptom of what came to be called the environmental crisis was the growth of road traffic. The number of vehicles on British roads, which had passed the 1 million mark in 1922 and had reached 5 million in the days of the post-war consensus, had by 1962 doubled to 10 million. It was (variously) projected to reach between 30 and 40 million by 2010, the year by which demand was assumed to have reached saturation point. The Buchanan Report, *Traffic in Towns*, published in 1963, translated these projections into physical terms and with irrefutable logic demonstrated that to accommodate even a third of the eventual demand for car-commuter travel to city centres would mean the demolition of half the physical fabric of the inner city. As the steering group's introduction put it: 'If we are to have any chance of living at peace with the motor car, we shall need a different sort of city.' The warning was explicit: unless public investment in roads and buildings could be brought to match the private investment now going into the mass production of vehicles, strangulation could be avoided only by locking up most of these vehicles in their garages. Taking a middle position between the extremes of demolition and restriction, Buchanan enlarged Alker Tripp's traffic-free 'precincts', unappealing-ly re-christening them 'environmental areas', and then threaded be-tween them a network of 'distributor' roads of different categories. The image that emerged of spaghetti junctions and multi-level, tower-and-podium, pedestrian-decked 'traffic architecture', first proposed by the Tatton Browns during the war, rapidly became the common language of city planners and commercial developers. It was not, Buchanan carefully explained, his recommendation: it was merely the least absurd of the alternatives. Society must choose.

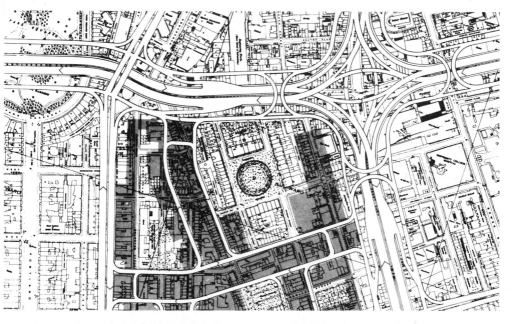

15 and 16. Traffic conduits and 'traffic architecture' applied to London's Fitzroy Square area in The Buchanan Report, 1963

The choice it made was not in the circumstances an unintelligent one. Given the emergent mixed economy of state socialism and take-over capitalism, the way to get the city centres rebuilt was thought to be Partnership between the two. This seemed the best way of belling the cat of commercial office development. Most of the big developers (Charles Clore, Jack Cotton, Harry Hyams, Lew Hammerson, Max Rayne, Harold Samuel) had made their names during the blitz and the post-war depression by picking up plum sites on main shopping streets dirt cheap and offering floor space at bargain rentals to the only tenants (bombed-out government departments and top-priority export industries) who could offer or obtain the privilege of inhabiting new buildings. The secret was always to be a jump ahead of the planning context. Indeed they had to assemble sites on the quiet if they were not to be hopelessly bid up, and they had to buy Green Belt land if they were to build cheap houses. Thus urban planning authorities, although they were under steady pressure from Ministers and from the Royal Fine Art Commission to be ready with their own policies for high buildings, in fact could have no idea where an application for one would turn up next – it would almost certainly not be in the places they would have chosen. And rural planning authorities saw their local conservation efforts overruled in the interests of irresistible regional population pressures which the developers had gambled on long before governments had finalized their regional plans. In those few cases, such as the LCC's South Bank development, where the planning exercise was carried out by the book and in good time, developers were apt to evince a second unpleasant characteristic: they became prima donnas and threatened to walk off the stage if they were not allowed to play the part in their own way, and they insisted that the project could not be financially viable unless they were allowed more cubic feet than the site should bear. Planning authorities seldom commanded the expertise or the political courage to argue with them. Lastly, and perhaps more academically, it was held against the developers that they picked up all the plums of urban renewal, leaving the local authorities to do the unremunerative chores. There was an unhealthy imbalance between their financial power and know-how and that of the local authorities who held the veto on their activities. At its best, this was a situation which was bound to lead to the overbuilding of sites; at its worst, it could create the conditions of corruption.

Two things were urgently necessary. The first was, generally by hiring planning consultants, to have a central area plan ready before developers' applications put one on the spot. The second (inexcusably delayed for political reasons) was to repeal the Third Schedule of the 1947 Act, which had sought to encourage post-war reconstruction by allowing a new building ten per cent more volume (and because of the spatial extravagance of old buildings this could be forty per cent more floor-space) than had previously stood on the site. By these means there was at last some hope of the public interest catching up with what had become a runaway private bonanza. The Partnership technique, as put out to planning authorities in Ministry circulars, called for land purchase by the city council, a three-dimensional model, and then the offer on building lease of appropriate sites for competitive bidding by developers. The result would normally be a brand-new inner relief-road feeding multi-storey car parks, a pedestrian shopping mall and the lettable office slabs that paid for it all, and the trick was to gain all this without squeezing developers' profits out of existence. At its best the technique could finance a vital road improvement such as the Euston Road underpass or the Notting Hill widening in London. At its worst it could wreck a cathedral city like Worcester, or exchange decent low-rented houses for unlettable shops, or (as in the notorious case of London's Centre Point) gain a traffic roundabout which was outdated by a new circulation pattern before it was even finished. And of course it never looked like operating on a scale that would give a city the new highway armatures postulated by Buchanan: neither public nor private capital of that magnitude was available. It was thought (hoped) that parking restriction plus taxation plus, as usual, better public transport would do the trick.

It was not only the traffic projections that were blown sky-high by the new population forecasts. The housing shortage also looked far more serious and prolonged than before, though it was not till 1964 that a new Minister, Richard Crossman, was able to persuade the Prime Minister that a target of half a million houses a year from all sources was technically achievable and would be a strong morale-booster at a time when the Wilson Government was being cruelly 'blown off course'. The figure duly appeared in George Brown's pie-in-the-sky National Plan in 1965, and set the seal on the great clearances and the system-built flats of the mid sixties. For it was obvious that traditional building methods as used in the New Towns, which were not vastly different from those used in ancient Egypt, would never deliver the numbers that were now needed in the cities: chronic labour shortage and the English weather would see to that.

A group of young architects that included Donald Gibson, Stirrat Johnson-Marshall, Roger Walters and Dan Lacey, together with a contemporary group of civil servants that included John Maud, Anthony Part and William Pile, were by now well placed to develop the new techniques of prefabrication that would be needed. The meccano-type structures first developed in Hertfordshire and then exploited in the necessary numbers by Gibson in Nottinghamshire and Johnson-Marshall in the Ministry of Education were more than

17. A Hertfordshire 'meccano' school of 1953

a technology: they were an ideology. Research, teamwork and feedback were seen as the triple key to a new England, with anonymity its pride, and with the architect's unique contribution, his capacity to visualize, no more than one component in a totality that included the user's enlarging capacity to think about human need and the councillor's power to get things done. Thus emerged, it was thought, the twentieth-century equivalent of the anonymous craftsman who had perfected the eighteenth-century terrace house. The seal was set on the achievement by the highest award at the Milan Triennale of 1960 (a year to which we shall be returning) to a run-of-the-mill CLASP School, not for its economy but for its beauty – rightly described by Reyner Banham as 'a gong for the Welfare State'. But it was clearly anomalous both technically and visually that the light-and-dry aesthetic of the schools and the wet-and-heavy aesthetic of the housing terraces should for ever quarrel in the same fields. It was obvious that the next move must be into housing.

It was easy enough to roll off complete dwellings; indeed the emergency housing programme had done just that at the end of the war. But for obvious environmental reasons this was unacceptable to architects, who were looking for a kit from which a humane variety of low-rise types could be assembled faster and cheaper than bricks and mortar could do it. They never succeeded. But what were available, mainly from France and Sweden,[14] were patented systems for the rapid building of multi-storey flats, which met the demand in continental countries. For Ministers and for housing committees seeking to beat all productivity records for new dwellings, this had to be the answer. A National Building Agency, managed by the severe and dedicated Cleeve Barr, was set up to help the urban housing authorities, the majority of which were wholly unversed in such matters, to find their way among the multiplicity of systems now on offer and to encourage them to group themselves into consortia. As early as 1961 Barr himself had warned of the dangers of monotony and an inhuman scale, but to no avail. Additional subsidies took care of the extra cost of tall buildings and of the far higher cost of inner-city compared with green-field sites. Indeed, successive Ministers provided that the higher the tower, the higher the subsidy per flat. The era of the sky-flat had arrived.

Everything was getting bigger – roads, car parks, lorries, multiple stores, office buildings, airports, hospitals, telephone exchanges. By the mid sixties both the context and the scale of the first-generation New Towns looked suburban. They were too close to their parent cities, too traditionally conceived as satellites, too concentrated in the south-east, too loose and anti-urban in form and philosophy. While the major historic cities bid for new universities, often setting up special promotion committees to present their case, the major conurbations bid for New Towns. Of the original fourteen New Towns, eight had been in a ring round London and had been planned to take a total of 400,000 people out of the city; the other six had resulted from regional studies indicating areas at present decayed, where industrial growth looked promising. The fifties only added one to the first fourteen, but this, Cumbernauld near Glasgow, was deliberately designed through its compact hilltop form, generous provision for cars and central megastructure to remedy what were thought to be their deficiencies. It is drily described by the Scots as 'popular with architects'. Another seven were designated in the early sixties, but they were still for the customary average 50,000 population, and in the customary satellite role. But with the shock of the population projections there was a radical rethink. Sites for genuinely New Towns in the original sense had been getting harder to find. The new Greater London Council, after a systematic trawl of the Home Counties, had lighted on an excellent one on land of low agricultural value around Hook in Hampshire, and had used their now world-famous expertise to produce a most enticing visual image, only to have the whole project rejected by a Tory landowner-dominated County Council. The GLC had to settle for expanding Basingstoke and Andover instead. This signalled the final rejection of the satellite concept. Henceforth the successful Development Corporation mechanism would be used to promote major population growth, generally tacked on to existing towns with first-class road and rail communications such as Peterborough and Northampton. The only two that could be said to be in the country, Milton Keynes and Telford, were each to house upwards of 200,000 people.

By now it had become evident that the 1947 planning machinery, struggling to cope with all these unforeseen pressures, was itself due for an overhaul. The first part to crumble had been the gallant attempt to solve the perennial problem of recouping from those who gained betterment from planning decisions in order to pay compensation to those who lost. The 1947 Act had bought out all development rights by a once-and-for-all payment to be financed by a development charge on every approval. The result had been no development at all and, after various tinkerings that only made matters worse, all attempts to collect betterment were abandoned and the lucky land-owner at last received the full market value of his land. The unlucky, denied planning permission, got nothing. Apart from its inequity, this dose of market economics put a severe strain on the local public purse and an equally severe strain on the integrity of planning officers and councillors, on whose say-so vast fortunes could now be made. The issue had become highly political, and was to remain so. Meanwhile the less contentious business of reforming the planning machinery could be got on with. The 1968 Act abolished the general-purpose Development Plans and the small-scale Town Maps, which it was becoming impossible to keep up-to-date, and made a sensible distinction between *strategic* plans, which required Whitehall approval in the light of the regional picture (now under the surveillance of advisory Regional Economic Councils), and *local* plans in appropriate degrees of detail, which were freed of Whitehall supervision and became wholly the responsibility of the cities and counties, subject to statutory 'public participation'. The urban Comprehensive Development Area became the Action Area, which meant much the same thing but did not have to be so rigidly defined. The general effect, given the local authority set-up as it existed in the sixties, was a more flexible and less paternalist environment. We could be said to be growing up.

The same could be claimed for the state of architecture. Until building licensing was abolished in 1954, architecture in the serious sense had been, as John Summerson had put it, 'an illegal profession'. The generation for whom Gerald Barry and Hugh Casson had been such adroit impresarios in 1951 had had nothing much to do once the South Bank show was over. Apart from the handful of pioneering public offices, the only private work available was minimal housing and an occasional factory or office block, the latter commonly entrusted to the sort of older firm that knew its way through the controls and did not waste time or money on 'architecture'. The result was one of the dimmest decades in our architectural history, enlivened at intervals by broadsides from J. M. Richards and the *Architectural Review* directed at such targets as the ham-fisted London office blocks built and leased to Government departments, the 'Failure of the New Towns' and the work of the elderly knighted architects still retained by the universities. In the case of the last mentioned, the *Review* lying on Common Room tables no doubt steadily infiltrated academic consciences, but what really got matters moving was the simultaneous appearance in the late fifties of a competitive market and a tougher streak in architecture.

The intellectual and moral leadership of the new movement came from two young architects, Alison and Peter Smithson, who in 1949, when he was 26, had won the competition for a secondary school at Hunstanton in Norfolk. Its design was avowedly inspired by Mies van der Rohe's Illinois Institute of Technology (completed 1947), but it carried the brutal exposure of its structural materials (steel, glass, bricks) and of its pipe-runs and conduits far further than the subtle Mies, whose real passion was for refinement of detail. While the school was building, the other seminal influence on the Smithsons and their followers was rising in a suburb of Marseilles. This was Le Corbusier's first *Unité d'Habitation de Grandeur Conforme*. Here concrete, which in the master's pre-war buildings had been plastered and whitened to sustain the image of a machine-age architecture, was allowed to proclaim its monstrous and ponderous character, responding to the rough formwork of semi-skilled Provençal and Algerian carpenters. *'L'architecture, c'est avec des matières brutes établir des rapports émouvants.'* The New Brutalism,[15] as it was inescapably called, had two aspects. First, it was a puritanical protest against the sentimentality, the effeminacy and the triviality of the Festival/New Town/ Coventry style. Second, it was a *rappel à l'ordre*, and the order (and scale) to which it recalled us was that of classical Greece, which had so profoundly moved Le Corbusier himself.[16] In both aspects, the movement called to mind the severities and the high intellectual tone of the eighteenth-century Palladians and the nineteenth-century Ecclesiologists, and its powerful impact on the young was comparable. But unlike those earlier reformers, the Brutalists were pulled two ways by their Classical ideology and their Romantic instincts, and these contradictions were never resolved.

In 1954, the year in which both Hunstanton and Marseilles were finished, the Smithsons fired a continental-style broadside at the English scene as they saw it:

We wish to see towns and buildings which do not make us feel ashamed, ashamed that we cannot realize the potential of the twentieth century, ashamed that philosophers and physicists must think us fools, and painters think us irrelevant.

We live in moron-made cities.

Our generation must try and produce evidence that men are at work.

Evidently Brutalism had much more on its mind than the rough surfaces with which it later became too narrowly associated. The Smithsons were passionate urbanists: at the CIAM congress at Aix-en-Provence in the previous summer, in alliance with a small international group that included the English architects W. G. Howell and John Voelcker, they had launched an attack on the simplistic slogans and the diagrammatic planning concepts which they believed had become a substitute for thought in the minds of the modernist establishment. Team X, as the new group was called, asserted the traditional English conviction that what mattered was not some Platonic ideal but the character and capabilities of the individual place. Still loyal (like latter-day Maoists) to the unpredictable Master himself, they had no use for the arid rigidities of the senior disciples. Their image of the city was a mobile and organic one. Above its old road pattern they would weave a web of pedestrian ways ('streets in the air'), and through its diseased quarters they would drive a grid of expressways, for the 'feeling of being trapped-in-a-jungle-of-irresponsibilities has made the car and its corollary, the urban motor-way, into necessities . . . they represent escape and freedom', and into its loosened fabric they would insert high-density 'clusters' of new architecture – the acupuncture that would reanimate the nervous system. It was the kind of heroic surgery by which Sixtus V had glorified sixteenth-century Rome and Haussmann had come to the rescue of nineteenth-century Paris. But could it be achieved? In the words of Aldo van Eyck, the most poetic of the Team X architects:

The capacity to impart order within a single thing – to make it rest within itself – is unfortunately no longer ours, and that's a terrible thing, for we can't do without classical harmony. The capacity to impart order at the same time to a multiplicity of things is just as unfortunately not yet ours, and that's a terrible thing too, for we can't do without what I wish to call harmony in motion.

Thus sadly the Team X Primer prefigured the experience of the sixties.

But for the moment the image was irresistible, and carried all before it at the A A and among the young graduates of the School who for ideological as well as bread-and-butter reasons were now happy to work in the drawing offices of those few cities which had had the good sense to appoint a progressive city architect, foremost among them London itself. This new consensus embraced not only the architects but also the planning committees and the commercial organizations on which they depended for policy decisions. Instead of trying uneasily, as Abercrombie had done, to accommodate the two extremes – English Garden City sentimentality and German *Zeilenbau* geometry – we could now consign them both to the dustbin. For the first time since Wren we had a technique for the rebuilding of cities not dependent, as the great Baroque vistas had been, on static view-points but kinetic, exploiting all the speeds and scales and levels of movement. For increasingly it seemed to this generation that mobility on the scale of the city region, so that the Londoner could walk in the Chilterns of a Sunday afternoon and carouse downriver of a Sunday night, would be the secret of happiness in the expansive second half of the twentieth century.

*

The year 1960, something of an *annus mirabilis*, ushered in the decade with a clutch of seminal buildings. The developers had by now become aware that informed opinion, anyway in London, was no longer prepared to wear the illiterate work of their earlier architectural associates. They sought out a new breed that had trained at the AA or at Liverpool and had the intelligence to master the system.

Three buildings of 1960:
18 *(top)*. Castrol House, London, by Gollins, Melvin and Ward;
19 *(above)*. Imperial College Hostels, London, by Sheppard and Robson;
20 *(opposite)*. The Engineering Building at Leicester University by Stirling and Gowan

So 1960 saw Cecil Elsom's no-nonsense Eastbourne Terrace facing Paddington Station;[17] Gollins, Melvin and Ward's Castrol House in Marylebone Road, an elegant but inevitably scaled-down version of Lever House in New York and the parent of a large and soon tedious curtain-walled progeny; and the very slim Centre Point, for which Seifert had hired better assistants and produced the first of his essays in precast concrete knitwear. Visits to Marseilles bore their first-fruits in the LCC's slab blocks at Roehampton, Richard Sheppard's Imperial College hostels in Prince's Gardens, and the Park Hill housing complex at Sheffield, originally an AA project by Ivor Smith and Jack Lynn and developed in the office of Lewis Womersley, the City Architect. Also derivative from Le Corbusier, but subtly gentrified, was Basil Spence's Sussex University. By now younger academics had become *aficionados* of modern architecture and 1960 saw at Brasenose College the brilliant infill which was to make Powell and Moya so sought after at Oxford and Cambridge. Denys Lasdun, infinitely the stronger for his breach with Lubetkin, completed in that same year the Royal College of Physicians and the St James's flats, both facing royal parks yet received with acclamation. Finally, 1960 saw at Leicester University the masterpiece of a short-lived partnership, Stirling and Gowan; James Stirling was later to go on to produce architecture that, unique in its generation in Britain, combined the wit of Vanbrugh, the formal originality of Soane and the outrageousness of Butterfield.

Of course one was best equipped to master the system if one had been a part of it. The move from the leadership of a public office into senior partnership in a private one (often combined with a university Chair) had been pioneered by the masterful Architect to the LCC, Robert Matthew, in 1953. In the decade around 1960 he was followed by Leslie Martin, Stirrat Johnson-Marshall, W. G. Howell, Richard Llewelyn-Davies, Hugh Wilson, Lewis Womersley and Walter Bor in that order. The causes, declared and undeclared, varied with individuals, but no doubt the root cause was the impatience of the creative half of the architect's mind with desk jobs which the overgrowth of public offices had made so largely administrative. Inevitably it presaged a decline in the quality of the public service and tougher competition and more professional management in the private sector. Unfortunately, this architectural brain-drain was not balanced, as it should have been, by an influx of major planning talents or by the recruitment of brilliant graduates, though there was a handful of exceptions that proved the rule. It was agreed on all sides that planning was now a highly sophisticated discipline, needing a rare mix of rational and intuitive skills and therefore properly taught at post-graduate level, in which one's own specialism would be transcended in the way that Abercrombie and Buchanan had transcended theirs. But in the sixties a vicious circle developed, in which overloaded local authorities, lacking senior staff of the right calibre, handed out major planning commissions to consultants, which made the private sector (temporarily as it turned out) still more attractive and the public sector less so. And as the scale of everything increased, the City Planning Officer's role, like the City Architect's, became increasingly administrative rather than creative and decreasingly attractive to architect/planners. As they moved out, geographers and sociologists and surveyors moved in, and practising architects became increasingly restive under aesthetic controls exercised by people they thought wholly unqualified to do so.

As the size of jobs escalated, management seemed more than ever the clue. The RIBA itself could not expect to be immune. At an angry General Meeting in 1958, which foreshadowed the much tougher environment of a decade later, the New Left led by Cleeve Barr and Anthony Cox launched its attack on this 'cosy club for elderly private practitioners'. The central demand was for election by postal ballot of all Council members, half of whom had hitherto sat *ex officio* as provincial presidents. Popular support was confirmed when Barr, despite his backroom personality, was returned top of the ensuing poll. A take-over had taken place. The first of a new generation of presidents was the widely acceptable and politically innocent Basil Spence, but the Left continued to meet regularly in Stirrat Johnson-Marshall's office to concert pressures for further reform. Particular targets were those firms that were either too large to be happy or too small to be efficient, and it was thought that the way to expose them was through a systematic survey of every firm in the country. This matured during Holford's presidency (1960–62) and delivered the answers that were wanted.[18] *The Architect and His Office* was the frankest professional self-examination to have been carried out in any country, and the RIBA, with its Commonwealth siblings, took considerable credit for being not only (improvidently) the largest but also the most progressive architectural institution in the world. The middle sixties saw a great deal of debate, wittily provoked by Oliver Cox, about the composition and relationships of the 'building team', now much more complex than the simple client/architect/builder trio of the past. Inescapably the architect's position was central in the

operation and there was no hesitation in claiming his central responsibility for the emergent urban scene. He could no longer afford to be
the shy inarticulate Spinlove who had safely left the detail to craftsmen trained in an immemorial tradition. He must translate vast social
programmes into building operations, learn the languages of new
technologies, take risks on inadequately tested systems and materials.
'You are an organizer, not a drawing-board artist,' Le Corbusier (artist
if ever there was one) had proclaimed, and the RIBA set itself,
through its control of architectural education, to produce such
people.

The Oxford Conference of 1958 was now bearing fruit. At this get-
together of leading figures at Magdalen College, the traditional system
of articled pupillage and centralized examinations run by the RIBA
received its final quietus. To the man who had learnt by doing we now
preferred the person who had been systematically taught, and this
must be on the basis of the 2 A-levels that were the minimum requirement of the learned professions. With architecture seen to be related
both to the social sciences and to the earth sciences, the place for this
must be the universities, and it was agreed that this was where the
schools of architecture recognized for exemption from the RIBA
examinations ought to be. Those which had grown up alongside a
college of art in a municipal environment were to be frowned on. But
as might have been expected the students of the sixties, with their
higher I.Q.s, failed or refused to meet their parents' expectations
and emerged not as organization men but as visionaries.

The consensus of the sixties was enlivened (it could hardly be said
to be disturbed) by argument within the profession between what
Leonard Manasseh in his 1964 presidential address to the Architectural Association called the Art Boys and the System Boys. We have
noted the strong conviction in official circles that only industrialized
building was going to solve the problem of productivity and achieve
a 'new kind of city' within a meaningful space of time. We have also
noted in the private sector the increasing expertise of the developers,
whose pet architects had by now made a smooth skill of manipulating
the planning authorities' parameters, the mass production of building
components (particularly curtain-walling), their own projections of
profitability, and Madison-Avenue-style presentation imported from
New York. A pincer movement from left and right could be claimed
to be closing in on the 'creative' designer, with his unique concepts
and his faith in the drama of the architectural competition as the
source of new young talent. 'Graph-paper architecture' (so drawn by

21. York, a system-built university

Steinberg in a famous cartoon) loomed ahead. The fight between art and systems was exemplified in the new universities, the plum jobs of the sixties. Sussex (Spence) and East Anglia (Lasdun) were major artworks by personalities referred to as prima donnas by the System Boys. Essex and York were 'cool', the first projected by Kenneth Capon of the Architects Co-Partnership as a growth pattern represented by a lego model, the second represented by Andrew Derbyshire (now third partner in the Matthew/Johnson-Marshall organization) by elegant diagrams like molecular structures and built in the CLASP system.

In fact this was, at this date, a sham fight. System Boys like John Weeks might claim that complete and honest attention to all the functional needs of a building, including the need for flexibility to meet the unforeseen, produced a resultant that was invariably a delight; but we know that if by chance it had not, it would have been scrapped. At the end of the day, how it looked was decisive, and both sides of this intellectual divide shared a common image of the world they were building. It was a world whose visual validity depended – though it went unacknowledged – on two features of the inherited world: great trees and old buildings. Diagrammatic architecture, whether in steel or glass like the Smithsons' celebrated Miesian School at Hunstanton, or in precast concrete wall components and tubular steel beams like York University, needed the eternal elms of the picturesque landscape, and needed old buildings, particularly elaborate Victorian buildings, for reflection in its glass walls. The same was patently true of the prima donna buildings in Oxford and Cambridge. And both sides saw the emergent city in similar terms. Down at the level of movement, it was to be a complex spatial 'experience' much influenced by the work of Gordon Cullen in the *Architectural Review* (but never as pretty as his drawings) and with much reliance on the right kind of commercial graphics as a substitute for architectural decoration, artfully populist, vacuumed, air-conditioned, musak-conditioned. And poised above this three-dimensional carpet, so transparently that they were almost a part of the sky, would be the glass towers. For the first time since the Victorians lost their grip on civic architecture over a century ago, this was a way forward on which both parties could agree.

If the answer in the argument between the Art Boys and the System Boys was that we needed them both, the same could be said of the concurrent argument between the Garden City Boys and the Urban Renewal Boys. In that same year of 1960 SPUR, the young Society for the Promotion of Urban Renewal, issued its first annual report. This was, in its own words, 'a group of professional workers and others who care about the condition of our towns'. Without proclaiming the fact, it had come together to resist pressures from the Garden Cities Association, recently renamed the Town and Country Planning Association, for the further dispersal of London and the other major cities. Its fear was that all the youngest and best were being drained out of the city, and its remedy was to deal with growth and reduce traffic congestion not by further green-field building but by spreading the load more evenly within the conurbations themselves – more office building in the loose outer suburbs, more housing in the inner core; the mechanism for this would be the now highly successful Development Corporation, and the slogan 'New Towns within Cities'. This 1960 report makes interesting reading in the light of what later happened.[19] As a statement of the consensus, it can hardly be bettered, and as the sixties taught their inescapable lessons, all of it in due course became official policy. SPUR itself, after the usual over-designed exhibition and four years of hard thinking, sensibly dissolved itself. Like MARS, its members were too busy to go on, and anyway the words Urban Renewal had by 1963 been appropriated by the developers and were no longer in radical currency, except satirically.

The decline in the quality of the public service due to the loss of many of its leaders in mid career went unnoticed until the late sixties, for two reasons. Firstly, the worker beneficiaries of the social services had not yet outgrown the traditional instinct to tell the boss what he wants to hear, of the cottager to tell Lady Bountiful that he's very well thank you, of other ranks to respond with silence to 'any complaints?' A brand-new flat with all mod. cons. was still a novelty, even a miracle; and the media had not yet come on the scene with their nose for disasters and their phone-in programmes. And secondly, local authority planners and architects ever since the war had been shielded by the consensus to a degree that was most striking, particularly to an observer from America where no such consensus existed.[20] Traditionally, politicians in local government saw themselves not as delegates but as governors, their role not to fight for the interests of their constituents but to search for and support the public good. Thus an LCC councillor is quoted as explaining:

One has to put the community first. A compromise approach might work in small units, but the County Council is dealing with matters of such large import that we cannot take the view of compromising with local neighbourhoods.

Party politics were strictly for election time. Thus Herbert Morrison:

Over a wide field both parties have been willing to consider many questions on the facts and on the merits.

If planning was not the reconciliation of conflicting pressures but the imposition of the higher good, the less publicity, the less fuss, the less deference to ill-informed opinions the better. It was strictly a matter of management, and by the mid sixties 'corporate management', by which was meant the formation of a development executive bridging hitherto jealously independent departments, was in vogue in many of the major cities.

Isolating it in this way, it is easy to be unjust to the post-war consensus. The very word looked suspect from the perspective of the seventies. Insecurely resting on 'funny money' and cheap oil, Swinging London by then looked a flash in the pan. Yet it was in material terms an unprecedented leap forward: the move from corner-shop to

22. Civic Trust Award-winning townscape at Norwich

supermarket, bewailed by some, transformed the working-class culture. If one compares photographs of the crowds at the South Bank
Exhibition – cloth caps and thick figures – with the denimed patrons
of the Brunel Centre at Swindon, one can see that the gap between the
architects' stage set and the costumes of the cast had been closed at
last. History will probably record the Beatle Age as a genuinely
creative moment, and British planning and architecture of the years
around 1960 as the most soundly conceived and the most healthily
various in the world.[21] It was admired not on account of its masterpieces, though these existed, but on account of its modesty. More
foreign planners and architects visited Harlow than any other single
project in the world, and it is doubtful whether any other industrial
nation could show infill jobs of the sensitivity that was annually
recorded in the Civic Trust Awards. History will also recognize (for no
one who has read Chadwick and Mayhew, not to mention Mrs Gaskell
and Charles Dickens, could not) that the stinking tenements of Glasgow and the cellars of Liverpool and the back-to-back terraces of Leeds
had to be destroyed, and that this had to be done comprehensively if

23. . . . , and at Lancaster

rebuilding was to be properly and economically planned. Even before the war had done a certain amount of the demolition, this was the central consensus of all. Thus the DIA Yearbook of 1929/30:

Our slums are a disgrace. Everyone has said so for 50 years, every party, every religion, every Society for this and that. Why then do we not demolish them and build healthy flats instead! Amsterdam, Hamburg and Vienna are not afraid of the problem. But in this country we build suburbs . . . too far from work to attract the slum-dwellers.

And Charles Reilly of Liverpool:

A block of new tenements here, another curly suburb there, will not be sufficient. Whole sections of the towns, now decaying and never anything to be proud of, must be destroyed, replanned and rebuilt, or new towns must be started and the old left to rot.

Many of the men of the consensus had indeed become architects and planners because of a decent determination that *this* time the long-awaited restitution for the sufferings of the industrial revolution would be achieved. This time, we would do it.

CHAPTER 2

Collapse

Building and rebuilding cities has always been a pretty brutal business, since new construction is only possible on the ruins of something else. For centuries it never occurred to the constructors that
they were not necessarily improvers. The contemptuous attitude to
the fabric of the old city that marked Le Corbusier's pre-war plan for
Paris and its imitators in other countries was therefore nothing new.
But the technology was, and this had brought with it an overwhelming change of scale, first seen on Manhattan in purely pragmatic,
unplanned form, and acceptable there because it was, after all, an
overwhelming spectacle and the pre-elevator city had been a very dull
one. But around 1960, in that same *annus mirabilis*, there began the
moral revolution which is the subject of this chapter.

England being what it is, there has probably always existed a
resistance movement against physical change, whatever its merits.
But, again characteristically, it was the landscape, not the cities,
that inspired the resistance. Wordsworth passionately defended the
wild landscape against the railway engineers, the most damaging
innovators in history, but nobody defended the cities, either as
environments or as the habitat of humble people. An occasional old
building found a champion, and there was much moaning about
the unstoppable advances of bricks and mortar,[1] but it was not until
William Morris founded the Society for the Protection of Ancient
Buildings in 1877 that an organized and architecturally educated
defence was put up. And it was not until 1935 that the threat to
Carlton House Terrace in London and the loss of Waterloo Bridge
and the Adelphi stung Lord Derwent and Robert Byron into setting
up the Georgian Group as an offshoot of the SPAB. Similarly, it
was the brutal destruction of the Euston propylaeum which led to
the foundation of the Victorian Society by Lady Rosse in 1958
(leaving poor William IV uncovered).[2] All three Societies dealt with
the particular, for architectural myopia had become a national
disease ever since the collapse of urban design a century earlier.
Only very gradually had the new enlightenment pioneered by
Geddes and Mumford penetrated the educated consciousness and
taught it to see the environment as a totality. In this work the
Architectural Review had consistently played the part of eye-opener,

seeking out the quirky and the unfamiliar, discovering born propagandists like Gordon Cullen and Ian Nairn, inventing Townscape, inventing Subtopia. But one should note that the targets of Nairn's special edition *Outrage*, published in 1955, were still spec builders, advertisers, gormless local officials and the general visual squalor of the twentieth-century scene. Architects were still immune. Indeed their leadership was now consistently conservation-ist. (This word, with its scientific affiliations, was more widely acceptable than the earlier 'preservationist'.) The highly cultivated Holford was founder member of the Historic Buildings Council, Basil Spence as RIBA President pioneered the campaign against the visual threat of urban motorways, while at the Institute's Glasgow conference in 1964 the newly published Buchanan Report was hailed not at all as a motorists' charter but as the best hope for the liberation of the hearts of the historic cities from the traffic that was already choking them to death. The proper attitude to old buildings was put like this:

> We must beware of contempt for old buildings just because, like old people, they can be frail, muddled and squalid. That contempt can easily become a sort of architectural fascism. Not all our slums are slums. Piecemeal renewal, each piece in scale with the place, is not necessarily a wrong answer just because it is an old one.[3]

These more sensitive attitudes to urban conservation were greatly reinforced by the rapid extension over these years of the network of local amenity societies. Duncan Sandys, as Minister of Housing and Local Government, had been made aware of the need for a Council for the Protection of Urban England as an eqivalent of the CPRE and, on moving to Defence in 1957, had been able to secure sufficient industrial patronage to set up the Civic Trust. This tiny but effective organization had earned its spurs leading the fight against Jack Cotton's naive project for London's Piccadilly Circus, and had gone on to sponsor, on the model of the pioneer project in Magdalen Street in Norwich, street 'face-lifts' all over the country that cost virtually no public money but did a lot for morale. By the mid sixties the Trust had some 700 affiliated societies of all degrees of size and sophistication. Even the most pin-striped of developers by now found it necessary to bone up on conservation.

Superimposed on this flurry of local and national spare-time activ-ity was the Royal Fine Art Commission. Its only power was to send for the plans of any project of national or major local significance and to comment on them, privately or publicly as might seem most effective

– but generally privately, so that it buried its successes: only its failures were conspicuous. The prestige of its membership had been designed to strike terror into the hearts of greedy developers and philistine councillors and in many localities it still did, and did good. But the proper denial to it of executive powers, and the waning repute of expertise and authority as such, made it vulnerable in more sophisticated circles. And there was the inescapable snag that to cut any ice with developers or their architects the Commission had to include leading figures in the profession, just the people whose own projects were often on the agenda. When it became evident that new and unpopular London landmarks like the tower blocks that now dominated the central royal parks had been pushed through despite its objections; that others had got by because it had failed to visualize some spoiled vista – or had been deceived; and that others had managed to escape notice until too late, the Commission was seen to be a leaky safety-net that would become redundant as planning authorities, which did have the powers, became better equipped to exercise them.

For this to happen, two things were necessary: stronger legal protection for historic buildings and areas, and a better deployment of local government. Between 1947 and 1974 Governments assumed ultimate control over the 230,000 buildings (in England alone) they had by then listed, and repair grants from the Historic Buildings Council were progressively stepped up, though they could never be enough and in many areas local authority grants were almost non-existent. Under Duncan Sandys's Civic Amenities Act of 1967, which introduced Conservation Areas, all buildings in such areas would now require consent for demolition. A strong local authority now had the powers it needed, if it could afford to or chose to exercise them. But few were interested. Few were large enough to be able to employ the essential expertise. By now few indeed were large enough to cope rationally with many of their functions – education, transportation, health, housing – for which it seemed that only a sub-regional authority could be effective. It had become evident that the nettle of local government reform had to be grasped and after some natural reluctance Richard Crossman decided to set about it.

Meanwhile, the consensus about housing, such as it was, had already broken up. One must remember how totally the character of our housing stock had changed in the half-century since the end of World War I. In 1919 council housing was a negligible proportion and owners occupied less than 10 per cent. Virtually the whole of the working class rented its homes from private landlords large and small, with the benefit of the rent controls introduced in the war. A generation and a second war later, despite the efforts of local authorities to build subsidized housing under the Addison Act, and despite the inter-war speculative builders' boom, over 60 per cent of the United Kingdom population still lived in privately rented accommodation. Only in the fifties and sixties, with the disappearance of the phrase 'working class' from official parlance and the assumption by the state of an overall responsibility for the housing scene, had the situation been transformed. Slum clearance and rent controls had ensured that by 1971 only 14 per cent of housing was still privately rented. Just over half the total was now owner-occupied, just under a third rented from housing authorities. It is true that these national statistics concealed considerable regional differences, of which the most noticeable was the persisting poverty and fear of responsibility in Scotland and the north, which held down private ownership far below the national average. But by and large it was the widespread aspiration to a mortgage which now gave tenancy a bad name and amplified public criticism of those who provided it.

Private and public sector landlords were held equally culpable. Of the private, a majority were too hard up or too tied down by the Rent Acts to maintain or improve their property; and a minority, exploiting areas of acute shortage, used strong-arm methods to expel tenants with a view to 'gentrification'. On the public side, the 'numbers game' had backfired on its well-meaning participants. By 1968, when the record of 414,000 completions was achieved, of which 204,000 were built by local authorities, numbers alone had ceased to signify. This was in contrast to the inter-war years. In both periods, after the immediate post-war rush to get some sort of roofs over heads, there had been a public-sector switch to slum clearance, and the private sector had been called in to swell the numbers elsewhere. But in the thirties low interest rates and low building costs had kept the output high right up to the war. By the end of the sixties, in contrast, slum clearance had begun to look like vandalism and the cry was for conservation. It was realized that what had been destroyed this time were not merely slums, but communities.[4] The ex-staff-officers who had managed the operation were made painfully aware that it had not been an operational problem at all, but a social one. When one had thinned out to the New Towns and to suburban extensions most of the growth industries and their skilled young workers, what was left behind? Leaking sheds of evacuated workshops, unskilled workers deprived by the slump of employment, pensioners, single-parent families unqualified for the housing list and black or Asian immigrants. The 'inner city' had become a social problem.

Anyone could see that the repair and/or improvement of old but usable houses was the clue, and in the mid fifties there were still plenty of them. Ever since the 1949 Act improvement grants had been available to landlords; but the Labour Government, intent on its new housing drive, had not promoted them. Not until 1953 did the Minister, by then Harold Macmillan, interest himself in the problems of the privately rented sector. But nothing that he or Duncan Sandys could do by way of de-controlling rents would persuade landlords either to repair or to improve their property. They saw no future in their invidious role and preferred to sell out. Improvement grants went not to the poor old landlords but to the rich young owner-occupiers. The privately rented sector, which for a century had taken care of the poorest and most vulnerable, which had above all provided pads for new arrivals, had collapsed. Homelessness was the inevitable consequence, and squatting became first a bitter necessity and then a life-style. When finally the 1969 Housing Act made it possible for local authorities to tackle the twilight areas comprehensively, the beneficiaries tended to be the better-off families on the housing lists; the poor still slipped through the net.

Conservation was now much more than a mandatory part of the vocabulary of planning officers. The amateur sector had been rejuvenated: it was no longer just old people who liked old buildings. They had become the protégés of the Ecology Movement, another stick for beating up the bourgeoisie, another count in the indictment of the crass materialism of the sixties. Often it was less the old that was loved than the new that was hated. Language became more violent: the Rape of Worcester; the Sack of Bath; the Vandalism of British Rail, of the University of London, of the Church Commissioners, even of the GLC. These previously reputable public bodies with the responsibility for modernizing transportation or education or housing might suppose they could doggedly carry out their statutory functions in the style to which for generations they had become accustomed. They could not. Something new had hit them.

Customarily we attribute to the Paris *événements* of 1968 the triggering of the moral revolution of the seventies for which we have no name. But like all such movements it was a convergence. There was to begin with a soft side and a hard side.[5] The soft side could be described as a reassertion, to a degree perhaps unique in western history, of the female half of human nature. Overt manifestations were Flower Power, unisex dress, 'Make Love not War'. Love extends to all creation, animals and plants, the fruitful earth itself, and to all in need of mothering – the Third World, racial minorities, the homeless, refugees. Space travel, which made it possible to see the beauty of the sapphire and diamond planet in contrast with the drabness of the moon, made it possible also to see the earth itself as our own precious spaceship with its life-support systems under urgent threat. The Club of Rome provided the evidence. The gurus of the soft side were Ivan Illich and Fritz Schumacher, their slogans Alternative Technology and Small is Beautiful, the activist spearheads Oxfam, Shelter and the Claimants' Union. Above all, conservation is itself female-oriented: the girl's instinct is to enfold the fallen fledgling, the boy's to raid the nest. Yet ironically it was Nietzsche who had put the principle in a nutshell in 1883:

> Once, the sin against God was the greatest sin; but God died and those sinners died with him. To sin against the earth is now the most dreadful thing.

The hard side was the aftermath of Vietnam. Extreme alienation among the American young was given definition by Dr Marcuse and exploited by Dr Leary. The first student sit-in had taken place in Sprout Hall, Berkeley, as early as December 1964, and lit a fire that spread across the world. The drug culture provided common ground for both sides and increasingly united them in a single great cry of protest. No aspect of 'late capitalism' was any longer acceptable.

An early casualty was the consensus that had protected town planners ever since they had come into official existence. The utilitarian notion that in a split society such as ours was said to be there could be such a thing as the public interest, the notion that a profession called town-planning could in these circumstances be trained up to and could claim to interpret it – all this was rejected. Planners were now seen as looking after no interest but their own. The conflict theory of urban society precluded the existence of the local community which planners had hitherto seen it as their role to protect and enhance. Belated attempts to create this community by exploiting the Boy Scout idealism of social development officers and to encourage its 'participation' in decision-making, officially sponsored by the Government on the recommendation of the 1969 Skeffington Committee, were written off as patronizing and paternalist. Perhaps the following advertisement for the Architectural Association postgraduate planning course conveys the change of climate as well as anything:

> The course includes urban and regional policy, Marxist economics, the historical and political economy of urbanism (internationally), and imperialism. This course responds to changing student needs. Opportunity exists to study the situation of women, the Welfare State, to take TPI exams and to develop other specific interests individually or collectively, such as involvement in local and other struggles.

In odd alliance with this Marxist polemic was the Old Right. The guru of the Old Right was John Betjeman. In 1931, as a staff writer on the *Architectural Review*, he had been able to go along with modernism as a new kind of Gothic Revival, backtracking no doubt via C. R. Mackintosh to Viollet-le-Duc. But he was no Roundhead, and he was out of sympathy with the austere and anonymous teamwork of even the best Welfare State architects. The worst, typified for him by Borough Surveyors and Planning Officers and symbolized by Col Seifert, were an irresistible target, for he had the unfair advantage of a marvellous sense of fun. Betjeman gathered to himself the overwhelming nostalgia of the English for better days, put it into endearing words, and so exacerbated the disease. Carl Strehlow, the pioneer German anthropologist, in his great work on the Aranada and Loritza aborigines of central Australia, writes:

> Since every feature of the landscape, pertinent or otherwise, is already associated with one or other of these myths, their forefathers have left them not a single unoccupied scene which they could fill with creations of their own imagination. Tradition has effectively stifled creative impulse: they are on the whole uninspired, not so much a primitive as a decadent race.

And so out of the woodwork came all those who had never liked the modern world anyway, and now could say so. It was a circumstance special to England that the intellectual establishment, which had gone some distance with contemporary art, thought it safe to be ignorant and contemptuous of contemporary architecture.[6] Surviving neo-Georgians like Clough Williams-Ellis and Raymond Erith found themselves overnight the heroes of the Young Right – a new generation of architectural historians and journalists[7] who enjoyed throwing at the post-war consensus the epithets it had itself used of the moribund styles of the thirties – and added a few more, the language of controversy having sharpened since those inhibited days.

Criticism from extremists to right and left would not have shaken the social-democratic centre if it had not been unexpectedly and devastatingly taken up from within the liberal consensus itself. This took the form of a barrage from across the Atlantic, starting in 1961. The big guns were Jane Jacobs, Christopher Alexander, Robert Venturi and Oscar Newman,[8] and though they fired from different positions their concentration on the target was impeccable and it is convenient to see it as a single assault. At the heart of it was the rejection of the hierarchical concept of the city, with its centrepiece ringed by subsidiary centres and districts, themselves divided into neighbourhoods each with their own little centres, with segregated industrial zones and open spaces, the whole bound together by a corresponding hierarchy of roads and a separate network for pedestrians. All this the Americans regarded as a travesty of the ways cities are actually used, of the infinite criss-cross of real movement, of the hour-to-hour need for passengers and pedestrians to change roles, of the mysterious interplay of market forces, social and racial groupings, job changes, school choices. And having thus childishly oversimplified the pattern, planners (they said) had set about transforming the city into their simplistic image, stamping with hobnailed boots on the intricate urban ecology. And for what? For 'prim dreams of pure order' that were neither desirable nor affordable – rents, taxes, electricity bills right out of reach. 'There is no place for the likes of us in new construction.' For the first time it was not just the neatly delineated conservation areas we were to steer clear of, but the whole crazy anthill – not just 'good' architecture, but 'bad' as well.

In the new ideology, those parts of cities that to the planner had seemed the worst, the 'grey areas', the run-down multi-purpose semi-

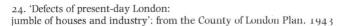

24. 'Defects of present-day London:
jumble of houses and industry': from the County of London Plan, 1943

commercial semi-residential low-rental inner rings, were the most fully humanized. And they were the safest. Those hard-won parks and play spaces whose soft green shapes diversified the geometry of new housing areas were death-traps, patrolled by gangs and addicts. Children rightly preferred to play in the street, and on the street, overlooked by the invisible eyes of residents, all of us were safe. So urban spaces should either be private and inaccessible or thronged with people. As to new architecture, the less of it in its present, off-the-peg, emotionally impoverished state the better: let new building infiltrate casually, cheerfully, unselfconsciously, the cells of the organism replaced as imperceptibly as in nature. If we wanted a model, let it be Las Vegas. The 'horrors' of the honky-tonk American highway, to which the *Architectural Review* had devoted a special *Outrage* number only a decade ago, were now thought a lot more alive than all those controls the English were so smug about.

Groggy from this, English architects were now shaken by a series of apparently unconnected external events. In the first place, post-war buildings began to come to pieces: they blew up, collapsed, leaked, burnt out, had their roofs blown off. The spacious new houses and flats that people could not afford to heat suffered appallingly from condensation. In the high flats, the lifts failed and there was no one on hand to repair them: in the sealed office blocks, the air-conditioning failed or the external cladding fell off. Those who had the courage to employ expensive *avant-garde* designers found themselves at worst ruined or at best embarrassed by experimental technology that went wrong. Those who were forced to employ the cheapest found 'cutting corners' could end in even more spectacular disasters. People began to look back with regret not only at the styles of the old architecture but at its comparatively safe technology. The symbol of collapse was of course Ronan Point (1968), from which moment, in an irresistible wave of unanimity, the nation decided that high flats should cease to be built in England.[9]

Simultaneously, the expensively and so liberally educated new generation for whom all this had been planned turned into 'vandals'. Here the archetype of failure was American – the 14-storey Pruitt-Igoe flats in St Louis, designed by Yamasaki, completed in 1955 in accordance with all the most enlightened and advanced thinking of the day, and given a national award by the American Institute of Architects, but mercilessly and repeatedly vandalized. On 15 July 1972 at 3.32 p.m., the 14 slab blocks were finally dynamited – an event as traumatic as Ronan Point. They were to be the first of many.

Vandalism perforce became a subject of urgent research. Younger liberals decided that it was an unforeseeable product of paternalism: if everything is provided by an invisible hand, by anonymous agencies set up by an educated elite that you have failed to get into, if no creative avenues are open to absorb your own aggression, you will take it out on your surroundings. Older liberals attributed the phenomenon to the decay of the nonconformist conscience, of the work ethic, and of the respect for property that these induced. Reactionaries blamed the general bloodiness of over-indulged youth. All interpretations threw a dark shadow across the Welfare State, which had been so large a part of the philosophy of the modern movement.

If the Vandals were the whipping boys of the Right, the Developers were the public enemies of the Left. Up to a point the attack on them was neither justified nor unanimous. Labour stalwarts on the LCC and elsewhere were sensible enough to remember that the best of London (as well as the worst) had been built by speculators, and this no doubt accounts for, though it cannot excuse, the blind eye that was turned on their easy money in the fifties. For ten years, from the abolition of building licensing in 1954 to the banning of new London office buildings in 1964, Conservative Governments to a degree that was unique in the world failed to exploit this rich source of revenue, or to deal with its abuses. When finally the necessary steps were taken in the mid sixties, 'the horse had bolted and the Government locked the stable door'.[10] Thereafter the seamy side of 'urban renewal' as practised by the property tycoons was conspicuous to all in the form of failed shopping centres, with peeling concrete and rusting steel and offices inhabited only by rats, and in the spectacular collapse of Poulson and his associates. It did not help the reputation of the profession that a City Architect and the head of a large private firm with international commitments were in gaol.

Meanwhile in the larger world the economic climate had utterly changed. In 1973, to the unaffected delight of Schumacher and the conservationists, OPEC quadrupled the price of oil. For some months, until they got used to it, people hesitated before taking the car out. And in the same year the population projections for the end of the century, which in the mid sixties had stood at 66·4 million for England and Wales, dropped back to 52·2 – roughly the forecast of the late fifties. All planning assumptions had once again to be revised. The atmosphere of optimism and the confidence in continuing growth and the assumption of full employment were gone, and with them all the economic forecasts they had given rise to. It seemed that the high-energy glass building must now be out. Alex Gordon's[11] slogan of the 3 Ls (Long Life, Loose Fit, Low Energy) indicated a reaction to the thick-walled, soft-centred, easily converted buildings that the modern movement had long since rejected. And the urban motorway, which in Europe as earlier in America had become the symbol of middle-class privilege, linking rich suburbs with downtown over the heads of the poor, plainly no longer justified its now colossal cost. Radical planners re-emerged to point out that the linear city, the natural expression of public transport, was much more egalitarian than the concentric one with its rings of wealth and poverty. Glamorous projects – TSR 2, Maplin Airport, Channel Tunnel – dropped out one by one. Only Concorde perforce survived as our ticket of entry into Europe. We were back in the threadbare, chastened world of the early fifties, but carrying the new burden of expectations that could no longer be fulfilled.

It was unfortunate that over this psychologically difficult time, when the urgent cry to planners was 'back to the drawing board', all their boards were being moved around in a widely criticized reorganization of local government. The Royal Commission under Sir John Maud, set up in the heyday of Big Government in 1966, and under the powerful influence of Dame Evelyn Sharp, the former Permanent Secretary of the Ministry of Housing and Local Government, had seen the City Region, the city with its rural hinterland or catchment area, as the natural unit of local government in the motor age. It was established to almost universal agreement that such regions, with populations of not less than 250,000 or more than a million, could best fulfil all the functions of local government just as the old county boroughs (on the whole, the most efficient units in the existing system) had done. Except in the case of three massive conurbations, where a London-type two-tier system was inescapable, any second administrative tier (particularly in matters like planning and housing) was firmly rejected. The cities and county towns were seen as the natural capitals of these 58 multi-purpose counties, which (plus the three metropolitan regions) would replace the 1200 miscellaneous units of the past. But when the time for implementation arrived, there had been a change of government, and Peter Walker was persuaded by party grass-roots pressures to revert to two tiers, with the Tory counties firmly on top. Thus, great cities like Bristol and Portsmouth became mere second-tier 'districts' within the counties of Avon and Hampshire, Sheffield was subjected to Barnsley, York to Northallerton, and it became necessary, against all experience, to try to shut off the strategic aspects of planning from its local implementation. The 1968 reforms, which had been predicated on unified planning authorities, now led only to time-consuming and demoralizing argument between the tiers.

In this administrative disarray and moral uncertainty, planners were in no state to resist our island version of the American broadside that descended on them in the later sixties. The protagonists were Reyner Banham, with his recent Californian associations, and Peter Hall, the professor of geography whose expansionist *London 2000*, written at the peak of the boom in 1963, had gone all out for the diffused, highly motorized city region that was rapidly coming to pass in the north-eastern United States. It was already, as we have seen, common practice in London to lament the destruction, now nearing completion, of the slums of the black north. The cry was now to call off the whole exercise, to abandon town and country planning as a failed experiment. This call was to be amplified in later years by the right-wing Institute of Economic Affairs to embrace the whole of the Welfare State in a generalized campaign for a return to market economics. In a special feature in *New Society* in March 1969 these two writers, with Paul Barker and Cedric Price, proposed the designation of whole countrysides of Non-Plan, released into a Texan free-for-all – the same speculators' paradise that was considered so obscene in the city centres. Planners were too demoralized to notice the contradiction.

The most implacable of the new guerrillas were John Tyme and Christopher Booker. Tyme, like some crazed Celtic chieftain resisting Roman centralized planning, conceived and executed the moral sabotage of new highway construction as such and succeeded in reducing the public inquiries that preceded it, which old-time officials took to be a time-consuming but necessary formality, to an unmanageable rough-house, so that it became virtually impossible to get motorways built any more. Booker, a journalist who was said never to speak to an architect if he could avoid it, ran a similar vendetta against high buildings and against their putative progenitor, Le Corbusier, whom he equated with Hitler. Characteristically late in the day, when much of the heat had gone out of the argument, the BBC in 1979 gave him two hours of prime television time, which he used to devastating effect.

There was of course an element of hysteria in all this, for it was all too easy to overdramatize the Rake's Progress of post-war architec-

ture. At the peak of the boom, as we have seen, decent modest building went on and imagination, not merely greed, had its triumphs.
Equally in the trough of the mid seventies, as we shall see, even in the
cities where things seemed to have gone most wrong, good new
buildings went up and worked. If one looks coolly at the critique of
architecture, it amounts to this. In the first place, the antipathy was
sensual. Old buildings had been 'soft': you could knock a nail in
anywhere, hang objects from a beam, replace a broken tile, move a
stud partition. Modest homes had consequently been casual, easily

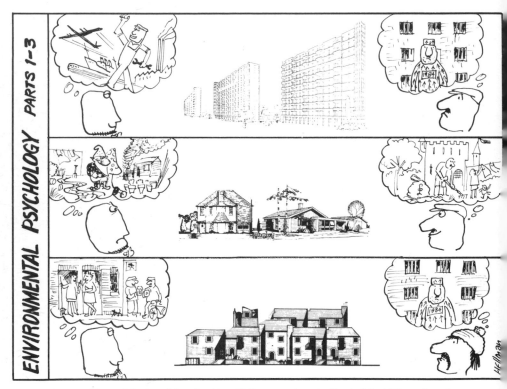

25. The architect and the client in a Hellman cartoon in the *Architects' Journal*, 1980

modifiable to take changes of taste or equipment, and this adaptability
had extended to the whole town and most notably to London, which
it was customary to compare with Paris in this respect. Converted
buildings seemed not only pleasanter but more functional than new
ones. This was of course a renewal of the generalized attack on
Machine Age architecture that had been launched long ago by the
Arts and Crafts movement. But the old targets of the nineties now
seemed cosy alongside the monstrous developers' egg-crates.

The critique then shifted from the architecture to the architects. First, their arrogance. Since its earliest days there had been a contradiction between the philosophical basis of the modern movement (human need plus technology) and the intellectual elitism of its leading figures. Even the unpretentious and humane Maxwell Fry had been moved as a young man to resolve to 'address ourselves only to those capable of understanding us, and let the rest go hang'. Highbrow contempt greeted Basil Spence's rash description of the architect as a tailor whose job was to measure up the fat man and the thin man and suit them both. Much more to the taste of progressive critics was the 'low-down cunning' which James Stirling admitted to using to get an exciting building past an unenlightened client. His History Library at Cambridge (1967), described by Charles Jencks as 'unquestionably the greatest piece of modern architecture now on view in Britain', and its younger twin, the Florey Building at Oxford (1971), were bitterly criticized in academic circles on functional as well as aesthetic grounds, and the 'masterpiece that leaks' became the regular burden of complaint. There was of course plenty of historical precedent, from Vanbrugh to Lutyens (who, when told that rainwater was falling on the dining-table, was said to have advised 'move the table'). And it was claimed by analogy that Grand Prix racing, with all its risks, was necessary to improve the performance of the standard model. The high-tech sci-fi fantasies that emerged from the schools of architecture under the influence of Archigram and the Japanese were seen as good exercise on similar grounds. But in the low mood of the late seventies, the stomach for this kind of adventure, as well as the money, had gone.

The second count of the indictment closely followed the first. It was that architects designed to impress their colleagues more than to please their clients. Again, they always had. But the tendency to speak a private language had been exacerbated by the indifference of the media. Of the two moments when public relations were called for – the unveiling of the project and the completion of the building – architects handled the first much better than the second: they had to. Each personality had his own technique for selling a design. Stirling presented his expressionist architecture in cool neo-classic axonometric, Spence in large and relaxed carbon-pencil and wash scenes that framed up splendidly for the Summer Exhibition, Casson by his witty and suggestive sketches, Lasdun by home-made balsa-wood maquettes that also gave the minimum detail, and the developers' architects by elaborate models that looked terrific from the air. But when the buildings were complete, what seemed to matter most were the photographs in the architectural journals, over which immense pains were taken by specialist photographers. The styles for these changed from strong shadows and black skies to hand-held colour slides with blurred movement, but the readership remained minimal. And when work dried up in the seventies, the new generation retreated into an even more esoteric underground, described by Peter Cook as 'Unbuilt England'[12] and closely related to conceptual art, much of it not merely unbuilt but unbuildable. It had for long been difficult to interest the media in anything but old buildings: *The Times* stubbornly refused to put architecture in its Arts page. Now it was impossible.

Behind these manifestations, and more serious, lay a deep unease among the young about the kind of social climate in which the architect was having to operate. Middle-class parents had encouraged their children to take up architecture in the image of James Spinlove,[13] and these same children had learnt to exchange this for a new image of selfless public service as the trusted doctors of the environment. Now this too seemed to have been mislaid, and architects found themselves cogs in huge impersonal plan factories, whether these were nominally in the public or the private sector. Charles Jencks in his *Language of Post-modern Architecture* (1977) admirably illustrates this totally unforeseen loss of status (*opposite*) as a result of which the very word 'architect', with its grand historical antecedents and still masterly associations, had become devalued. Writing in anger after many years' service in the RIBA, Malcolm McEwen[14] vividly describes the collapse of social idealism into bureaucracy hedged about by Byzantine codes of procedure and brutal cost yardsticks; and he quotes the *Architectural Review* of March 1973 for its physical embodiment in 'badly fitting buildings, grotty concrete steps, cheap twisting aluminium trim, rough precast concrete panels, like giants' breakfast food, thin broken plastic infill panels – the whole unclean and uncleanable, unloved and unlovable, the architecture of greed and carelessness'. In this indictment, the architect is seen not as tyrant but as slave.

To the left of McEwen, an activist cell called the Architects' Revolutionary Council gave birth in 1965 to the New Architecture Movement, a direct attack on middle-class 'professionalism' and specifically on the RIBA itself. As in all such groupings, there was some tension between the Trotskyist wing, for whom the revolution must come first, and the Owenite or Anarchist Community Archi-

		SYSTEM 1 — PRIVATE private client is architect user	SYSTEM 2 — PUBLIC public client and architect users differ	SYSTEM 3 — DEVELOPER developer client and architect users differ
1	ECONOMIC SPHERE	**Mini-Capitalist** (restricted money)	**Welfare-State Capitalist** (lacks money)	**Monopoly-Capitalist** (has money)
2	MOTIVATION	aesthetic inhabit ideological use	solve user's problem housing	make make money money to use
3	RECENT IDEOLOGY	Too various to list	progress, efficiency, large scale, anti-history, Brutalism, etc.	Same as System 2 plus pragmatic
4	RELATION TO PLACE	local client user architect in place	remote users move architects to place	remote and absent changing clients draughtsmen
5	CLIENT'S RELATION TO ARCHITECT	**Expert Friend** same partners small team	**Anonymous Doctor** changing designers large team	**Hired Servant** doesn't know designers or users
6	SIZE OF PROJECTS	"small"	"some large"	"too big"
7	SIZE/TYPE OF ARCHITECT'S OFFICE	small partnership	large centralised	large centralised
8	METHOD OF DESIGN	slow, responsive, innovative, expensive	impersonal, anonymous, conservative, low cost	quick, cheap, and proven formulae
9	ACCOUNTABILITY	to client-user	to local council and bureaucracy	to stockholders, developers and board
10	TYPES OF BUILDING	houses, museums, universities, etc.	housing and infrastructure	shopping centres, hotels, offices, factories, etc.
11	STYLE	multiple	impersonal safe, contemporary, vandal-proofed	pragmatic cliché and bombastic

26. Charles Jencks's 'three systems of architectural production.
The left column shows the implications of the old, private systems of production,
while the right columns show the two modern systems.'

tects, who believed in cooperative enterprise in which designers, craftsmen, apprentices and tenants would sink their identities in self-build housing or rehabilitation. The RIBA sought to neutralize these fissile elements by giving support and money to a Salaried Architects Group to raise the status of the cogs in the plan factories, and to a Community Architecture Working Group to help promote co-operative action in areas of housing stress. Similar motives inspired officially non-political charities like Inter-Action and Shelter, both of which under brilliant leadership were able to raise substantial public and private funds for community arts and activities in the same areas. To all such, bureaucracy was the enemy, and they made no distinction between the capitalist bureaucracies which had destroyed the city centres and the socialist bureaucracies which had destroyed the working-class communities. This made possible a working alliance with the critics of the Right, such as the historian David Watkin who researched the Communist leanings of the pioneers of the modern movement in the thirties, not excluding the hitherto impeccable Nikolaus Pevsner.[15] By 1979 one of the original proponents of the International Style, Philip Johnson, the one-time partner and disciple of Mies van der Rohe, and the epitome of the elegant Bostonian, giving the RIBA's Annual Discourse in Portland Place, could merrily join in the attack and advocate a return to those '57 varieties' of style that Frank Lloyd Wright had so magisterially denounced while speaking in that same place exactly forty years earlier.

It was no answer that these criticisms were self-cancelling, because the evidence was there, on the ground. Few historic cities could not show a street or space ruined in their eyes by the arrogance of highly regarded designers – Brighton sea-front, St Stephen's Street in Norwich, King Street in Bath, Longwall in Oxford, George Square in Edinburgh. And of course London, as we shall see, could show many. In ages of optimism people are blind to this kind of damage. If they were not, nothing of lasting value could be built. But in the nervous breakdown that now afflicted Britain, the adventurous role of the city was required to yield to the protective one. Architects were expected to minister to a nation that had run out of self-love.

It was in the great cities, those cities that were now seen as either the cause or the symptom of a collapsing culture, that their capacity to do this, to play a part unrehearsed by architects since the Middle Ages, was now to be tested.

CHAPTER 3

London

A. The Octopus 1740–1940

John Rocque's great map of 1745, which shows virtually every building in the London region, is as good a launching-pad as any. Even then, at a high point of European planning, there is no discernible pattern. The rebuilt City is still a medieval jumble, and only the squares of Mayfair, which has just reached Park Lane, show signs of civilized order. It is plain that such thrust of growth as exists is east–west – Roman Oxford Street emerging out of the slums of Holborn and supplementing the curving Strand that connects the commercial with the administrative capital. Across the flat fields between Finsbury and the hamlet of Paddington the New Road, the first British by-pass, is nearing completion, eventually to develop into Westway – the first and still the only effective fragment of an inner ring.

Everything else is ribbon development along the Roman radials, supplemented by some improved medieval tracks; new building is mainly for artisans and immigrants in the east, mainly for gentry in the west, nothing much going on in the north, and the south bank only accessible by the picturesque and hopelessly congested London Bridge. Along the northern edge of the old City are its hospitals, madhouses, prisons; south of the river its playhouses, brothels, squatters. Earl's Court and Bethnal Green are still in the country, and of course further out some of the more salubrious villages like Hampstead and Richmond show red-brick gentlemen's houses and an occasional speculator's terrace. Conspicuous in the quiet patchwork of hedged fields are Mr Child's French-style park at Osterley, Lord Burlington's villa at Chiswick and Lord Tylney's Palladian Wanstead, as are the market gardens and weekend cottages of Chelsea and Fulham. Seen from Westminster, the city still looks new, with its red houses, tiled roofs, cobbled streets and white classical porticoes and steeples. Yellow brick was not used externally until the second half of the century; nor were slate roofs.

Rocque's plan was drawn during a pause in development, before the great landowners and the turnpike trusts got busy in the second half of the century. But it is already apparent that, with the sea for its moat and no longer needing its walls, London's relaxed sprawl would bring problems as well as benefits: there was no ready-made *Ringstrasse*, no central imperial axis. Growth was either tentacular or cellular, and wholly uncoordinated. The 'improvements' proposed by Gwynn, and those later achieved by Nash, were cosmetic, not surgical. With the greatest ingenuity, Nash opened up new vistas and improved the settings of older buildings, neatly inserting Regent Street to shut off spacious Mayfair from squalid Soho. But this first north–south axis of more than local significance was blocked by parks at both ends; in this sense Edwardian Kingsway was more useful. The five new bridges built between 1750 and 1820 did, it was true, suggest to the turnpike trusts the fingers of an open hand, with its palm at St George's Circus, and new main roads were laid out accordingly, producing an inevitable bottleneck and difficult triangles to fill in. North of the New Road one or two other new radials were built to take the strain off the Great North Road, but the railways intervened and killed all road building before a viable north-eastern exit had been achieved, and it is still missing.

The Municipal Reform Act of 1835 imposed representative government on all the major cities of England, except London itself, which outside the City was still managed by a medieval patchwork of parish 'vestries', whose powers and duties were defined by no less than 250 separate Acts of Parliament. Over ten thousand self-appointed commissioners tried to make the system work, with only the police and the drains under metropolitan control. Yet when in the fifties a Royal Commission at last examined reform, London was thought to be too big for local democracy, and a Metropolitan Board of Works, manned by delegates from the vestries, was recommended. Duly enacted by Parliament in 1854, the Board gradually accumulated, over the area fortuitously defined by the old Sewage Commission, powers to control building, lay out parks and build roads. But such road improvements as the Board achieved in the thirty-three years of its existence were tactical in character and inadequate in scale – a matter of driving sixty-foot bus routes through slum areas here and there and of lining the new roads with 5-storey workshops and tenements for some of the displaced inhabitants. Victoria Street and Charing Cross Road were typical examples. Alone of European capitals, London failed to provide itself with a system of wide boulevards in the days when the victims still made no sound. So High Victorian London disposed its grand architecture and displayed its imperial role on a framework of communications that was notoriously insufficient. As the eleventh edition of the *Encyclopaedia Britannica* (1911) magisterially put it: 'One of the most serious administrative problems met with in London is that of locomotion ... the police have powers of control over vehicles and exercise them admirably: their work in this respect is a constant source of wonder to foreign visitors. But this control does not meet the problem of actually lessening the number of vehicles in the main arteries of traffic.'

We were of course by then a railway-dominated culture, and nobody could accuse the railway promoters of short-sightedness. On the contrary, their scale of operation was nation-wide, and they charged across London blissfully unaware of the new and unalterable armature they were inserting into the expanding city. This cut the tight patchwork of workers' terraces to ribbons, displacing in the second half of the century some 76,000 people from their homes, generally by deep cuttings to the north and by brick-arched viaducts south of the river. To the north, the New Road provided a natural and correctly recognized location for and link between termini; it would in any case have been politically and financially impossible to invade the superior residential districts to the south of it. To the south, the absence of any such ring road and the centripetal pattern of the radials tempted promoters to make a dash for the centre, thereby destroying Canaletto's image of the Thames for ever and substituting the smoky one that so appealed to Monet. In 1863, when it was decided to build an Inner Circle subway to link all the main line termini, it too inevitably stayed north of the river, and south London remained starved of other than makeshift orbital communications.

The centre was, in the eyes of the world, what mattered, and in the second half of the nineteenth century the scale of its buildings was almost exactly doubled: it was as though a taller species had come on the scene (and indeed Mayfair man was nearly a foot taller than the man in the Mile End Road). 'The conversion of the vast and shapeless city which Dickens knew – fogbound and fever-haunted, brooding over its dark, mysterious river – into the imperial capital, of Whitehall, the Thames Embankment and South Kensington, is the still visible symbol of the mid-Victorian tradition' (John Summerson). It was not to be expected that the undemocratic and possibly corrupt Metropolitan Board of Works could long satisfy this high-minded as well as tall generation. In 1888 a Conservative Government created the London County Council, and in 1899 another at last killed off the vestries and created in their place the twenty-eight London boroughs as a second tier for local matters. The LCC, which many had feared would develop quasi-parliamentary aspirations, indeed did so, became rapidly politicized and came under continuous pressure from the 'gas and water socialism' of the Webbs. Under their influence it rejected the trappings of authority and remained studiously subfusc, disdaining that 'union of modern jobbery and antiquated foppery', as John Stuart Mill had described the City Corporation.

Meanwhile, London continued to be shaped and expanded by the railways, as the main lines began to recognize the vast potential of commuter traffic. The effect that the siting of suburban stations must inevitably have on the settlement patterns of the region (not to mention its land values) took another half-century to penetrate. To begin with, decisions were strictly commercial and competitive, the attractive south and south-west, for example, getting far more attention than the north-east, where development was mainly confined to the cheap ticket-holders whom the companies were obliged by Parliament to provide for as a condition of demolishing East End cottages – though in fact, for the urban poor, the trams turned out better value than the trains, offering in the early 1900s mobility and escape at twice the speed and half the price of horse-drawn vehicles.

Steam-age transport and horse-drawn buses produced fairly widely-spaced and compact suburbs. Electrification and tramlines closed them up, and the motor age filled in the spaces between them. By then, the underground had taken over from the railways the pioneering of the main thrusts into the Home Counties. The first tube railway (an invention necessitated by the absence from London of the great boulevards that made cut-and-cover possible in Paris) at last gave London its east–west transportation spine when the Central Line opened in 1900. By 1919 the Bakerloo had reached Watford, and by the early twenties the Northern Line had reached Edgware. Thereafter the new London Passenger Transport Board, by coordinating its underground and surface services, became by pure chance the prime agent of London regional development.

The inter-war roads achieved nothing of the kind. By-passing historic bottlenecks here and there on cheap backland, they were meanly designed and immediately exploited by house and factory builders and even shopping developers until the Restriction of Ribbon Development Act put a stop to the nonsense in 1935. By then it was too late and it was obvious that the by-passes would have to be by-passed.

Meanwhile, the character of London housing had totally changed. The first comprehensive London Building Act of 1774, which classified terrace housing (like men-of-war) as first-rate down to fourth, had codified the double and characteristically English process of standardization combined with firm class distinctions. It was not until the end of the Victorian era that the semi-detached house (first seen in St John's Wood in the 1820s) and the widespread reaction against the monotony of terrace housing really took hold and the Garden Suburb asserted its ideological supremacy. Flats by then had a bad name, being associated with the grim mid-Victorian tenements put up in slum areas by the Peabody and other charitable trusts. The first (and still unexcelled) LCC 'cottage estates', such as those at Roehampton and White City, were designed under the influence of Unwin and Adshead in the best Hampstead manner and using the best available red brick. The colour of London, it was hoped, would revert to what it was in the days of Queen Anne. The yellow brick and slate of Bloomsbury and Islington, the stucco age inaugurated by Nash, the High Victorian polychromy for which we have to hold Butterfield responsible, and which had lasted from 1850 right through till 1914 despite the efforts of Morris and his followers – none of this was acceptable. By 1914 this London elite had reached a fairly high point of planning awareness and housing expertise, and the effect of the war was to stiffen their determination to get it right. 'You cannot expect,' proclaimed Richard Reiss, one of the pioneers of Welwyn, 'to get an A1 population out of C3 homes.' Yet the inter-war LCC sadly failed to get it right. The challenge of numbers was, as we have seen, not met, despite a feckless sacrifice of miles of first-class farmland. Becontree, for example, which spread across the featureless arable of the Thames flood plain, a so-called cottage estate to which 80,000 people were exiled from the hugger-mugger East End, was a bleak come-down after leafy Roehampton.

In 1940 this was the picture of the thirty-mile-wide conurbation. Islanded in the great sea of semi-detached metroland were the old village centres, now expanded by cheapjack terraces of shops and neo-Georgian banks and pubs. Into this surrounding sea stretched peninsulae of older, prosperous suburbs laid out in the Romantic manner, from smug Wimbledon to high-minded Bedford Park. Thence inwards to the great trapped Victorian capital, already starting to decay around its northern fringes where the tall crumbling terraces in a great arc from Earl's Court round to Islington had now fallen into multi-occupancy – a much sadder scene than the raffish and fogbound East End, long inured to squalor and self-help. Hard by lay the dark square-mile of the City itself, solemnly mid-Victorian in

character, with here and there new white head offices in the more
scholarly Banker's Georgian that had proved at least cheaper than
Edwardian Baroque. The Georgian and still residential West End, on
the other hand, was disintegrating rapidly under commercial
pressures. The myopia which sanctioned the Queen Anne front and
the Mary Ann back still blinded architects to the totality of the urban
scene. With it went a self-interested but still extraordinary insensitiv-
ity to London's historic buildings. Having in the twenties demolished
Nash's Regent Street, the Crown Commissioners planned in the thir-

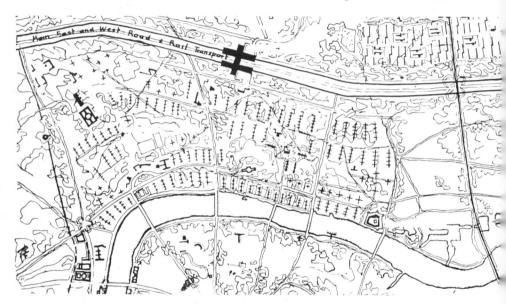

27 and 28. Extremism of the Left and Right. A small section of the MARS project of 1942
showing the rebuilt City. The Royal Academy's bird's-eye view of a new Piccadilly Circus.

ties to replace Carlton House Terrace with a Portland stone façade by Sir Reginald Blomfield. Robert Adam's Adelphi was replaced by a modernistic office building, St Paul's Cathedral obscured by the backside of Unilever House and beyond it by a neo-Georgian telephone exchange. Still worse was the cruel masking of Wren's steeples of St Bride's and St Magnus by the flanks of new office buildings a few feet from them. The building boom in Mayfair and St James's led to the replacement of Adam façades by travesties expanded upwards or sideways, to the domination of Berkeley Square by a moronic ginger-brick office block and to the virtual destruction of Portman Square. In Chelsea and St John's Wood, elephantine blocks of luxury flats were allowed to obliterate whole streets of little houses, all of which would now have been listed. Conversely, the tall stucco terraces of the Church Commissioners' Bayswater estate began to be replaced by 3-storey houses in brick and tile. It was evident that late Georgian and early Victorian London was considered expendable. There was, we must remember, no machinery by which historic buildings (as opposed to earthworks and ruins) could be protected: if you owned one, you could do what you liked with it.

Though they were published in the war, two sensational plans for a new London typified the myopia and schizophrenia of the thirties. The left-wing MARS plan was a futurist fantasy, which virtually destroyed the conurbation and started again. The right-wing Royal Academy plan was a period piece of academic nostalgia incorporating every cliché in the *Beaux Arts* repertoire. Neither had the slightest feel for the complex visual organism that London had become, or for the attitudes of the ten million people who lived or worked in it.

B. The City Region 1940–1970

Fortunately for London, three personalities capable of rising to the situation were now to appear upon the scene. Patrick Abercrombie came from an outstanding generation of Liverpool men. Energy, enthusiasm and intuitive good sense were delightfully combined in him, yet he always had a shy independence of London, retaining only a minimal and rather slapdash organization there: continually on the move and no administrator, he preferred to rely on officials for his research. His successor as Professor of Civic Design, first at Liverpool and then at University College in London, W. G. Holford, more complex, more intellectual, remarkably handsome, committed himself on the other hand totally to the city of his adoption (he had been brought up in South Africa) and had the mental equipment and the historical knowledge that would be needed to think through the intricate problems of its rebuilding. Robert Matthew came of a Scottish architectural family and was in an essential respect complementary to the other two, sharing their sensibility and their charisma but having also the capacity, which they lacked, to manage a great organization and to get his way.

Abercrombie was an Edwardian – a generation older than Holford and Matthew: he had been Professor at Liverpool from as long ago as 1915. So his training was classical, his tastes Arts-and-Crafts. But with his wide culture, his curiosity, his vivid literacy, he was a Renaissance man in the wider sense, and like Mumford he had absorbed first from Patrick Geddes and then from geography and social science colleagues at Liverpool the image of the urban region as the one meaningful receptacle for twentieth-century society – the theatre of modern life. This was the specific Anglo-American contribution to the lore of the modern movement, and it transcended Abercrombie's unregenerate and unsophisticated architectural predilections.

The London of the forties to which they came, a patched-up wreck, was aware that its wartime endurance had become a cliché yet was sustained by the legend through the exceptionally cheerless years of the return to peace. Labour had for long been its 'natural party of government', and the tone of decent if threadbare social democracy had been firmly set by such indigenous figures as Latham, Morrison, Stamp, and Denington. But the impetus behind the *County of London Plan* (published in 1943) came, as such generally did in the worst days of the war, from Reith as Minister of Works, and it was he who proposed to the LCC the appointment of Abercrombie to work in conjunction with Forshaw, their architect, and his staff. While the county plan illogically preceded both the regional plan (1944) and the City of London plan (1946), there were valuable overlaps both of time and personalities between the three. Much of the work on Abercrombie's regional plan was done in Holford's research unit in the Ministry of Town and Country Planning, and the City plan, after an unimaginative attempt by Guildhall officials, was entrusted to Holden and Holford over the same period. It is convenient to look at all three as a single package.

Since the overriding assumption of the forties was 'No Immigration', either of people or jobs, the structural problem of the metropolitan region was simply what to do with the overspill – the Londoners, that is to say, who could not be got back into the old built-up area at contemporary standards of density, of social provision and of open space. To arrive at their numbers one had first to establish the standards, and Abercrombie went at them with a will. Residential density was in any case an obsession of the period. It was something you could get your teeth into: the mathematics were elementary and the flats-versus-houses controversy was familiar and affected everybody, whereas the real determinants of the future – economic forecasting, population projection and the price of urban land – were not within the know-how of town planners, or even, as it turned out, of economists.

Unfortunately, despite its comparative simplicity the planners got it wrong. They realistically set up a scale of density stretching from the city centre to the outer suburbs, but stretched it too far in both directions. In the West End the existence of the Royal Parks was thought to justify a density of 200 persons per acre rising to 300 in small areas, where 'the City clerk, the West End shop assistant and those working in the East End', provided they had small families or none, might be expected to live. In the commuter belt (though the expression contradicted the philosophy of bicycling to work and was never used) it would fall to 30. More critical statistically, and more regrettable in the future, were the next figures inwards. For the whole of central London from Camden Town to Brixton and from Notting Hill to Tower Hamlets the density (where not higher) was set at 136, for the outer suburbs and the New Towns (where not lower) at 50. The former figure, high enough for example to rehouse on site that half of the 200,000 pre-war population of Stepney and Poplar that had hung on through the war, would permit only one third of it to live in houses. But a relaxed view was taken: it was a strong sellers' market and it was anyway clear that most preferred to live within easy reach of their work and families rather than be exiled beyond the Green Belt. But the East End, where not overcrowded, had originally developed at 100 and it was retrogressive to go higher. At the other end of the scale, the suburbs were let off their fair share of the outward movements. (Where their existing density exceeded 75 it was even proposed that they be 'thinned out'.) And the New Towns should have been required to (and later did) exploit their huge infrastructures more intensively.

The planners were at some pains to justify proposals which they well knew would not give inner-London families what they needed –

a proper home. It was claimed (without evidence) that to reduce the figure to 100 would require the decentralization of more industry and business than could reasonably be expected, and Abercrombie pointed out that if you took the region as a whole, 8·5 million could still have houses and only 1·5 million need be in flats. But elsewhere he admitted the converse: that if inner London had been allowed its traditional 100 (with 85 per cent in houses), the overspill from the metropolitan area would have increased only from 1,033,000 to 1,232,750. This surprisingly small difference was due to the fact that large numbers were having to move anyway, not because their old housing was too congested but because their old neighbourhoods nowhere near met the new standards for open space. This was another obsession. The National Playing Fields Association, obviously an interested party, was treated as authoritative in demanding ten acres of parks and playing fields for every thousand people: this would mean that a town of 30,000 people, with a built-up area of 1,000 acres, would need 300 acres of parks and goal posts. In inner London this was a fantasy, and it was scaled down to 4 acres per thousand, but even this meant colouring substantial areas of old housing green, and it was never achieved. The men of the forties, who saw your working man as a Saturday footballer, had not anticipated that the future lay in watching sport, not playing it.

Abercrombie proposed to provide for his million-plus overspill by eight satellite towns each of 60,000 people and by enlarging existing towns in the 'outer country ring' by 260,000, by placing 125,000 (surprisingly) in the Green Belt and by exporting the remaining 260,000 out of the region altogether. His thinking was conditioned by another assumption that was almost an obsession: he thought in 'rings'. Perhaps it was the Green Belt that started it. This high-minded effort by the LCC to contain the growth of London had started with the purchase by the City Corporation of Burnham Beeches in 1880, and other patches all round London had been added under the Green Belt Act of 1938. It was now seen that planning rather than purchase was all that would be needed, but the concept had become sacrosanct. The conurbation was mapped as an annular structure with five rings: the Centre, the Inner Urban, the Surburban, the Green Belt, and the Outer Country. In fact, any diagram of the built-up area in 1945 reveals it to be not annular at all but tentacular – an ink-blot spreading out along its main road and rail radials. Only by chopping off the tentacles could the rings be given credibility. Perhaps unconsciously influenced by Clough Williams-Ellis's successful *England and the Octopus*, Abercrombie could not see any octopus as benign, and gave no consideration (as the Danes were doing for Copenhagen) to fairly high density tentacular growth as a concept that could be as valid as the planet-and-moons concept he adopted and which might have avoided the overloading of the Outer Country belt, particularly in Hertfordshire.

Ring-mindedness equally dominated the thinking about roads. Here too there were pre-determinants. The thirties had seen the beginnings of the North and South Circular roads, and in 1938 the Bressey-Lutyens Report had proposed a complete set of rings and radials. Abercrombie did not look into alternatives – for example the 'bent grid' which was to become fashionable in the Buchanan era – and developed the Bressey structure into a tidy pattern of ten radial motorways and no less than six rings. Between the main motorways were lesser radials, and here trouble was taken not to thread shopping centres or to break up the organic communities of London in whose existence Abercrombie profoundly believed. As for the rings, later to be the subject of infinite acrimony, the innermost (A) passed just east

29. Abercrombie's image of the organic communities of London, 1943

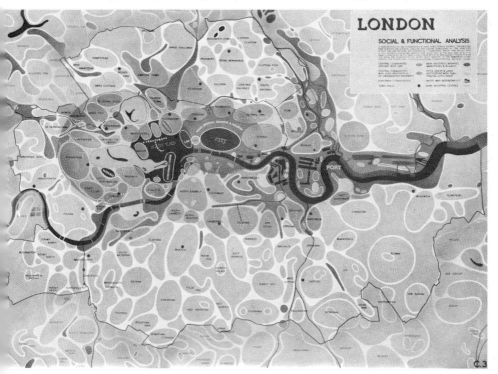

of the City, tunnelled the Thames by Tower Bridge, ran west to Vaux-hall Bridge, cut across Chelsea, tunnelled Hyde Park and then picked up the old New Road of the 1750s past Paddington, Euston and King's Cross. The B ring, north of Regent's Park, south of Brixton and Camberwell, was later to achieve notoriety as the Motorway Box. Then came C, the long-delayed North and South Circulars; D, an orbital motorway roughly fencing in the built-up area that was to remain on the drawing boards until 1970; and finally E, a rural 'parkway' that still survives as the M25. North of London there was even a shadowy F, far out beyond Luton and Bishop's Stortford.

The whole giant spider's web was intuitive and unsupported by traffic surveys or projections, as was inevitable in wartime; and in later years, as such surveys and projections multiplied and contradicted each other, it was to seem none the worse for that. What sank it, or most of it, was not a lack of science but a lack of cash, and in particular a failure to solve the problem of urban land values. Even where strips of property were reserved for it in areas of obsolescence and low values, 'planning blight' was to afflict them almost as cruelly as the road itself. One by one, the reservations had to be abandoned. Later, when the homework could be done and the implications of a scientifically based transportation system for London could be seen, it became apparent that such a system would never be achieved in a participatory democracy, and people looked back with some nostalgia at Abercrombie's comparatively modest four-lane roads and round-abouts. They would have been a lot better than nothing.

Road planning and social thinking combined to favour that master concept of the forties, the residential neighbourhood or its inner-city equivalent, the precinct. These were the bricks out of which the future structure would be built. A New Town would have six neighbour-hoods of 10,000 people; a London suburb such as Islington or Clapham might have ten or more; a historic precinct such as the Inns of Court or the medical enclave around Harley Street could be comparatively tiny – only a few blocks wide. In all cases the reasonable hope was that their protection from through-traffic would secure their identity and hence their architectural character. Yet this organic, even medieval, concept of the city conflicted with the *Beaux Arts* principles and the neo-Georgian vernacular in which Abercrombie, Forshaw, Holden and Holford had all been educated. When the bare bones of the London plans were given flesh in the form of sample layouts and bird's-eye views, the conflict became apparent. The ideas for 'ceremonial London', though less explicit and grandiose than those of the Royal Academy, were in their image, with 'cornice heights' treated as critical, as though all buildings had attics. Forshaw was given his head with the South Bank, an industrial eyesore now to be a cultural and civic showpiece, and proposed a stodgy assemblage of symmetrical edifices confronting Paris-inspired road bridges which, in fulfilment of an old dream, were to replace the Victorians' monstrous railway viaducts. And across the water, Westminster was to become a precinct bounded by new sweeping boulevards, which would involve the destruction of the best pre-Georgian street in London, Queen Anne's Gate. But for the housing areas, both in the East End and in the putative New Towns, a different image was projected. Here Garden City symmetries were abandoned in favour of monotonous rows of parallel flats and terraces on continental *Zeilenbau* lines, no doubt at the instance of the younger members of the team. It was of course a mistake, though a natural one, to propose detailed layouts for such huge areas. Smaller contracts, local accidents and assorted architects would in due course ensure a more human diversity.

It was in the more detailed plans for the square mile of the City that these conflicts of architectural principle were eventually to be resolved. Already in 1943 Allen at the Building Research Station had demonstrated that holding down cornice lines and setting back attics were not the only way to get daylight into city streets, and Crompton in the Ministry had invented a geometry which would achieve equally effective daylighting control with much higher buildings. The uniform corridor street, in other words, had already lost its functional justification. In 1945 the alert *Architectural Review*, aware no doubt that Holden's cornice-height preconceptions were the same as Forshaw's, proposed a new urban aesthetic on Picturesque principles, which would exploit the admirably picturesque ruins of Wren's churches and every accidental glimpse of St Paul's (*overleaf*). Hugh Casson's enticing sketches were featured to show what a jolly mix you could get of glass office blocks, black seventeenth-century stonework and restaurants in what was soon to emerge as the South Bank style. Clearly the serious and horizontal Renaissance city was on the way out. Ten years later Holford, working on the new setting for St Paul's, not without an inner struggle, jettisoned Duncan Sandys's preferred mini-Bernini piazza and bravely proposed an asymmetrical solution which retained the piecemeal exposure of the west front as one ascended Ludgate Hill. But in an unfortunate tactical error he set back the building line on the left before allowing it to break forward again to its original alignment, and so made the last building seem an outrageous intrusion. For this, and for the dullness of the developer's architecture, he suffered severely.

But on the whole, fortune favoured the London plans of the forties. In the explosive sixties they looked obsolete, but by the seventies reduced expectations made them seem about right in scale, and recent

30 and 31. Holford's asymmetrical treatment of the St Paul's precinct (*right*) was a fulfilment of the *Architectural Review's* 'picturesque' proposals of 1946 (*below*)

attempts to systematize and computerize city planning had failed so abysmally that Abercrombie's intuitive methods had come back into fashion. However, it could not be denied that, confined by the context of their time, they were invalidated by two weaknesses: a natural inability to foresee financial constraints and opportunities that would affect London far more profoundly than the work of planners, and a failure to project architectural solutions that would attract the allegiance of the rising generation.

This was now to be the role of a rejuvenated LCC under the architectural leadership of Robert Matthew, soon to be joined as

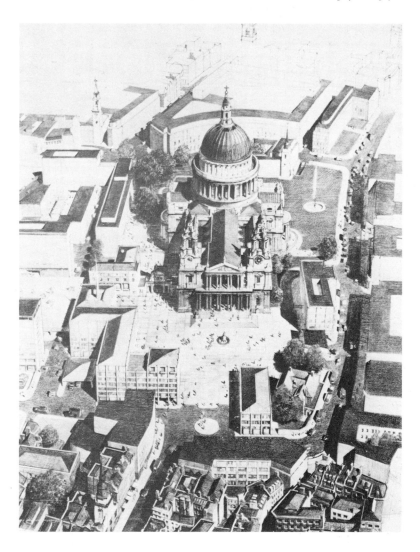

deputy by Leslie Martin, whose high seriousness and *avant-garde* artistic affiliations were in many ways complementary to Matthew's more pragmatic nature. In 1946, on the eve of Matthew's appointment to succeed Forshaw, when roofs-over-heads were the first priority, responsibility for housing was transferred from Forshaw to Walker, the Valuer – an emergency decision that certainly worked in terms of output, which rapidly reached 10,000 dwellings (of a sort) a year. But its architectural first-fruits, revealed at Woodberry Down in 1948, were deplorable, and a campaign against the new set-up was mounted by J. M. Richards. In 1950 the issue came to a head over the first housing project at Putney Heath. Matthew, who admired the half-modern, half-vernacular housing constructed in Stockholm at the end of the war, proposed that Swedish-type 11-storey 'point blocks' be used; Walker remained faithful to the familiar LCC balcony-access slab. The decision, in which Mrs Evelyn Denington played a key part on the Housing Committee, went to Matthew, and with it went the restoration of the Architect's responsibility for housing (he was already responsible for planning). This was the signal for which the young had been waiting. Ex-student militants, veterans of the AA School *événements* of 1938 (when one of them, required to produce the regulation measured drawing of some important building, had chosen to measure up an artisan's dwelling in Fulham), flocked to the colours.[1] Service in a great organization dedicated to the rehousing of the people of London met their political as well as their architectural aspirations.

While the architects got to work on new types of house and flat and maisonette, the planners under the leadership of Arthur Ling had to translate the Abercrombie–Forshaw proposals into the official 1951 LCC Development Plan. In the process 'realism' inevitably made its appearance. The 4 acres of open space per thousand people came down again, to 2·5, and at the same time densities in the central area went up, though it was hoped to compensate later. And the ring roads, under Ministry of Transport pressure, almost disappeared, to be replaced by 'cross routes', which sounded more up-to-date but were in fact mainly improvements of existing roads. For London no longer seemed the *tabula rasa* of a few years back, and people and industries were flooding back into anything habitable. So it was urgent to press on also with the re-planning of the major areas of war damage, of which by far the largest was the 2,000 acres of Stepney and Poplar. In 1949 the energetic Percy Johnson-Marshall, newly arrived from Gibson's wartime team at Coventry, was put in charge, and work went ahead in a spirit of unity and optimism.[2] At the Plan density of 136 p.p.a. it was to house 100,000 people and be divided into a dozen neighbourhoods, and it was decided that the first would be named after George Lansbury and that its first section, together with the Royal Festival Hall, would be the LCC's main contribution to the 1951 Exhibition. Since the point-block issue had not yet been resolved or the new designs approved at County Hall, the assorted flats and houses and the new market-place were mostly done by private architects in the bland and safe domestic style that was to be the hallmark of the early New Towns.

Now that a common front in face of that *bête noire* the Valuer was
no longer required, LCC architects could afford the luxury of argument, and a rift emerged in the housing department that was to cast
a long shadow into the sixties. It could be said to be symbolized,
though it was never explicit, in the different temperaments of Matthew and Martin. Oliver Cox later labelled the two parties the Soft and
the Hard. If cottage Lansbury was the prototype of the Soft, Churchill
Gardens, the great Pimlico riverside housing project won in competition in 1946 by two young architects only just out of the AA.
Powell and Moya, modest and urbane though it now seems, was the

32. Powell and Moya's Churchill Gardens, Pimlico, won in competition in 1946,
is the most successful high-density project in London

prototype of the Hard. No village, but an anglicized Gropian *Zeilenbau*,
it seemed to show that in the right conditions even the 200 p.p.a.
density could be made to work. But the Soft party in the LCC had
sold the point block to the Council on the model of Gibberd's 1951
brick tower at Harlow[3] and went right ahead with them at Alton East,
Roehampton, mixing them with 4-storey maisonettes and conventional red brick and tile houses.[4] The ambience was middle class, with
enclosed and prettily tiled entrance halls to the flats. 'Mixed development' was the watchword of the Soft side, preferably at 100 p.p.a. and
among old trees. Contemporary with Lansbury, in a green oasis just

33. 'Mixed development' by the L C C, using Victorian gardens at Roehampton

off the rackety Stoke Newington Road, Gibberd had admirably and unpretentiously demonstrated how at that density the whole of the East End could have been rebuilt without going above three storeys.

The Hard side could not rest content with what they saw as mean utilitarianism. Suckled on the *Ville Radieuse*, weaned on Le Corbusier's recourse to the sculptural use of concrete, in close touch with the Smithsons' New Brutalism, their concern was less with the assumed desires of consumers, whether they were councillors or residents, than with the totality of London. They knew that it was thus, and only thus, that the great urban images of the past had been realized. Whereas the Soft party had been content (in Cox's words) to humour and persuade, the Hard men were ready to confront and amaze. Lazy English eyes, they believed, could be opened. Inevitably such attitudes alarmed committees, and inevitably too the planners, closer to market realities, were drawn to the Soft side. There was ample evidence to support them, for example the great success with the middle class of the Soft housing designed by Eric Lyons, despite its being at double the density of pre-war equivalents. But by force of conviction the Hard men won.[5] Alton West at Roehampton was the turning-point. Using maisonettes (to save money on lift stops) in great 11-storey slabs, they were able to reproduce the Marseilles *Unité d'Habitation* on a (reduced) English scale and with the benefit of romantically planted English parkland. But this they still saw as a Soft approach. Their vocation was not to exploit rich Victorian gardens but to rebuild the slums, and they believed in higher densities and higher buildings (for which there were obvious economic arguments). As the fifties advanced, the great projects – Loughborough, Brandon, Elmington, Pepys – advanced with them, eastwards across south London into dead-flat Bermondsey and Deptford. A great sight, but to the tenants they meant board-marked concrete instead of coloured tiles in the entrance halls, black bricks instead of red, and, for many, life at high altitude.

The story is easily dramatized, but should not be. For a start, Cox's 'hard' and 'soft' are knowingly tendentious and proclaim the side that he was on. If 200 p.p.a. and even 136 seem high densities, it should be borne in mind that for the civilized Chinese in Hong Kong we were building at 2,000. The development of policy in County Hall was in no sense a revolution but strictly a development, governed by the scale of the need, the scale of the land-take and the economics of building. One should not, in other words, overstress intuitive factors. First, from the mid fifties, with Cleeve Barr in charge of a new Development Group, research into building economics led inescapably to

34 and 35. Corbusian slabs of the Loughborough estate
photographed in 1958 and 1978

tower blocks that were both thicker (six flats per floor instead of the
original three) and higher – not only for maximum economy in the
use of their most expensive component, the lift, but also to clear the
ground for play-space and (increasingly) car-space – not, sadly, for
the romantic greenery imagined by Le Corbusier and achieved at
Roehampton. Secondly, continuous development work was done in
all the components – frame, cladding, windows, internal fittings –
with a growing tendency to resort to proprietary systems: with
builders increasingly attracted to commercial work after 1954, this

36. 26-storey LCC point blocks in Stepney

was the only possible way to get the required productivity. And third-ly, the new housing, both the LCC's own and the central London boroughs', was sensitively monitored by Margaret Willis, the only qualified sociologist so employed. Recording attitudes to high-rise living, to maisonettes, to noise and aspect, to different environments, to play-space, she found (in 1955) that 'the overwhelming majority of families living on the upper floors in 8- to 12-storey blocks of flats like living there in preference to moving lower'. But then, the over-whelming majority still liked what they had, whether they overlooked a noisy bus route or a school playground or lived above a terrace of shops or even alongside a main railway line (provided it was electrified). The young LCC architects were not, as they saw it, designing for elderly Mr Wilkins of Bethnal Green, but for their own generation, capable of seeing the point of a brave new world. Just after a war, the error was pardonable.

As it turned out, the most conspicuous example of the movement from the Soft into the Hard was not in housing at all, but on the South Bank. The whole long bend from Vauxhall Bridge down to Southwark Bridge had been declared a Comprehensive Development Area after the war, and it was seen by all as the test of our capacity to do something splendid in the heart of London. The 1951 Exhibition had demonstrated that Architecture can be Fun, in styles that varied from Machine-Aesthetic to New-Look Rococo, and its sole permanent legacy, the work primarily of Leslie Martin and Peter Moro, was an admirable exemplar of the Soft school. The Royal Festival Hall as we now see it has ironed out some of the more whimsical detail of 1951 and now dates much less cruelly than the adjacent *béton brut* townscape of 1963, whose designers, given too free a hand in line with LCC notions of shop-floor democracy, have remained sensibly anonymous.[6] Who would guess that these gloomy bunkers were built to celebrate the pleasures of the senses? But the saddest failure on the South Bank is the Shell complex. Percy Johnson-Marshall, the LCC

37. The Hayward Gallery on the South Bank, 1963: London's most unloved new building

planner who made the master model in 1953, had recently been in Rio de Janeiro and had 'envisaged that the whole complex would be built in a light, airy and graceful manner ... something that would express frankly the structural techniques of today'. Howard Robertson, the architect for Shell, had recently been in New York and envisaged no such thing, but rather the monumental manner of the Rockefeller Center (but without the height). As a recent RIBA President and current member of the Royal Fine Art Commission, no power on earth could move him. And more ominously, the promoters got away with a higher floor-space-index and taller perimeter blocks than either the LCC planners or the Commission had wished. The property boom was already audible.

If the South Bank was the shop window, the City must be the showroom, and ten years after the last V2s the situation seemed pretty dismal. The LCC, now formally the planning authority, had to defer to an unimaginative City Planning Officer who had already permitted some fast movers to erect, luckily not on sites of major importance, old-hat office buildings of quite incredible ugliness. And south and east of St Paul's, where the Holden/Holford plan rightly tied down the height of new buildings, Holden had established old-fashioned academic guidelines (plinth, string-courses, cornice and so on) which few could believe came from the designer of the pre-war tube stations. Red brick with Portland stone dressings was the recommended costume – a red rag to modernist critics. In a later age, after the total victory of modernism, these few products of the Holden regime were generally seen as 'rather nice' – not least Richardson's *Financial Times* building, in front of which the student Anti-uglies had organized a pioneer 'demo' in 1959. For much bigger beasts were ready to pounce. The Douglas-Home Government had not only neglected to deal with the abuse of the Third Schedule of the 1947 Act. As late as 1963 a White Paper declared that any kind of Government control over the building of offices in central London would be impracticable. The consequent bonanza surely could not last (and indeed one of the first acts of the Wilson Government in 1964 was to introduce, first in London and then more widely, a system of Office Development Permits similar to that which already controlled the location of industry). But while it did, the developers went all out to take advantage of it.

And so the skyline of London was transformed in the years around 1963 by two agencies, the public housing authorities and the commercial developers, neither of whom had made any such impact in the past because all London buildings had been held down to the height (100 ft) that could be reached by the fireman's ladder. With modern construction and amended escape clauses, the Shell tower had been allowed to break this barrier, and the myth that London clay could not carry tall buildings followed it into limbo. Henceforth building economics proposed though the planners disposed, and it became urgent to have a philosophy which the LCC could defend on appeal. Some work was done on this in consultation with the Royal Fine Art Commission, with height contour-lines drawn across the map of London, the general idea being that tall buildings should be encouraged, indeed if possible clustered, at important traffic nodes and alongside major open spaces, and discouraged where they would obtrude upon historic silhouettes. For a variety of reasons, it never worked. Lacking the gridiron plan which, projected into the air, gave American skyscrapers a fortuitous but intelligible relationship with one another, London's tall buildings just heaved up in odd places, and the play-safe economics of British office planning made them too thick for their modest height.[7] And the 'major open spaces' were not necessarily a good location. The curvaceous Millbank Tower on the Thames (1963), designed in the same office as the neo-Georgian Farmers Union building at Hyde Park Corner, was generally thought to provide a good full stop to the upstream prospect from Westminster Bridge; but the Hilton on Park Lane (also 1963), imposed on the shocked LCC and RFAC by a dollar-hungry Cabinet, was a disaster – the first of several that were soon to mark out the boundaries of Hyde Park, in which sheep had grazed as late as the twenties in a landscape that seemed limitless. The garden of Buckingham Palace was now overlooked by the Hilton on one side and by a rather Germanic grey office block on the other. St James's Park was equally oppressed, first by Matthew's New Zealand House (1963), justified to the planners as a closer to Cockspur Street but wholly inappropriate in the classically conceived purlieus of Waterloo Place, and then by the black-topped slab taken over by New Scotland Yard, which exploited the Third Schedule to secure a plot ratio of 1:7 – twice the planned figure for Westminster. It would have cost the LCC £7·5 million to refuse it. This granite-faced hulk was eventually to be satisfactorily masked from the lake by Spence's white stone-roofed Government offices, the last of the encircling Whitehall palaces, elephantine at close range but nothing like as scenically damaging as was foretold by the violent opposition he now habitually encountered.

38. Sir Basil Spence's design for what is now the Home Office,
here seen from St James's Park, was bitterly attacked when it was published in 1972

One must not forget the monster it replaced, a glum stack of late
Victorian flats whose height so offended Queen Victoria and oppressed
the heart of ceremonial London that it led to legislation to control the
height of buildings. In the end the most popular of the West End
towers was neither flats nor offices but a slim glass cylinder housing
telecommunications equipment and topped by a stack of horn aerials
– a piece of pure futurism that would have delighted Sant'Elia, so
abstract and aloof that it did not hurt Regent's Park.

In fact the towers were often less damaging visually than the slabs.
The Commission failed to anticipate the fatal effect on the lacy silhouette of the Palace of Westminster, seen from the South Bank, of the
three austere slabs of the government offices in Marsham Street, or
the destruction by the BBC extension of the vista up Regent Street

of Nash's little steeple of All Souls. In the City, there was much agoniz-
ing in the early fifties over Bucklersbury House, the first major depar-
ture from conventional street-line infill, though by later standards of
size this dull pile, characteristic of its decade, seemed of no significance. Thereafter, except in the immediate vicinity of St Paul's,
stubby skyscrapers became the norm, the first out of the ground being
the curved green glass tower in Drapers' Gardens, put up by the
Centre Point team. The best, and indeed the only towers of the sixties
to approach Chicago or New York standards, were the two in Leadenhall Street, masterminded by Sir Colin Anderson of the old Orient line
and designed by Gollins, Melvin and Ward.

The Great Fire of 1666 had laid waste 437 acres, three quarters of
the City. The fire raid of 26 December 1940 destroyed rather over half
as much, but it was well concentrated north and east of St Paul's,
stretching up into Finsbury, and the LCC planners were determined that the free-for-all that was inevitable in the far less damaged
banking and insurance district to the east should not be allowed to
happen here. Relations with Holford were easy, with Mealand the City
Planning Officer less so, and a foretaste of the inter-authority wrangles that were to become a regular feature of London government
ensued. But eventually the best thinking of the day triumphed in all
four of the areas into which the great expanse divided itself. Holford
himself (who presented his proposals for the Precinct in 1956) had the
most difficult passage because he was working closely under the eye
of a Minister of powerful convictions, Duncan Sandys, whose predilections for a classical solution were, as we have seen, only overcome
with reluctance when they received no support from the series of
aesthetic pundits he privately consulted. This was not the only issue.
Holford, bitten no doubt by the skyscraper bug now rampant, had
rashly proposed a 250-foot office tower to give 'scale and interest' to
his main piazza. Several pundits were shocked by this, and Sandys
was able to cut it down. But further north in the Barbican area,
traditionally the City's back yard, such constraints could be forgotten:
indeed the Corporation had set up an open competition for the
15-acre Golden Lane housing site on the border with Finsbury as
early as 1952, and had had the courage to give the young winners
– Chamberlin, Powell and Bon – their head. The saucy roof sculpture
with which they crowned their central tower block became a subject
of puzzled discussion at City luncheons.

South of Golden Lane the willow herb waved as far as the silhouette
of St Paul's, and no plans existed for the wilderness except that it was

39. The Commercial Union Tower in Leadenhall Street
in an aspect typical of the City

to be bisected by an east–west ring road labelled Route 11. Presumably office buildings would line it on either side. Then in 1954 a group of private architects galvanized the authorities by submitting a wild futurist project called New Barbican. The city fathers now agreed, first, that the LCC planners collaborate with their own on a model for the business sector lining Route 11 and, second (under some pressure from the Minister and the LCC), that 35 acres between this business zone and Golden Lane be reserved for high-density middle-class housing. Cripplegate ward, which had had 14,000 residents in 1851 and in 1951 only 48, would be back to 7,000. Chamberlin, Powell and Bon were to prepare a scheme for the 35 acres. The two zones, business and residential, closely interlocked and laid out on a single axis, emerged (after ten years of argument) quite different in character, deriving from different exemplars in the *œuvre* of Le Corbusier. The business zone was scaled-down *Ville Radieuse*, smooth glass towers evenly spaced and lightly poised on an upper deck bridging London Wall and extensible some day into the eastern recesses of the City. A similar set of towers, at closer spacing, had lately been built in Stockholm, always a respectable precedent. The residential zone had in turn borrowed from the *Ville Radieuse* its grandly scaled *lotissements à redents*, but the architects were also strongly influenced by the later Le Corbusier, the concrete sculptor. The two great squares were capped with barrel-vaulted aedicules and overlooked by three triangular 43-storey monoliths that would be the tallest flats in Europe. There were echoes, too, of Boullée and Ledoux, of the surrealist cityscapes of Chirico and Delvaux. The great pale courts and crescent, the generous public buildings, the wide lawns and pools and terraces, the glass pyramid conservatory, promised a civilized environment on the scale of the Palais Royal or Carlton House Terrace, and unseen since.

For years the beautiful model was all we had: one of the sad features of the Barbican operation was the time it took. The LCC's first model was produced in 1954 and the first glass tower opened in 1960. This was reasonable, and thereafter the business zone rode the boom at a fair pace. But the residential sector lacked that jet propulsion, was riskier and more unorthodox, and when it did get under way it was dogged by mismanagement and consequent labour troubles which were exacerbated because it was thought to be for the rich. Eccentric detailing later led to horrific maintenance costs and lawsuits, the burden of which diverted the City's resources from the completion of their equally arty but better built Guildhall extensions.

40. The Barbican model from the west, with Golden Lane on the left,
the 'Route Eleven' glass blocks on the right

Still, the achievement is there, a credit to the boldness of the City's
notoriously conservative establishment. In the lunch hour, on a blue
and white day of early summer, or in a warm November dusk when
the office lights come on, when shadows or darkness conceal the
stained and cracked precast slabs, heading for a deck-level pub across
London Wall, the spaciousness and the achievement, after the
claustrophobia of the inner City, after all the makeshifts and accidents
along Gresham Street, are exhilarating. But even then there is never
enough traffic below (the intended ring road being corked up at both
ends) and never enough humanity above. The figures that had enlivened the geometry of the architects' perspectives have never
materialized: all we have is the geometry. Spaciousness is mere space
if the crowds don't take to it, and it seems doubtful if they ever will.
The City's deck system got off the ground only because the scale of
post-war reconstruction facilitated it. In the spacious sixties the intention was that it would stretch all the way from the steps of St Paul's
to Liverpool Street and from Golden Lane to the Tower, ramifying en
route. Then it was dragged down into disrepute by the collapse of the
tower-and-podium ideology that had sustained it: the old lanes and
esoteric short-cuts now seemed the far better answer. With the con-

41. The Barbican flats and one of the three towers that overlook
the sixteenth-century church of St Giles, Cripplegate

servationist counter-revolution and the listing of the majority of the City's surviving Victorian buildings, the deck system, which had to be extensive to be effective, became unattainable as well as unwanted, and the planners retreated to a Minimum Walkway Network knitted into the old ground-level alleys. Among the casualties of the change of mind was to be the new Museum of London, designed with their usual competence by Powell and Moya but impossible to find one's way into from street level.

In the residential section of the Barbican the deck system is justified by the massive stacking of cars below the main pedestrian spaces. Perhaps because of this, but also because of its sombre colouring, the effect is hard and severe to the point of oppressiveness. Footsteps echo down interminable perspectives, scary after dark, and the pools and cascades, so pretty on a drawing, feature the usual muck and scum. Views into lower depths are of Stygian gloom; but those up to the immense sculptured towers, which stand uncompromisingly on the elevated pavement, are of Piranesian grandeur. Inside, the flats interlock with delightful ingenuity. It is quite unlike anything else in London, and the fact that, contrary to intentions but not to experience in other capitals, only senior executives and the like can afford to live in it does not seem socially intolerable. It has certainly injected into the City a sophisticated electorate, which one must hope will not only accept with good grace the daily invasion of schoolgirls, tourists, music students, artists, performers and audiences of all sorts, but will also help manage the institutions concerned.

It had become possible by the mid sixties to assess the largest scheme of all, the great 2,000-acre wedge of Stepney–Poplar, which had been started in such high hopes in the early fifties to house 100,000 people of the old East End. Its timing turned out unlucky. The threadbare fifties feebly failed to buy it all while it was cheap, or to set up the kind of inter-authority management team, or better still development corporation, that could have prevented the usual London inter-tier squabbles. So it never came together as a grand concept that could be apprehended, for better or for worse, as a totality. Yet it was largely rebuilt too soon to benefit from the skills in rehabilitation and in the knitting together of old and new that were painfully learnt in the sixties and given legislative sanction in 1969. The ten neighbourhoods Abercrombie had proposed, later increased to twelve, do not register as such, and his great swathes of parkland, deprived of continuity by the usual snags and obstacles, are still bleak and uninviting and often hard to distinguish from the blocks of cleared but unbuilt land, which burst into green life in June but for the rest of the year are intermittently used by fairground operators, totters, drayhorses, transport undertakings and protest groups. Victorian pubs, habitual survivors, stand up here and there shorn of their supporting terraces, together with cut-price community buildings, littered terraces of shops, architect-designed churches, and quite a few unregenerate slum terraces and boarded-up tenements. Thus the casual, hand-to-mouth, scrap culture of the old East End reimposes itself on the dream of a new order. Architecturally the result is a dusty museum of changing ideologies stretching all the way from the sub-Shaw tenements of Boundary Street (1895) via neo-Georgian King's Mead (1938) to the Festival/Swedish of the fifties and thereafter to all the systems of the sixties, culminating in the three mighty and much hated 26-storey monoliths of the Wellington estate in Hackney and the St George's towers that loom up south of Commercial Road. What makes this most extensive of London's post-war environmental failures so gratuitous is that it all began so well. Lansbury's architecture may be bland but its staying power has been proved, now that the trees have grown and the stock bricks have weathered. It feels snug, good to enter, and even the clutch of 11-storey point blocks seem cosy compared with their inflated successors (one of which, called Balfron Tower as though after some Hungarian economist, looms up grimly behind Crisp Street Market). The fringes of Lansbury have succumbed to traditional East End squalor, Gibberd's 1951 pioneer of pedestrian centres is scandalously ill-maintained and unhygienic, but the centre of the neighbourhood, dominated by the fortress-like Catholic church that once seemed so old-fashioned and is now so functional, holds firm. This simple answer of 1950, at the old density of 100 p.p.a., is entirely relevant in 1980, even to its chimneys. But in the whole of the East End, perhaps the pleasantest and best-run housing belongs not to the great socialist authorities but ironically to the Crown Commissioners. Christchurch Square and its environs, just north of Victoria Park, are proof that even in supposedly difficult areas none of the problems of weekly-rented housing are insoluble.

If the new East End, seen as a whole, looks a failure in the terms in which it was conceived, it may not necessarily appear so through the eyes of the eighties. No Bloomsbury, no Pimlico, no Bedford Park, it could yet be a Camden Town – an adaptable, loosely woven old coat which may suit the do-it-yourself culture of the post-industrial age.

42. Lansbury: private enterprise moves in

43. Christchurch Square near Victoria Park in east London

The slow-coach exploitation of the evacuation of the docks was a failure of a different kind, common to London and Liverpool. Unforeseen by Abercrombie, the gradual emergence of this great opportunity of housing large numbers in inner London without unhousing others passed unnoticed in the LCC while it still had the power to call the tune. The Docklands Joint Committee of the GLC and the five riparian boroughs was not set up until 1974 (in a very different climate), and was hardly the ideal vehicle for overtaking a situation in which infrastructure costs (whatever the infrastructure might be, and this was far from settled when the DJC issued its report in 1976) had by then soared to a staggering figure per dwelling. Not until 1979 – to anticipate – did the new Government set up an Urban Development Corporation on the lines recommended by SPUR in 1960, and this inevitably had a hostile reception from all the bogged-down authorities in the area.

By the time the LCC Development Plan came up for review in 1960 it was already apparent that things were not going according to Plan. Political necessities had put housing way ahead of roads as a national priority, so that the great swathes of land purchase similar to those which had unhoused so many thousands a century earlier, and which were the only hope of getting the ring roads even programmed, could never be achieved. And the influx into the region which had so troubled Barlow had started up again, with a population gain in the fifties of over a million, of which one third were new arrivals – the very circumstance that Abercrombie had been briefed to exclude from his calculations. Many of these people had taken jobs in the expanding consumer-durable factories in the western suburbs, in a great number of minor extensions which were either individually not significant enough to engage the attention of the Board of Trade, or were valuable enough in terms of exports to be connived at. Others, perhaps a third of them, had got themselves office jobs over which there was as yet no control at all. Fifty million square feet of post-war office space could take in a lot of people. Most of them occupied brand-new speculative housing in the Home Counties, where the planning authorities had zoned housing land capable of accommodating nearly a million people more than the Abercrombie ultimate target of 11,298,000. Of this huge increment a good half was due to the unforeseen 'baby boom' of the fifties.

There was now, of course, a critical shortage of housing land in the south-east. The Government's *South-East Study* (1964) projected a regional population increase of 3.5 million by 1981,[8] and for the first time the expression New Towns had to be officially amended to New Cities. South Hampshire, West Berkshire (where Newbury seemed a natural crossroads of east–west and north–south traffic routes) and North Buckinghamshire were the preferred locations (of which only the last was to materialize as Milton Keynes). Major expansion was also proposed for Stansted (now facing its first threat as the third London Airport), Ipswich, Peterborough, Ashford, Swindon and Northampton, plus a dozen less dramatic extensions. All this, with a 'limited amount of housing in the Green Belt', would together take a million plus, and more would have to follow. A circular went out to housing authorities urging them to step up residential densities and generally cooperate, a thing which few of the Conservative ones were keen to do. And within the conurbation the search for usable housing land was intensified. Croydon and Hendon airfields were pressed into service, plus surplus railway and other often uninviting public utility land wherever it could be found. But the most spectacular decision was to use 1,300 acres of the windswept Erith marshes on the southern bank of the Thames estuary, an apparently hostile environment of power stations and giant pylons and sewage outfalls, for an aquatic New Town to house 60,000 people. In 1962 a comparatively modest group of square 'Kasbahs' ornamented by pencil-slim towers had been projected for the easier inland stretches of the site and romantically presented by Norah Glover in a group of delicate water-colours that reached a high point of unreality. By 1965 the thinking had become bolder and more comprehensive. The master plan now showed a network of canals and lakes and a hierarchy of roads culminating in the trench down which Ringway 2 would plunge into its tunnel under the river. Three big contractors were invited to offer building systems that would include a factory on the site for the manufacture of the structural components, the competition being won by Cubitts with the Balency precast concrete system. The whole project was then set forth in the other Great Model of the sixties. Protected from the wide-open north exposure by miles of tall curving terraces in a manner later to be brilliantly exemplified on a smaller scale at Newcastle, the white-walled towers and terraces and yacht harbours promised the kind of *douceur de vivre* that the French were busily building, in a rather more auspicious climate, on the coast of Languedoc.

The great asset of the project was that land costs were low – about a tenth of the cost of inner-London sites. On the other hand, infrastructure costs were immense. The marshes consisted of mud and lagoons overlaying deep layers of peat, so the foundations even of low buildings had to be piled sometimes to great depths. Habitable buildings were restricted to a band of good air that started eight-foot six above Newlyn datum (to avoid flooding) and finished a hundred

44. The Thamesmead model, with long walls of flats and central yacht harbour

45. System-built housing at Thamesmead, showing the 'dead' ground storey

and fifty feet above that (to avoid high air-pollution from the power stations). So a 'decked' scheme, with all the disadvantages of a 'dead' ground floor, was mandatory (though with later experience it was abandoned). Moreover, to consolidate the land for surface works, immense quantities of sand dredged from the North Sea had to be laid upon it. So the scheme must be dense and boldly scaled, to reduce unit cost and also, as the architects saw it, to stand up to the vastness of the windswept site.

The Balency housing of the early stages is indeed perhaps the most handsome industrialized project ever achieved in England. The linear blocks are highly sculptural but without brutality, and the towers, after the excesses of inner London, are human in scale. Above the first boating lake a café floats in mid air, and a smart shopping piazza overhangs children's islands. Great steps reminiscent of India descend into the water. The whole layout has a firm rectangularity that helps to orient one on the huge plain. But it failed, as all the systems did, in both economy and speed, and the hope that Thamesmead might.

unlike all the other English New Towns in their elmy pastures, be readable as a totality died with it.

In 1972 the inevitable reappraisal took place. In the first place, the projected average density of 100 p.p.a. was obviously not going to be achieved. Since 35 per cent of housing, occupying over half the housing land, was to be private development at perhaps 40 p.p.a., the density of the rest would be pushed impossibly high. Taking this and other factors into account, the target population dropped from 60,000 to 45,000. Secondly, the pace had to be slowed. Not only were the shells taking longer, but the finishing trades were hard to attract to this inhospitable spot. So instead of 17,000 dwellings in 15 years it would now be 13,000 in 22. (Even this was twice the rate ultimately achieved.) The loss of momentum and the loss of scale were by the end of the decade not viewed too tragically. Smaller contracts had practical advantages, and slower growth had social ones. The GLC's overall output of housing had collapsed so spectacularly that in 1979 Thamesmead's modest 400 per annum was nearly half the total; all the rest (other than the still hypothetical Docklands) was to be phased out. So it was a privileged survivor; but by now of course it consisted of brick-and-tile villages, interlaced by canals, wrapped round old moated islets and thickly planted. The main shopping centre (jealously eyed by neighbouring Woolwich and Bexley) was out for developers' bids, and so was the big marina on which the fun of the place had always been predicated. One had come to accept that a small town does not have to be a work of art.

Through these years of apparent triumph, indeed of triumphalism, the days of the LCC were in fact, as its leaders well knew, numbered. The County of London, unlike the city of Paris, had long been a geographical anomaly, and Harold Macmillan was too astute to lose the chance of reforming this mighty nation within a nation, with its safe Labour majority. The Herbert Commission set up for the purpose in 1958, to which Labour councillors were not invited to give evidence, duly recommended an enlarged County which would take in the Conservative suburbs right out to the inner edge of the Green Belt. To the 28 boroughs (excluding the City) within the old County would be added 24 outside it, with average populations of 100,000 and with increased planning powers. In fact when the London Government Bill reached the Commons in 1963, this unwieldy total of 52 small boroughs was reduced by amalgamation, to loud protests from several, to 32 in line with the larger-scale thinking of the sixties. The new boroughs would now have populations equivalent to sizeable provincial cities like Portsmouth and Newcastle, with ambitions and capacities to match, while the distended GLC, a strategic authority yet not a regional one, would find itself under pressure from both below and above. Politically now evenly balanced, and swinging damagingly from side to side every four years, it would never again have the same prestige or the same freedom to plan with some hope of fulfilment. Nor would it ever again have the same appeal for young architects, particularly since planning was now taken out of the Architect's Department and set up independently under a surveyor-planner who did not command their enthusiasm. It was some consolation that at the eleventh hour the RIBA was able to persuade Sir Keith Joseph, the responsible Minister, to make the appointment of Borough Architects a statutory obligation, and some of them, like Lambeth, Camden and Hillingdon, went ahead and acquired the architectural sophistication that Westminster had always had. Others postponed meeting the obligation as long as they could.

City-region enthusiasts like Peter Hall were bitterly disappointed that Herbert had failed to embody their concept in a regional government, which would in fact have had to deal with one third of the population of England. The trouble was that even this, the new south-east economic planning region, did not cover the magnetic field of London in an age when cheap fuel and motorways encouraged commuters to travel in from Peterborough and Swindon. And anyhow, the Government had briefed Herbert not to get into problems of regional government, which would have nation-wide and, as it later proved, supranational political repercussions. So the GLC was confined within the built-up conurbation, which because of its Green Belt could at last, unlike the old LCC boundary, be regarded as permanent. With the creation of George Brown's short-lived Department of Economic Affairs in 1964, planning responsibility for the south-east devolved upon the new regional Economic Council, under the eye of Whitehall.

The last five years of the old LCC (1960–65) were the heyday of the Architect's Department, when it could fairly claim to be not merely the largest but the best design organization in the world. Leslie Martin had left in 1956, wishing to shed the heavy administrative burden the post increasingly carried, and had been succeeded by the West Riding County Architect, Hubert Bennett, a tough-minded and businesslike man who relished it. The political consensus still held, and Bennett was well equipped to reassure it. And the boom held, at any rate till 1964, when Crossman was at pains to protect housing from the cuts that followed the sterling crisis. The only limiting factors were the capacity of the building industry and the competition of the more profitable private sector, and these, as we have seen, were to be

46 and 47. GLC Towers of the sixties: the Warwick estate in Paddington . . .

increasingly taken care of by prefabrication. The era of the great Corbusian slabs, which had begun in Bentham Road, Hackney, in the early fifties and culminated in Alton West, Roehampton, at the end of that decade, was now over, and the era of the high towers, slimmer, less oppressive, more flexible, and of course more highly subsidized, had begun. In the decade from 1964, 384 of them were built by the GLC alone. There were three main phases. The first, as in the attractive Warwick estate adjacent to Little Venice, merely stood the Corbusian slab of 2-storey maisonettes on its end. The second, of which the Canada estate in Southwark is the archetype, was that of the indented 21-storey towers, notable townscape objects, notorious subjects of alienation and vandalism. The third featured the ingenious but socially disastrous 'scissors' maisonettes, and is best seen on the

and the Canada estate in Bermondsey

Pepys estate at Greenwich, where the three towers go up to 24 storeys. Interleaved were brave experiments in prefabrication, of which those used on the Elgin estate in Paddington and the Watney estate in Stepney, with their lightweight railway-carriage aesthetic, are the most elegant (if far from trouble-free) example. However, none in the event secured the savings either in time or in money that were expected of them.

Analysing the storm that broke over these towers in later years,[9] Kenneth Campbell, who had been in charge of LCC and GLC housing design between 1959 and 1974, attributed it to three 'total weaknesses'. First, the lifts were too slow, too few, too small – all false economies – and were easily put out of action with appalling human consequences. Second, the young couples who moved into the towers

48. Terrace into Tower:
cartoon by John Walters

could not forcibly be moved out of them as soon as they had children, so that a time soon came when 14 per cent of LCC tenants with children were found to be so housed. Third, the mere size of the Director of Housing's organization (particularly after 1965) made management and maintenance disastrously slow to react. The tradition of the concierge did not exist in Britain and it has taken years to build it up. And yet, as he went on to point out, we cannot regard these great projects as a mistaken investment in the long term. The popularity of high flats in the private sector has never been in doubt, and in a country 60 per cent of whose households are without children it cannot possibly be a bad thing that (in 1971) 2·5 per cent of the local authority housing stock (6·4 in London) consisted of high flats. It would emerge in the future that the real social problems of alienation and vandalism were created not by height but by mass (specifically by massed children) – indeed, that by and large the slabs turned out worse than the towers.

At Kidbrooke, in a verdant valley behind Blackheath, two LCC estates separated only by a chain-link fence epitomize the change that had overtaken London in fifteen years. Brooklands Park is a group of brick terraces and a few little 5-storey point blocks standing among immense trees on a lawn that slopes down to a darkly wooded little lake. Across the fence, the Ferriers estate, a classic of the orthogonal precast-concrete era, has the aspect of a major hospital complex, with a hard-to-grasp circulation system and ranges of high-level bridges – an elegant essay in grey geometry. The contrast seems to prove the point that logical aesthetic consistency is no high road to popularity.

Well before Ronan Point, indeed by 1965, the tower blocks had vanished from the drawing boards at County Hall, though the long lead-time of large projects (up to ten years from brief to feedback) ensured that they were still being built at the end of the decade. The reaction towards 'low-rise high-density' was more than a mere rebound from the tower block. For one thing, the generation that had been overwhelmed in its impressionable youth by the squalor and smog and above all by the unutterable dinginess of the slum streets of east and south London, that had seen fresh air and wide views and green spaces as the way out, this pre-war generation was itself on the way out. For the young there was no rationale in 'mixed development' with its ill-assorted building blocks of tower and terrace that could so easily and indeed frivolously be stood on their sides or their ends in pretty patterns. What mattered was the identity and uniqueness of the individual household, symbolized by its own front door, and the tension between privacy and neighbourliness that was the stuff of urban living. The need for new urban patterns to dramatize a revulsion, a revolution, against the old or to symbolize a victory of the powers of light over the powers of darkness was no longer felt. People's houses now seemed the most inappropriate possible components for the making of monumental statements. On the contrary, with the Street making its comeback under the influence of Jane Jacobs, and with the rehabilitation of old houses now increasingly on the agenda, what must now be sought was a reintegration of the urban fabric, an intricate knitting job, and the smaller the pieces the better.

It was now that the London boroughs began to make the running. Hitherto they had rarely had the financial resources or the expertise to assemble sites with the speed and scale the LCC could command. And without in-house architects, they had had to use private firms for design. But from 1965, with smaller projects and larger powers, the boroughs were able to attract good people from the great team at County Hall, until now so remarkably united. The City of

Westminster of course had long since achieved special prestige with Powell and Moya's Churchill Gardens. Now, just round the corner in Vauxhall Bridge Road, another open competition produced another milestone – Darbourne and Darke's intricate, chunky, red-brick complex around Street's solemn church of St James the Less – 218 p.p.a. with nothing above nine storeys. At a price (for prices were rising fast), it seemed that the reign of concrete and the rule of repetition could be ended. Soon Southwark and Lambeth, Wandsworth and Hammersmith, Camden and Haringey, came up with bricky courtyard dwellings close in scale and in texture to the old Victorian tenements, but of course having to use infinitely more ingenuity to accommodate car storage, safe pedestrian passages, sunny balconies, children's play-space and forest trees.

Leslie Martin's research staff at Cambridge had argued that residential densities as high as those required in central London could be achieved by the theoretically elementary expedient of laying four tower blocks on their sides round a rectangle of open space. In 1968, on the Foundling estate in Bloomsbury, this Cambridge team developed the theme further, in combination with the stadium section Martin had earlier used for his Caius College student hostel. This achieved a high density of mixed uses, but in a glaringly hard and austere environment reminiscent of a decade earlier. The stadium section, in the wake of admired figures like Lasdun and Stirling as well as Martin, now became instantly fashionable, even in old towns like Cambridge where its orthogonal severity was cruelly indigestible. In London its most dramatic example is to be found on the northern fringes of St John's Wood – Camden's wildly expensive kilometre-long white concrete 'grandstand', backing on to the long curve of the main line to St Pancras. Early in the thirties the intellectual enclave atop Hampstead Hill had sheltered the first swallows of the modernist spring, and now in its high summer a brave Borough Architect (Sidney Cook) and a radical Planning Officer (Bruno Schlaffenburg) were determined to enlarge the tradition. Talented young architects like Neave Brown and Gordon Benson were engaged and every fragment of unbuilt land, however unpromising, was exploited. But the season was far advanced, and before much was completed the cold winds of inflation had begun to blow. Technical snags and threats of bankruptcy prolonged the agony. By the time they were finished, Camden's smart white council homes were costing upwards of £100,000 apiece to build, including the cost of their often expensive sites.[10] It seemed that soon new housing, like new roads, would be unaffordable.

49. Darbourne and Darke's housing in Vauxhall Bridge Road, won in competition in 1961,
is in red brick to match Street's Victorian church. Shrubs and even trees grow on the balconies

50. Camden's 'grandstand' in St John's Wood, the longest terrace in London

The great thing in the late sixties was to squeeze in as many people as you could as close to the ground as you could get them. This, of course, had been the philosophy of the Victorian slum – too simple an answer. It was soon evident that a total rejection of tower blocks was just as silly as a total commitment to them. High-density low-rise in practice meant mobs of children in echoing bricky courtyards, and mobs meant vandalism, which could be even more dispiriting in the close-up viewpoints of these tight little schemes, where every broken pane was conspicuous, than in the windy spaces of the old 'mixed development'. They became 'hard to let'; i.e. lettable only to the poorest and most disorderly families, who seldom had cars to occupy the now mandatory basement garages, and whose children wrecked the few they had. So these vast black caverns had to be abandoned to rats and refuse and became scenes of Dostoyevskian horror, images of the next war. This happened at all scales, from Wandsworth's bleak York Road estate to Fulham's abortive little deck scheme in Reporton Road, originally intended as a prototype for several acres but wisely abandoned after a couple of tries. By 1980 Lewisham, whose management policies were by then exceptionally enlightened, was in the process of demolishing the concrete car-stacks in its two high-density Deptford estates as part of a humanization programme which it was desperate to protect from the Thatcher cuts.

The lesson of the late sixties was that there is a happy mean, often of density, but always of scale. Few of the boroughs achieved it. Southwark, with an ambitious borough architect and going all out for numbers, signed the biggest single housing contract of all for the giant Aylesbury estate in Peckham – magnificent, but not London. At World's End, Chelsea felt justified in going for the highest density in London (350 p.p.a.) and in order to sell it to the Government ingeniously engaged Eric Lyons, who had made a unique reputation by designing beautifully planted terrace houses for the professional classes on the most delectable sites in south London. Lyons, using a hexagonal grid he had first tried in a cedar-shaded garden in Weybridge, evolved a handsome group of brown brick towers, which would have sold well alongside the East River but has been ill-used by its extremely mixed tenantry and ill-maintained by a council that could afford better. At the other extreme, Merton developed a cool, white, vitreous enamel shell for 3-storey terraces of great elegance, achieving a density of over 100 p.p.a. with generous acres of green space (on which children are sadly forbidden ball games). At Water-meads, Mitcham, in a romantic setting of oaks and cedars and an

51. World's End, by Eric Lyons with Cadbury-Brown

artificial lake, this housing is a last reminder of what the modern movement was all about, and of its affiliations (so strongly urged by Giedion) with the landscape tradition of Georgian Bath. In the end, perhaps the most successful of the inner-London borough projects of the sixties was Battersea's nicely scaled and handsomely landscaped Winstanley Road, designed for them by George, Trew and Dunn. This, given its brief, still seems a civilized answer for the inner city.

Right through the decade, the pressure of population seemed relentless. To many, it was the challenge of vitality. The high point of positivist and optimistic planning was reached in 1967, when the regional Economic Planning Council issued its *Strategy for the South-East*. It was now expected that the 17 million inhabitants of the region would grow, largely by natural increase, to 19 million by 1981. By the end of the century, accepting the assumptions of George Brown's abortive 'National Plan', another 4 million would be added. Within the region, if Greater London was to be held below 8 million, its own natural growth of 1 million would also have to be accommodated. Consequently an area equal to Greater London itself would have to be urbanized, and the *Strategy* signalled the abandonment of the satellite image and the whole-hearted adoption in its stead of the tentacular image fashionable among foreign metropolitan planners. The thickest tentacles were aimed at the proposed new cities of Swindon (via Reading – the Newbury notion had been dropped), Northampton (via Milton Keynes), Peterborough (via Stansted, the Government's 'firm' location for the third airport), Ipswich, Ashford (and on to the Channel Tunnel) and South Hampshire. Thinner ones projected each side of the Thames estuary and via Crawley to Brighton. In addition to the radial highways threading these tentacles, four orbital motorways would need to be completed by 1981 (despite a projected serious shortage of labour). This report devoted a whole chapter to office development, which had grown by another 20 million square feet to nearly 200 million (over half the national total) since it had come under control in 1964. It was hoped that most of it would go to the new cities. So should as much as possible of the region's highly mobile industry. Croydon, which had through local initiative become a major commercial centre, was not thought to be the right answer.

In 1970 there appeared the third regional plan of the decade, the *Structure Plan for the South-East* (SPSE), which was essentially an amplification, with a major input from Whitehall and local officials under the leadership of Wilfred Burns. This was a significantly more professional and therefore more cautious affair. It refused to call itself

52. Classic housing at Watermeads by the Borough of Merton

53. Battersea's Winstanley Road, with maturing landscape

a master plan, more a discussion document, with the main role of providing background material for the statutory county Structure Plans (though the GLC's own was already out). Alternative growth philosophies were proposed and evaluated, and there was an emphasis on flexibility, and a new-born concern for the social problem of the inner city – the ominous words 'multiple deprivation' making a significant appearance. So had an estimated 40,000 'second homes'. The tentacles had disappeared, but the concentration on 'counter-magnets' was still there, the highest priority being given to Southampton/Portsmouth for which the Buchanan team had produced a dauntingly abstract concept. As a result of a great fight by Essex, the problem of the third London airport had now been passed to the Roskill Commission, and since it was expected to generate a new town of between a quarter and half a million this was a major element of uncertainty. So was the size of the voluntary exodus from London, which it was feared might bring its population down to 7 million by the end of the century. That this had become a fear rather than a hope was an early sign that the American urban heart-disease might be on its way.

The GLC's own *Greater London Development Plan* (GLDP) had appeared in 1968, and it too had shown a new tentativeness – and some unresolved dilemmas. Like those of the SPSE, its accompanying diagrams were abstract to the point of impenetrability, perhaps to obfuscate the anti-motorway lobby. Again, the fact that the young and ambitious, and particularly the young families, were voting with their feet against living in London was now the central concern, and more so for the GLC which feared for its rateable values. The dilemma was that in mere physical terms this exodus, which Abercrombie had planned for and the SPSE showed could be accommodated, theoretically provided elbow room for lower densities and the long-sought new parks. But far from sighs of relief, there were cries of pain at the prospect of labour shortages in expanding industries like the over-subsidized hotels now springing up for package tourists, so densities must be held high (in the RIBA view they ought to have been higher still). Pious (unfulfilled) hopes were uttered that the outer boroughs would do their bit by increasing densities in a concerted effort by all the planning and housing authorities in London 'to stanch the outflow'. A manifest gap opened up between the GLC's plan to encourage commercial concentration in six major suburban centres on the Croydon model and the Burns team's desire to draw it away to the new cities on the fringes of the region. As for the motorways, the Abercrombie Rings, now renamed Ringways One, Two and Three – alias the Motorway Box, the North and South Circular and the old C Ring – made their customary bow, but to a new and very different audience. They would cost £2,000 million, it was now thought, take twenty years to build, and unhouse 2,000 people per mile in the very areas where 'housing stress' and the plight of immigrants both black and white were becoming a public scandal. The GLDP was full of unexceptionable sentiments in regard to such social problems, but it was no longer in a position to solve them.

All the same, as the decade ended, the plans were there, the need for such strategies seemed incontrovertible and no sensible person could see how the great City Region, the apex of the Golden Triangle of north-western Europe, could remain prosperous or even livable without them.

C. The Retreat 1970–1980

The turn of the decade fairly closely coincided, as we have seen, with the emergence of what was curiously described (as though it was temporary) as the Environmental Crisis, and its two interwoven strands, conservationism on the one hand and the reaction against high technology and high mobility on the other, are nowhere better illustrated than in London. The two most scandalous demolitions of the post-war years were the destruction of the Euston 'Arch' in 1961 and that of the Coal Exchange in 1962. Both lay in the path of improved transportation and were the work of public authorities; both were the decisions of Conservative Ministers, then notably philistine in such matters. Pevsner characterizes the first as 'villainy', the second as 'stupidity', the first correctly. But the second could only have been saved by slicing off the certainly less interesting (but at the time more highly graded) backside of the Custom House. In fact the Hobson's choice between Custom House and Coal Exchange was a true dilemma, for the road that did the damage was genuinely necessary, since it turned out to be the only east–west by-pass the city would possess in this century. But the 'Arch' could unquestionably have been rebuilt as a grand frontispiece to British Rail's minimally functional new station. The cost, even on Government estimates, was a mere £190,000 and could have been less. This could have been offset ten times over by the profits from office development above the new station, but the GLC, bound by their deal with Joe Levy down the road, refused to agree to what would have been a competing project. With the uninterested Brooke as the responsible Minister and with populist Macmillan (who had downgraded planning by that mere appointment) as Prime Minister, the outraged protests of the artistic establishment were blandly swept aside. Even the demolition contractor was shocked.[1] Because historic London was now so largely Victorian, it was the Victorian Society (rather than the SPAB and the Georgian Group, whose cases were more often outside London) that bore the brunt of the fighting, and its bitterness was directly attributable to the shabby story of these initial disasters.

With the seventies the previously conservative and even aristocratic character of the conservation movement was modified by the arrival of reinforcements in the shape of the New Left. The occasion for this uneasy, but while it lasted far more formidable, alliance was Covent Garden – the name given by planners to the congested district east of the West End and west of the City, bounded by Kingsway, Holborn, Shaftesbury Avenue, Charing Cross Road and the Strand. It had two poles: to the south-east the Inigo Jones piazza and church of the 1630s, the first piece of Renaissance planning in England, and to the north-west the little *étoile* of Seven Dials (1693), a Dickensian relic held in planning blight by the long wait for the removal of Covent Garden Market to Nine Elms. This was now at last to happen in 1972,[2] giving actuality to the problem of what to do with this famous slum and beloved haunt of Dryden, Garrick and Samuel Johnson, birthplace of Turner, and burial place (in the churchyard of St Paul's) of the *literati* and theatre people of two centuries. The GLC's answer was to set up a 'consortium' with Westminster and Camden, advised by a young and highly intelligent joint planning team, which reported in 1968.

There were three main objectives in the official mind. First was the need to clear out a small amount of actual slum and a much larger amount of depressing and now redundant warehousing and office space and some archetypically gloomy Victorian tenements. Second was the opportunity, at a time when such objectives seemed within reach, to improve the heavily trafficked main streets surrounding the area: it even seemed an option to duplicate the Strand along the line of Maiden Lane. The third and most exciting was to wrap round the historic core of Covent Garden an architectural backcloth which would rehouse and augment the indigenous population, together with the theatres, arcades, hotels, boutiques, bars, restaurants, which the old West End now so squalidly accommodated. 'Multiple use' was the prevailing watchword and 'partnership' between the public and private sectors the technique, whereby the profits of the latter would go some (though not all) of the way to carry the burden of the former.

The team's report was a sophisticated and glossy example of the high planning of the late sixties. Careful surveys were set on foot to discover what sort of dwellings the locals wanted, though it never occurred to anyone to ask whether they would prefer to stay where they were, looking out on tarmac courtyards at an indecent density of over 300 p.p.a. The ragbag of tiny industries – violin makers, coppersmiths, theatrical costumiers – the 34 bookshops, 26 stamp dealers and 124 publishers, printers and engravers, not to mention the Opera House and 17 other theatres, all were happily recorded by young clipboard callers who had read Jane Jacobs and knew a rich urban tapestry when they saw one. Urban structure and visual character were analysed after the manner taught by Kevin Lynch and Gordon Cullen, and pedestrian routes and habits and frustrations carefully plotted. All must be protected, none driven out. 'The interdependence of existing activities must be recognized and special care taken to avoid their accidental loss', even if they 'may need special accommodation in terms of design, location and rental levels'. But much more would be added. 'One of the most exciting prospects is the opportunity offered by the removal of the market to cultivate experimental activities and new possibilities in urban living ... small laboratory theatres, new combinations of indoor entertainment, small informal galleries combined with books and the modern equivalent of the old coffee-houses, linked with artists' studios, experimental film units ...' The residential population would increase (from 2,347 to 7,000) as would space for hotels and entertainment, while office and warehousing floor-space would be reduced. Vehicular traffic of all sorts would vanish underground, pedestrians radiating freely in all directions, often under cover, from a 3-acre garden that would replace the grim chasm of the ironically named Floral Street. The whole project, illustrated by expressionist drawings that curiously combined the graphic styles of Munch and Mendelsohn, was uninhibitedly positivist: this would be the new heart of creative London.

The draughtsman was a young Merseyside radical called Brian Anson, whose socio-political interests complemented the systems-analysis slant of Brian Nichols and the architectural background of Geoffrey Holland, the lone survivor who was to endure all the brickbats and become a familiar and respected figure in the back streets of

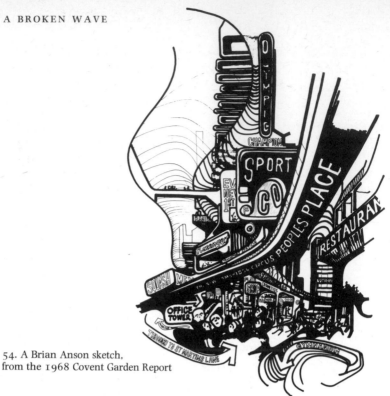

54. A Brian Anson sketch,
from the 1968 Covent Garden Report

the Garden right through to the triumphant opening of the Market building in 1980. But by 1970 the gale of the world, roaring across the Atlantic and the Channel, had blown Anson out of the team. Now a dedicated revolutionary, he made it his business to stir up the hitherto apathetic inhabitants against the intentions, not to mention the ideology, of his colleagues. In the Reverend Austen Williams, Vicar of St Paul's, he found a sympathetic listener, and together these two unfurled the banner of the defenceless poor and old, of the shy craftsman in his low-rent attic or cellar, threatened by the overwhelming might of big business and bureaucracy. London now had its own version of the People's Park in Berkeley, California – a conveniently accessible battleground for AA and LSE students, 'advocacy planners' and assorted activists from all over. In 1971 the Covent Garden Community Association, composed of street representatives democratically elected, met in a mood of high euphoria. Its chairman was Austen Williams. Press coverage from adjacent Fleet Street was lavish: it was the start of the build-up of the Planners as public enemies.

By now the GLC/Camden/Westminster consortium had come apart, splintered by internal political tensions, and the GLC assumed the strategic responsibility (in consultation with the boroughs) which had been specifically reserved for it in the London Government Act. A Covent Garden Committee was set up, and it was thought a good move to appoint as Chairman the elegant Lady Dartmouth, until now the enthusiastic Chairman of the Historic Buildings Committee. It turned out not to be: unpopular policies were not her natural *milieu*. And she was soon at odds with the planners, desiring for example to remove the Victorian glass-and-iron roofs from the Georgian Market building. Her resignation in a blaze of publicity was a further blow to the beleaguered GLC team in their corner shop in King Street. It brought to the side of the left-wing CGCA the powerful support of right-wing aesthetes and liberal conservationists. Against such a background the result of the 1971 public inquiry was predictable: the Secretary of State, Geoffrey Rippon, gave the GLC its compulsory powers over the area, but at the same time listed the great majority of its buildings and decreed that conservation was to be the central object of the operation and that 'full public participation' was to be the technique. We consequently saw in Covent Garden the first thorough-going 'exercise in public participation' (to use the unconsciously cynical phrase that became habitual in planners' jargon) and one of the most successful because of the high motivation of the participating parties. The mechanism for this was the Forum, deliberately not a GLC creation but constituted 'from below' to represent by election all the interests in the area, including the Community Association, whose chairman took charge. The ends of the political spectrum were admirably represented by John Wood on the one hand, the proprietor of Rules Restaurant, and by George Clark on the other, peripatetic militant and squatter leader. From the summer of 1974 this remarkable cross-section of an inner-London community, with its tenement tenants, theatre managers, publicans, craftsmen, property owners and shopkeepers, continued through the years to meet in public every three weeks – long evenings devotedly burnt up by all concerned, including Geoffrey Holland and his team who now had what planners and public architects long for: direct contact with the real client.

While the planners churned out discussion papers, slide shows and questionnaires, and organized even more meticulous house-to-house surveys, the new attitude to Covent Garden took shape – an attitude rather than a plan. It amounted to a change of consciousness. The epithet 'obsolete' was now as indecent for a building as for a person; and within this quite fortuitous square kilometre bounded by six ugly general-purpose streets, the time-honoured notion that knocking down worn-out buildings and replacing them with something better was a useful and often a profitable occupation was ruled out. It was no doubt very English that the decision to mothball a particular group of buildings at a particular moment in their history should be made too late for Portland Place or for Smith Square or for Berkeley Square and should now be accorded to this 'dear old slum', but this was because none of those had been urban villages of the kind that commanded a ferocious loyalty that transcends class, and none had lasted into the age of protest.

Protest is addictive. The Community Association did not last long inside the Forum. Its natural habitat was opposition, and even planners in white sheets were still planners. In a characteristically grumpy commentary on the emergent Plan (*Keep the Elephants out of the Garden*, September 1976) the CGCA complained that the GLC still adopted a too broad-brush approach to rehabilitation, and meticulously added up every semi-derelict tenement or warehouse in which more living space could be found. 'Housing gain' had become an obsession on both sides, despite the incurable deficiencies of schooling and the almost total absence of green space in this congested area. The official target now was to raise the resident population from 2,417 to 5,274 (with 1,000 children under 15). The inflexible CGCA position was the defence of the village against the cultural and tourist invasion. Thus, the GLC's now minimal 1·5-acre central open space 'is not wanted by the people of Covent Garden ... We ask that there be no galleries or studios in the principal shopping streets ... no more museums ... no Conference Centre ... no more hotels, with loud coachloads of singing Germans arriving at 6 a.m.'. Covent Garden must simply 'provide living, shopping and leisure facilities for the people who work in the entertainments industry, rather than tourist attractions ... COVENT GARDEN IS NOT PART OF THE WEST END'.

For their part, the GLC's Covent Garden Committee, chaired through three difficult years by the cheerful and accessible Lord Ponsonby, could not be expected to neglect the unique asset it would have in the rejuvenated Market buildings. The piazza was going to be one of the jolliest things in Europe, whether the locals liked it or not.[3] When the Plan after five years of intensive participation was finally printed in 1978, it was, if not a ridiculous mouse, a nice kitten, affectionately received by all, including the Forum's new (and equally accessible) chairman, Mark Patterson. All the shibboleths of the sixties were swept under the carpet. Density: 'Few residents express

55. The Market building, Covent Garden, 1980

dissatisfaction with their present accommodation on grounds of lack of privacy, shortage of external space, or noise ... Covent Garden residents, in common with those from other parts of the city centre, have a long tradition of urban living and the concept of density is not significant in their conception of a living environment; the value of plot ratios to control building bulk and employment density is limited.' Zoning: 'The Council considers that a mixed-use approach to development control will provide the best possible way of achieving the Plan's total aims ... interpreted as flexibly as possible in order to respect the delicate relationships' etc., etc. Traffic: 'The most heavily trafficked of the through-routes is Monmouth Street/St Martin's Lane which carries 1,100 vehicles per hour through the working day.' (It also carries them charging one-way downhill through a local shopping centre with practically no pavements and through the pedestrian crowds converging on four big theatres, one of them the largest in London.) Architecture: The change of view here is perhaps best shown by the labelling of Basil Spence's and Andrew Renton's Thorn House of

1959, described by Pevsner in his 1973 guide as 'one of the best office buildings of its date in England', as a 'disruptive element'.

Averting the eye from the intractable urban conflicts that had been the stuff of planning – the conflict of motor car versus pedestrian, the conflict of new structures versus old environments, the conflict of high commercial demand versus low-rental socially desirable uses – planning had here become estate management: making the best of what one has got. Geoffrey Holland could claim that he had never had to use compulsory purchase: all renewal sites had been negotiated. Covent Garden and Seven Dials now took their inevitable places as Conservation Areas designated as 'of outstanding status'. Cheek by jowl with other Conservation Areas – Whitehall to the south, Soho to the west, Bloomsbury to the north and the Strand to the east – they were now part of the strange fact that virtually the whole of central London, which had reached its present form through continuous change, was now one big Conservation Area.

The defeat of planning in Covent Garden was not primarily a con-servationist victory, though it was so described in appropriate circles; it was a political one, won by working people under skilled middle-class leadership. Its central theme was that people are more important than architecture. Even the planning establishment was in process of conversion. Thus F. J. C. Amos, President of the Town Planning Institute through the period of the battles in the Garden, could confess in a lecture at the Royal Society of Arts: 'I am not very worried if what we call the geographical inner area becomes a waste of derelict bricks. If we solve the social problem, I am quite happy to let the physical problem either not get solved or take our time over it.'[4]

In that same lecture, Amos admirably analysed the origins of multiple urban deprivation in well-intentioned and at the time un-questioned liberal housing policies – the manifest necessity for comprehensive reconstruction in the post-war decade, the pressure to raise densities so that as many people as possible could stay with their jobs in the inner city, the consequent recourse to high flats and the consequent moves of young families to new jobs and nice houses beyond the Green Belt. What had not been foreseen was that to this increasingly elderly inner-city population, most of them employed in small workshops which were themselves vulnerable to slum clearance, would be added new elements unknown to Abercrombie: the rootless young and the immigrants. As the clearance of the dilapidated terraces of North Kensington round to Islington proceeded, the rooming-house culture, moving continuously ahead of it, was progressively compressed. Even when clearance was abandoned in favour of rehabilitation, the result was less accommodation and higher rents, and the pressures on new arrivals unqualified for the housing lists mounted to the inevitable climax of homelessness. Simultaneously other factors conspired to undermine the physical and social environment. Industrial relocation, properly and expensively embarked upon to improve residential amenities, often ended in the extinction of marginal enterprises, and even those who hung on found themselves increasingly threatened by legislation properly conceived to improve the environment. Increasingly, cleared industrial sites became unlettable. Other sites cleared to accommodate the lavish space-standards for new schools, parks, playing fields and other social services became wastelands when their programmes had to be cut back. Corner shops found they could no longer make a living out of the thinned-out population and closed down. Gallant Asian replacements were vandalized. Police, social workers, teachers, street cleaners, overstretched and disheartened, applied to be posted away. The East-Ender who had told Wilmot and Young in 1957 'I was between two thorns: I didn't want a flat but I didn't want to leave Bethnal Green' in the end was glad he had.

For the social geography of London was in a state of flux. The Victorian 'two nations' of the East End and West End had since World War II redeployed themselves. Now, it could be roughly generalized, the workers lived along the four arms of a hollow cross oriented north–south through the City, with the middle classes in the interstices. Within the cross, 'gentrification' in boroughs like Islington and Lambeth had infiltrated here and there.[5] And even this more complex pattern was not the end of it, for it was pock-marked by the black blobs of the areas of housing stress, many of whose victims were not working class in the old sense at all. Many, of course, were black. The 1971 census showed that over half of the male black unemployed lived in Brixton, Lewisham, Hackney, Willesden, Tottenham and Holloway, where 1,200 out of 12,000 were out of work. Of London's teenage unemployed, one third were black. The pattern of movement had also become more complex, with considerable reverse commuting to suburban offices and industries. In other words, the stereotype of an impoverished 'inner city' and a prosperous suburbia was equally oversimplified. Thus the exodus of a million and a half people from inner London since 1945, far from producing the easement and simplification Abercrombie had anticipated, seemed to have had the reverse effect. For it was the conventional 'families' who had gone, and the old and the single young, the white one-parent households and the big immigrant families who had stayed or arrived – a much more confused minority to which few of the old generalizations applied. The political consensus about housing policy was now unkindly redefined as 'a way of keeping the majority of the community happy ... while the weakest suffer'.[6]

It was over this period of collapsing confidence in our capacity to cope with urban problems that the GLC had to go through the long haul of the Greater London Development Plan. It was to be longer than anyone had imagined. After two years' work the planners were confronted with the White Paper (1967) giving effect to the recommendations of the Government's Planning Advisory Group, under which their role was to produce a 'Structure Plan' only – a socio-economic framework within which the enlarged boroughs were to do the real work of physical planning. This went hard with the GLC, many of whose members and officers had grown up with the old LCC, which had long been the supreme planning authority. Its staff were largely *town* planners,[7] not urban economists or sociologists, and its habit was to run London. Pioneering the interpretation of the word 'structure', the GLC naturally sought to enlarge it while the going was good, so as to assert its traditional supremacy. Consequently, another two years went by while detail that would later be held to be supererogatory was accumulated and all the boroughs (as the 1968 Act required) were brought into consultation. When it finally appeared in 1969, the GLDP was a disappointment. At a time when the *How* of planning was beginning to seem more significant than the *What*, much of the Plan was platitudinous. Thus, whether the rate of decline of London's population was a bad thing as the GLC maintained, or a good thing as the South-East Economic Planning Council believed, there was plainly very little the GLC could do about it. Similarly, the GLC's desire to lower densities in the inner boroughs and raise them in the outer might well be a good thing, but there was no prospect of so persuading the outer boroughs. Most conspicuously of all, the by now traditional spider's web of new roads, with its thirteen radials and three ringways (as they were now renamed), scarcely seemed meaningful if it would cost £3,000,000,000 at 1972 prices and not be completed till the end of the century.

All this and much more was rubbed in with brutal clarity by the marathon public inquiry which the GLDP had next to undergo.

This was conducted by an expert panel presided over by Frank Layfield QC. It occupied almost two years, had to deal with 28,392 objections, and finally reported in 1973, the year of the oil crisis. There was consequently a tendency in Whitehall to treat the whole exercise as a sick joke, which it by no means deserved. For it was in fact a masterly analysis which permanently transformed (as its authors were determined it should) the intellectual standard, and polished the language, of planning discussion. In so doing, it had a good deal of quiet fun, not without a certain legal arrogance, at the expense of the GLC. It rewrote much of the 'Written Statement', refused to accept the Metropolitan Structure Map at all because it was too precise to be 'structural', and so produced not a mere commentary but a substantially better plan. Much of this was agreed by the GLC, which found itself repeatedly and embarrassingly constrained to modify its policies as the monster inquiry proceeded. In particular, the panel had been deeply disturbed by the Milner-Holland Report of 1965, which, with others that followed it, had concentrated on the wretched state of the privately rented sector and on the plight of the homeless. It found the GLDP chapter on housing 'thin and unconvincing', doubted whether the GLC even knew how much it could build by 1981, considered that Green Belt land would need to be used if adequate numbers were to be housed without resorting to what it considered the GLC's excessive densities, and above all recommended that the production and distribution of London housing, as opposed to its management, would never be effective without a 'strategic housing authority' (such as the old LCC had been). This of course meant an authority with the power and the will to force the outer boroughs to accept higher housing densities.

But it was the roads controversy that hit the headlines; it was indeed the road proposals which the GLC blandly considered 'undoubtedly the key features of the Plan'. That 75 per cent of all the objections were to the GLC Primary Road Network confirmed that this was so. These objections were brilliantly 'orchestrated', the anti-motorway lobby now emerging as the formidable force it was to be through the seventies. The arguments were to become familiar: the network would cost as much as Maplin, Concorde and the Channel Tunnel combined; it would destroy upwards of 30,000 houses at a time of severe housing stress; it would break up communities, wreck beautiful scenes, shake and deafen riparian populations, encourage more people to take to their cars, choke the secondary network, and anyway be obsolete long before it could be completed. There was also of course a political aspect. Generally, Conservatives supported the motorist lobby, indeed were said to pour vast sums into it via the Roads Federation with its powerful contracting interests; Labour voters were more dependent on public transport. Parochially, Ringway One ran through the mainly working-class areas of housing stress (indeed the panel made no bones about it: 'Ringway One will assist in the planned redevelopment of some areas of poor housing'; this was one way of putting it). Ringways Two and Three threatened the mainly Conservative outer suburbs. The leading inner-London anti-motorway organization, LATA, led by Douglas Jay whose Battersea constituency lay in the path of Ringway One, was a far more effective force than the scattered pressure groups further out, whose members were torn between self and public interest.

Rising above such considerations, the panel decided that the case for a major primary network was incontrovertible, but that it could not be quite as major as the GLC proposed: it would be too expensive and, more important, would take too long. So two of the Ringways must go, and so must the whole of the in any case unworked-out Secondary Network (a distinction the panel thought meaningless). It opted for Ringway One, the notorious Motorway Box, because this came out better on cost/benefit testing and would do more to relieve central London. Ringway Two through south London must go, though its northern half, the largely existing North Circular, could stay 'because it was there'. So must Ringway Three, its place taken by the orbital M25 outside London. But the panel made a point of putting the motorways last in its sequence of thought. Of the four interlocking and integrated components of a transport policy, the radical improvement of public transport (far more radical than the GLC's vague and anodyne declaration of faith) came first, traffic management and restraint second, measures (admittedly expensive) to safeguard riparian amenities third, it was calculated that these cuts would reduce the capacity of the network by a quarter, its cost by a third. This was immense enough, but we could manage with no less.

Well, we shall have to. While the Department of the Environment brooded over the 1,142 pages of the Layfield Report, and 1973 passed into 1974, and 1974 into 1975, the campaign against the Motorway Box was intensified. The RIBA joined the fray, unearthing an apposite comment from the *Builder* of 1869: 'Any means which could be devised to diminish the vehicular traffic in the City would be more successful than endeavours to accommodate it.' There was time for

LATA to set up a volunteer research group and to commission a book on its findings, and for Stephen Plowden to write another.[8] Both were totally opposed to Ringway One, despite the fact that the Government in an attempt to take the issue out of politics had committed itself to it. But in 1974 the Heath Government collapsed, and it was plain that Ringway One had collapsed with it. The Wilson wage explosion of 1974–5 and 25 per cent inflation settled the issue. When at long last, in the autumn of 1975, Crosland issued his decision letter, while accepting most of the Layfield recommendations, he could comfortably say that 'new primary roads are no longer acceptable to the Greater London Council'.

Five years later, with inner London wracked by Euro-juggernauts, with decent Victorian residential streets like Redcliffe Gardens and Gunter Grove martyred by designation as lorry routes, and even Cheyne Walk scarcely habitable, with no one daring to hurt the London motorist, and with a consequent steady deterioration in the bus service on which all depended, matters did not look so straightforward to a Tory GLC.[9] Westway, the one fragment of an urban motorway that had actually got built, once money had been spent on riparian rehousing, no longer seemed the 'obscenity' it had formerly been labelled, and did not (contrary to expert prognoses) flood its feeder roads with unmanageable traffic queues. It now seemed that to have bought the Motorway Box when it could have been afforded would have been the most civilized of investments. Like the City's abortive Route 11, which had been laid out across the blitzed Barbican on a foolish alignment and then feebly abandoned, it would not have done everything, but it would have done something. But it was no longer an option.

Thus in the seventies planning in inner London became politically impracticable. In the same decade, out in the region, it became technically suspect. The occasion for this was the long saga of the Third London Airport, 'the largest piece of transport investment this country has ever seen'. Here too the last recourse was to an expert panel, in this case a non-statutory Commission chaired by Mr Justice Roskill and set up in February 1968. Essex County Council having (as it thought) won its great fight against the Government's choice of Stansted, the front runners were now a strip of elmy country in mid Buckinghamshire, obliterating among others the village of Cublington, and a remote saltmarsh on the Essex coast off the island of Foulness, of interest to naturalists. When in 1971 the Roskill

Commission's report, which had cost over £1 million in exhaustive computerized cost-benefit analysis, finally appeared, it contained to everyone's embarrassment a Note of Dissent by the best-known personality among its members, Professor Colin Buchanan, which succinctly described his colleagues' choice of Cublington as 'an environmental disaster'. The issue was a simple one. To the majority, 'no single factor can dictate our answer'. Cublington might destroy quiet pastoral landscapes and a Norman church, might overturn the planning of Milton Keynes, but it was cheaper by £86 million, it was operationally preferable, and its comparative proximity to Heathrow would give the latter (and its deafened surrounding populations) far more relief. It must win on points. To Buchanan, after weeks of painful self-examination, the urbanization of the last great tract of peaceful countryside between London and Birmingham was absolutely unacceptable. 'Villages and hamlets, churches and chapels, country houses and cottages, farms, woodland, roads, footpaths and antiquities would all go, as well as the community life gradually developed around these features over centuries'. Scientifically organized analysis which came up with such an answer made a nonsense of science, and must submit to the moral imperative of conservation. Buchanan's authority and eloquence were irresistible; and in yielding to it and so accepting the enormous extra costs of Foulness, the Government paid a tribute to subjectivity which grievously damaged the repute of objective planning, and exemplified, in the words of the Roskill Commission itself, 'a national tendency to forgo economic gains and to prefer other goals'.

Indeed, by the mid seventies the GLC had virtually abandoned its strategic role, and planning in London had ceased to exist in any other than a regulative sense. Public participation must be either a fake or, if taken seriously, a veto on action of any kind, because all action could be blocked by one or other of the powerful lobbies that had now set themselves up to speak for it. The residents' lobby had killed the roads, and now the motorists' lobby killed the only alternative way forward – the control of the private car. In an abject and threadbare set of pamphlets, with pathetically funny pictures, issued in 1975 under the tired title *London is for People*, the GLC spoke like a brainwashed prisoner.

The Council believes that, with the completion of an outer orbital road, London will have a road system which, taken in conjunction with surface and underground railways, will provide an integrated and efficient transportation system, suited to modern-day needs. Within this, wholesale building of new roads and widening of existing roads will not be required ... The reactions and views of Londoners [it proclaimed] are vitally necessary before any decisions can be taken ... Public transport is the cornerstone of the Council's transport strategy ... Should the GLC have powers to control the use of private car-parks in offices and to charge people to drive to congested areas?

The answer from the car lobby was predictable. On another bone of contention, heavy lorries, the pamphlets had announced:

A lorry route system for London would have to make use of existing main roads and divert lorries from less suitable ones. On this basis the Council has been preparing proposals for a network of lorry routes and has sought the views of the London Borough Councils and other bodies. There will be full public discussion before any decisions are taken. If generally acceptable, a lorry network could start to be put into force by the end of 1975.

It was not generally acceptable. On pedestrians and cyclists, the under-privileged so desperately in need of protection:

London can change only slowly and there are great problems to be overcome in improving the environment for pedestrians and cyclists in what will always be a crowded city. Progress cannot be fast ...

The moral collapse of planning under these economic pressures and technical inadequacies was as nothing compared with the moral collapse of modern architecture. This was mainly brought about by a group of able London journalists, often briefed by young architects of the counter-culture. While Nicholas Taylor, who was not only an architectural writer but also Chairman of Lewisham's Housing Committee, eloquently defended the charms of suburbia, Simon Jenkins first in the *Sunday Times* and later as editor of the *Evening Standard* was well placed to lampoon the leaders. When in 1975 a bricky and romantic design by Casson, Conder and Cadbury-Brown for the Royal College of Art was rejected on appeal in favour of some mediocre Victorian houses that existed on its site in Queen's Gate, and a letter in support of the architects appeared in *The Times* signed by Denys Lasdun, Peter Chamberlin, Philip Dowson, Norman Foster, Stephen Gardiner, Frederick Gibberd, Erno Goldfinger, Philip Powell and Richard Sheppard, Jenkins, using the fashionable device of dubbing them 'The Camden Town Nine', commented: 'The architects' rage reflects insecurity on the part of the older generation of modern architects ... these men now see the conservation movement as a threat to their livelihoods ... they are unlikely to find much sympathy either from their clients or from the public'. This was comparatively mild. According to Paul Johnson of the *New Statesman*, 'all sensible and sensitive people know that modern architecture is bad and horrible, almost without exception'.[10] For Roger Scruton in *Encounter*, after references to 'the ravings of Le Corbusier' and 'the gibberish of modernism', 'the ugliness of the Smithsons' project at the Elephant and Castle[11] is not separable from the contemptuous conception of life's value that it conveys'. Conrad Jameson, another journalist, developed a technique of intervention at architectural conferences, and there advocated the abandonment of any attempt by architects to design housing: Georgian pattern-books would be preferable. Even the BBC's sensitive music critic Antony Hopkins felt able to join in: 'Future generations will look back with disgust and disbelief at the architectural heritage we have left them which manages to combine shoddiness and indestructibility in the most depressing manner.' We may take Michael Church, *Times* television critic, to round off this brief anthology. 'If there is one thing on which all Londoners would now agree, it is that the planners and architects who occupied positions of municipal power in the sixties should be put in the stocks, and that when all the available rotten eggs have been thrown they should be made to live out the rest of their miserable lives in the concrete hells they have created.' This was written at a time when British planning and architecture were the most highly regarded in Europe and British architects the most frequent winners of international competitions.

Epicentre of the whole upheaval was the hitherto impeccable GLC itself. Over the years of the wearisome and embarrassing GLDP inquiry the Architect's Department was in even deeper trouble. Again, the attack came from both sides. From the left, as the slump bit more deeply, the NAM and the SAG[12] pressed for unionization and the closed shop. The quiet, liberal Roger Walters, who had taken over from Hubert Bennett in 1971 after a brilliant Whitehall career, found himself the 'grey man' at the head of a vast bureaucracy of administrative officers, buried under which the NCOs – the job architects, the actual designers – found a devastating champion in the *Architects' Journal* cartoonist Louis Hellman, who had himself for a time been one of them. The more concessions Walters made to shop-floor democracy, the more 'red' became the department's image. With the Conservative victory in the 1977 elections the fat was in the fire. In its liberal innocence, the RIBA invited George Tremlett, Chairman of the GLC Housing Committee, to give the keynote address at its 1978 Conference.

The fact that I have made no secret these past twelve years of my disrespect for the architectural profession's work in inner London makes me a surprising guest. I am personally of the view that the architectural profession has debased London in recent years, and in the process has debased itself . . . You more than any other people with your professional training should have known that the high-rise developments and the styles of building that you were getting approved by your councils were almost unspeakable in their ghastliness . . . The architects designed them, and their basements have become haunts for thieves, drunks and dossers. In those developments sit trapped somewhere around 80,000 people, many desperately anxious to escape, imprisoned by municipal vandalism . . . Has it ever occurred to you what horror it must be not to be able to step out of your door at night and gaze at the stars? Has it ever occurred to you how miserable it must be never to hear the song of a bird or the waving of leaves on a tree because there, 20 storeys high, no birds sing and no trees reach . . . YOURS WAS THE HAND THAT SIGNED THE PAPER THAT FELLED A CITY.

Above all else we will not lend our name to any architectural project which is not sympathetic to the environment. We will not build high-rise blocks. We will not build high-density developments. We will not demolish whole communities. We will not permit the GLC architects to carry on doing the things to inner London that we have resisted them doing for so long to outer London. And if that makes us unpopular, and that we clearly are, judging by the outpourings from our Architect's Department, then so be it.

Thus, in her characteristically crude way, Nemesis overtook the Hard men of the fifties. The campaign against the tower block as a symbol of oppression meanwhile continued unabated. Ten years after Ronan Point *The Times* still carried letters such as that from which a few sentences are here extracted:

I live with my wife in a GLC tower block. This is situated at the intersection of two motorways: the Westway and the M41. The noise is sickening, it is impossible to read, think or listen to music. We sleep fitfully and wake with a huge din of traffic in our heads. Our air is contaminated by fumes and lead. These conditions are the result of GLC planning. Our block, which is similar to many others in this area, was consciously planned and built with foreseeable results: *specified*, that is, as uninhabitable. I must confess that the vandalism which is slowly eating away this particular estate elates rather than horrifies us. If to destroy these places is some sort of crime, to have built them is worse . . . Factory farms for psychosis and barbarity.[13]

That the GLC had long ceased building tower flats was no answer: they were there. Nor was it much of an answer that living in an old terrace on an inner-London lorry route or in a new house on the so-called South Circular was as bad or worse: the GLC had been set up to solve the environmental problems of London, not merely to move them about.

Newly arrived in the centre of things, Tremlett must have been aware that it was too late for his speech to be more than a polemical gesture. For what was actually being built in the seventies was not like this at all. In the field of public architecture, this was the decade of the boroughs. There were now, as we have seen, thirty-two of them (excluding the City of London), each the size of a small city. It soon · became customary to think of them in two groups – Group A, the thirteen high-density inner ones where the problems were, and Group B, the sprawling outer suburbs, Betjeman's Metroland, largely built between the wars. Most of the inner boroughs were now elongated wedges, of progressively lower density and lesser stress as they spread outwards to the old LCC boundary where they marched with their new and generally richer neighbours. Of these Lambeth is typical, hanging like a pear from the South Bank opposite Westminster.

Created with all the others in 1899, Lambeth was a mere geographical expression, given the only dignified name available within its boundaries – that of the Archbishop's medieval manor house. Like its neighbours south of the river, Lambeth was nothing but a smoking sea of close-packed slate-roofed houses and workshops, overlooked by the occasional board-school and threaded by long straight roads on which dignified late-Georgian ribbon-development survived, dead flat until at Brixton the long slope starts, and with it, as is customary in south London, a better class of residence. Clapham with its wide common and Streatham with its views had been favourite commuters' villages since the eighteenth century, and on the ridge at Norwood, looking south over Croydon, the borough ends.

It was the second-largest of the metropolitan boroughs, with 155,000 inhabitants in 1939 which doubled when it took over a large slice of Camberwell and a small slice of Wandsworth in 1965.

Ever since the eighteen-nineties, housing authorities of all sorts had been busy in the northern and poorer half of Lambeth. The Prince Consort's model dwellings for the labouring classes had been re-erected in Kennington Park after the Great Exhibition, and close by was the delightful Courtenay Square quarter, designed for the Duchy of Cornwall by Adshead and Ramsey in 1924 and still a model of how Londoners would wish to be housed. From then on the LCC had been building in Lambeth in a big way, with projects of all vintages culminating in the three great Corbusian slabs of the Loughborough estate, now painted white to mitigate their grimness. Yet despite all this effort the new borough's housing survey of 1967 painted a depressing picture. Of nearly 94,000 dwellings containing 121,000 households, 56 per cent dated from before 1914 and 60 per cent were in various stages of decay, including 10 per cent (housing 14,000 households) which were beyond repair. Altogether 40,000 households lacked a separate dwelling.

The borough, which like the rest had hitherto had no architects on its staff, using private firms to turn out a mere 150 flats a year, decided that the annual output of new dwellings from all agencies must now leap to 2,000, with 1,000 from the conversion of larger homes and a further 1,000 from rehabilitation. To head the new Department of Architecture and Planning it appointed a young Londoner who had distinguished himself in the Schools and Housing Divisions of the LCC. Edward Hollamby had grown up in Hammersmith, the locale of William Morris's utopian fantasy *News from Nowhere*, and on qualifying had moved with a friend into Morris's celebrated Red House at Bexley Heath, where he was to live with his large family ever after. Staunch social democrat and conservationist, he was not among the hard men. Indeed, when in the mid fifties Leslie Lane (who had succeeded Ling as Chief Planner) persuaded the old LCC Housing Committee that alongside the great white towers of the Brandon estate in Southwark some terraces of old houses should be rehabilitated, Hollamby had been put in charge of this part of the

56. New and old in Vassall Road, Lambeth

57. Lambeth's pentagonal towers and terraces off Clapham Park Road

contract. So from now on, rehabilitation in Lambeth ceased to denote mere hand-to-mouth repair with an eye to roofs-over-heads and became the careful restoration of listed (or potentially listed) houses with an eye to a richer environment.[14] When this could be combined with the excision of rubbishy buildings, with the neat insertion of new houses and with the replanning and replanting of the surrounding spaces, hard and soft, the result was winningly attractive. The pioneer project in Vassall Road and Cowley Road, which won a Heritage Year award in 1975, was followed by an even more intricate and extensive operation at Clapham Park which produced a delightful mix of the low-rise housing fashions of a hundred years, with a tall board-school and a fine old pub thrown in. We had of course always known, and at Lansbury had demonstrated, that this was the answer all along, and by the mid seventies, by which time the numbers game was over and the high-rise projects had done their necessary brutal work, it became possible to revert to it.

But back in 1965, when Hollamby took over, numbers still looked

58. Wates towers in Lambeth

critical. No local government that came to power in that year could
resist Whitehall pressure for higher output and higher densities, and
there was in any case a strong desire in the inner boroughs to show
County Hall, which for seventy years had had all the powers, all the
expertise, and all the land it could digest, that they meant business
and had the capacity to emulate GLC design skills and scale of
operation. In Lambeth two teams were put to work on the two inevitable answers; towers and slabs. Under Hollamby's influence, both
came out comparatively humanized. The pentagonal towers were of
moderate height, romantically castellated in silhouette so that they
are an ornament to the townscape, and mainly for two-person
families. Only seven of them were built on four sites, and they still look
and let well. And when they had to be supplemented by eight of
Wates's 22-storey brown concrete prefabricated towers, these too
were handsome to look at and have not been difficult to let. The great
'slab' scheme was Stockwell Park. This also was originally to be built
of prefabricated concrete components, but was mercifully changed to

59 and 60. Low-rise Lambeth housing at Tulse Hill and Loughborough Park

yellow stock brick in the aftermath of Ronan Point. Compared to
Southwark's neighbouring Aylesbury estate, which has a continental
insouciance and immensity, Stockwell is comparatively cosy. Of course
the subterranean garage is a write-off – the usual pitch-dark acre of
devastation – but there is no reason why the long decks and landscaped courts should not be recivilized some day when the present
plague of wild and destructive gangs has become a part of history.[15]
In the late seventies the weak and the old have lived in a state of siege,
confined to barracks after dark, their front doors reinforced against
kicking-in, a reproach to our society.

Supposing in all innocence that Ringway One was to take the line
of Loughborough Road, Lambeth duly designed a 'barrier block' to

wall it off on the south, as recommended by Buchanan a decade earlier. Started in the year the Ringways were finally abandoned, it was still building in 1979 – the whitest of elephants – with a brown brick village nestling in its lap. But this was *retardataire*. Elsewhere through the seventies the domestic scale was carefully maintained, sometimes in white brick, sometimes in black, sometimes using old yellow stocks from demolished buildings, sometimes cool and

geometrical like Central Hill on the steep wooded slope at the far end of the borough, sometimes warm and informal like the snug village that lines the west edge of Brockwell Park along Tulse Hill, one of the nicest small schemes in England. The proper modesty of scale of each of these projects should not conceal the fact that cumulatively they were working a beneficent transformation of the atmosphere of south London.

Lambeth had sufficient deprivation, and sufficient enterprise, to claim and secure one of the three Inner Area Studies commissioned by the Department of the Environment in 1972 and published in 1977. Lambeth's was run by Shankland and Cox, who chose Stockwell for their survey area. They found that the main complaints 'were directed against "outsiders"', on grounds of colour or because they were 'rough' or 'problem families' (the survey found that 1 in 40 families could be so regarded). There was also criticism of the behaviour of children and young people, and fear of vandalism and crime. Lambeth, they noted, was short of skilled workers yet flooded out with unskilled ones, trapped in inner London. Clearly many more training schemes were needed, as was a reversal of the post-war decanting of small industries. But the central recommendation, characteristic of the political innocence of architect-planners, was that the unskilled unemployed (a large proportion of whom were 'coloured') should be evacuated into private housing compulsorily acquired in the outer boroughs, and into the Green Belt.

Right up to the end of the decade, and beyond, while the GLC threw in the sponge, Lambeth with so few natural or financial advantages went on doggedly building, repairing, struggling with its rich jigsaw of unstable communities. Of course the grand aims of 1967 were never achieved. In the following six years 4,360 new dwellings were built (one third of the aim), but 7,067 had to be demolished, and many of these had to go not because they were unfit but because they interlocked with those that were. The whole operation made sense only because over the same six years there was a gain of 5,125 from conversions and because the population was fortunately falling fast – from 341,625 in 1961 to a projected 250,000 in 1981. But no sooner did the pressures on the London boroughs appear to have finally eased through the exodus from London, which seemed to justify the Thatcher Government's radical cut-back of subsidized housing, than the cost of mortgages went through the roof and threw large numbers of young people out of the private sector on which everything now depended. Simultaneously, the scrapping of Parker Morris space standards encouraged all concerned to invest in what were quite obviously bad-buy houses. Housing authorities who felt that at last they knew what to do were once again without the means to do it.[16]

The great years of the boroughs as builders, 1965–80, covered exactly the same span of time, fifteen years, as the great years of the LCC that had started in 1950. By 1980 housing had ceased to be the major determinant of the look of London and become a social rather than an architectural activity, picking up the casualties of the urban battlefield – the old, the handicapped, the immigrants, the homeless young – and knitting the little dwellings that met their needs into the great patchwork so that the join was as neat as possible. We were back with the 2-storey cottages from which the adventure had started a century ago.[17] With the Conservative victory of 1979 the huge territories of the housing authorities, to degrees of enthusiasm or obstruction that reflected their political complexion, were in dissolution and their financial resources in decay. In Lambeth an administration described by Labour stalwarts as Trotskyist stripped Hollamby of his power as environmental supremo, setting up a separate planning department under the influence of a Royal Town Planning Institute which had lost most of its architectural element. Politically, all over London things were falling apart.

Not only in the dining-rooms of town halls and the smoking-rooms at Westminster but even within the walls of Conservative County Hall, it was now being freely said that London could do without the GLC, highly unlikely though it was that any Government would take up this gratuitous legislative burden. What could be done was to slim it down, in particular to give away whatever chunks of the great housing empire the boroughs and expanded towns could be cajoled or if possible forced to accept. By 1980 a hundred or so new projects had been stopped and sold off and new housing confined to Thamesmead and Docklands. The thankless task of confronting the redundant planners and architects fell upon the broad shoulders of Frederick Pooley, perhaps the most individual of the County Architects of the sixties, who had left Buckinghamshire in 1974 when his pet project for a New Town built by the County was taken over by Milton Keynes. Appointed Controller of Planning and Transportation, he was prevailed upon to become Architect to the Council as well when Walters resigned in 1977, rather in the spirit in which Mountbatten was sent to Viceroy's House. In February 1979 he went up to Portland Place to say what could be said to reassure the profession. His address, suggestively entitled 'The Ulysses Factor',[18] was a watershed. The watchword was 'opportunity planning' – not concepts, not strategies, not projections into the future; Pooley did not disguise his contempt for all three. But of course 'opportunities' had been the springboard of those who had the power and money to use them ever since London had existed; they were not 'planning', and one did not need the huge apparatus of planning to take advantage of them. In another sleight-of-hand, he offered the ludicrous Dutch word woonerf as a description of what in English practice had hitherto been called General Improvement Area as though it denoted something new, and hoped there would be within ten or fifteen years be a thousand of them in London. The bare cupboard of transportation planning was decked out with £500 million to be spent over fifteen years on the 500 'extraordinarily difficult junctions' in the old road system, presumably by little flyovers and underpasses. But it had to be admitted that the only surviving motorway, the orbital M25, supposing it were to be finished in the foreseeable future, would only take 4 per cent of the traffic out of London. 'Management' and 'restraint' would have to do the rest. The lecture was well received; none of the critics present liked to give a tweak to the Emperor's clothes. And anyway, they were on his side. There seemed no point in arguing over the dead body of planning.

The smoke of battle having cleared, we can finally take a view of the London we now have. Operationally it obviously works no better than it did forty years ago. Movement is no easier, bus queues no shorter, squalor no less (though this last has largely been removed from the private realm into the public). That this is so is the fruit of national policies and preconceptions we have already touched on and will return to. But especially damaging in London was the failure to buy up the land needed for the 1951 road system while this was still possible, as the bomb-damaged provincial cities were able to do. Even in the East End, where the bombing was heaviest, and even for housing, with its much more popular backing, land assembly was patchy from the start, with two disastrous consequences. The first was the temptation to build at too high a density, and too high, on the sites that existed: there was no space to lay the towers flat on their sides. The second was the virtual failure to build primary roads at all while it was still financially and politically practicable – and by this no one now means the whole network, but minimally one *autoroute périphérique* (in London's case probably the North and South Circular) such as Paris and every other continental and even British major conurbation has been able to build. So the shortest way through London for heavy transport is still straight down Piccadilly, and unhappy thousands have to endure the misery of living on makeshift lorry routes. It was a wretched result of Britain's class-conscious two-party system that transportation policies became politicized, with cars as Tory and buses as Socialist; and when for the old Labour LCC London exchanged a GLC that changed colour infallibly every four years, any possibility of a long view had gone for good.

To this worst failure of post-war planning in London many people in the late seventies would have added the policy of decentralization,

which was held to have drained the life-blood out of the city. But this
is much more debatable. Abercrombie adopted his excessively high
densities precisely in order to minimize overspill, and this remained
the policy of Governments and of the LCC and GLC right through
to the mid seventies, by which time the exodus from the County had
reached proportions which made them no longer necessary. This
exodus was of course the largely voluntary one of both people and
businesses which only a dictatorship could have stemmed. No doubt
low-rise low-density housing would have tempted some people to stay
in town and enabled the heavy subsidization of high flats to be diverted to better uses, but the loss of population would have been no less,
possibly more. In this field, the real failure was the political one of
inability to persuade the outer boroughs to accept higher densities,
with the result that inner-city housing cost almost twice as much as
outer.

The critics of decentralization are generally, absurdly, also the critics of the towers. It was not, of course, a city of towers at all that we
acquired, but an assemblage of matchboxes, and this was as disap-
pointing to their architects as to their critics, since both inherited the
inborn northern image of the city as a silhouette. Somehow to
contrive a 'vertical feature' was a genuine, if psychologically obscure,
compulsion to the post-war architect. But the idea that point blocks
could 'punctuate', could do for the twentieth-century city what Victorian steeples had done for the nineteenth, turned out to be naive in
the extreme. Le Corbusier had no such romantic aspirations, taking
a robustly Mediterranean view.

> As you go north, the crocheted spires of the cathedrals reflect the agony of
> the flesh, the poignant dramas of the spirit, hell and purgatory, and forests
> of spires seen through pale light and cold mist.
> Our bodies demand sunshine: there are certain shapes which cast shadows.

Equally naive was the idea that a conurbation the size of London
could have an overall silhouette at all. Only a handful of English cities
– Sheffield, Bath, Durham – are any longer comprehensible as
totalities, and since the thirties the dominating skyline features
(though the eye tends to ignore them the way it ignores riderless
horses in the Grand National) are public utilities like power stations
and gas-holders. These until recently occupied the foreground of the
famous silhouette of Oxford from Hinksey Hill. Even York, a small city
of similar size, has long ceased to live in the ambience of the largest
cathedral in England. The skylines that matter in London are the

multiple short-range ones of a mile or less, and it is the takeover of these by palisades of high flats or office blocks that constitutes the post-war revolution in the look of London.

Of course there were errors and transgressions, some of them already noted. If there were to be high buildings at all, some views were bound to suffer; but making all allowances the vista-control supposed to be exercised by the GLC and watched by the Royal Fine Art Commission was pretty feeble and easily subverted. Conspicuous casualties were the views from the central parks, the view down St James's Street, the view up Regent Street and across to Westminster from the South Bank. But others survived, and there were gains. Boring Victorian thoroughfares like Tottenham Court Road, Euston Road, Notting Hill Gate and Victoria Street all gained from high or higher buildings, and visually so did the whole southern arc of inner London from Deptford round to Wandsworth, Lambeth conspicuously so. Great stretches of London that no tourist had ever penetrated were now better visual value than Mayfair, their picturesque qualities enhanced by the total absence of rectangularity in their street pattern.

Of all the short-range silhouettes the most celebrated is the view of the City from Waterloo Bridge and points west. The tide of commercial

61. City silhouette in 1980 from Hungerford Bridge

building had been rising round St Paul's for a hundred years and the worst wave, with Faraday House of 1932, had been the last. Of the 51 Wren churches that we see in the Goodwood Canaletto 25 had already gone before 1940 (more than the war destroyed) and only three or four were now just visible. In other words the silhouette had greatly deteriorated, and perhaps the present cluster of grey-black rectangles within which the hemisphere of the dome takes its central seat can fairly be said to be not much worse. Well away to the right, Seifert's 50-storey Nat West Tower, voted to that height in an extraordinary plebiscite held in the Royal Exchange, relieves the monotony without hurting the cathedral, and if, as seems possible, we soon achieve the removal of the offensive top of Faraday House, it might seem a fair exchange. Upstream and down, outside this particularly sensitive reach, the towers unquestionably improve the river views, and we could do with more of them.

One has to penetrate the innermost recesses of the City to feel more warmly about its present state. We can now see that the worst period

62. In the heart of the world's financial capital

in its architectural history was the 1950s, a period of unique impoverishment of design as well as of material. City architecture traditionally runs the gamut from luxurious reticence to rich vulgarity, and impoverishment, especially when tricked out with cheap gimmickry, is the one failing it cannot tolerate. Luckily it did not last long. By the mid sixties the old gang of City architects had begun to yield place to more sophisticated outsiders,[19] and the Commercial Union tower was the signal for a curious reversal of the familiar aesthetic by which the old commercial palaces had been black, the new white. Now, with the clean-up of Victorian London, the old were creamy white, the new fashionably black or bronze. And bronze glass, cliché though it soon became, is a marvellous reflector of the newly revealed intricacies of the old façades. The half of the City that has resisted all planning, particularly the banking and insurance district east of the Mansion House, is now one of the richest urban puddings

63. Fragments of three centuries near the Bank of England

in the world, and the high blocks which may look dull at a distance come into their own here, introducing a surrealist scale and uplift into the tiniest lanes and alleys. The very fact that each generation – the High Victorians, the Baroque Edwardians, the neo-Georgians, the blue-glass and chromium modernists, the concrete Brutalists etc. – were hit over the head by their successors, or by a war or a slump,

64. Nat West Tower

before they could do too much has kept the ingredients in perfect balance. Long may the process continue.

Considering the scale of the rebuild, there was far less 'civic improvement' than there should have been, least of all in the tourists' London north of the river. Compared with the provincial cities, virtually nothing was done to pedestrianize shopping streets or plant trees. Even the widening of Oxford Street's pavements was done on the cheap and without imagination. The de-industrialization of the South Bank could hardly fail to be an improvement, but it too received no bouquets in an age which hardly ever congratulates itself. In their perverse way, Londoners preferred to jam themselves into old spaces rather than spread themselves over new ones. This was partly climatic. Sheltered Covent Garden is a perfect resort on a chilly summer evening, and the South Bank will never emulate it until it too is glazed in and stuffed with bars and boutiques. But then the change in the character of London over these forty years has been far beyond the realms of planners and architects. When the period began, all men wore hats or caps in shops and picture galleries as well as in the street; horse-drawn vehicles obstructed traffic everywhere; the wood-paved main streets were without white or yellow lines; the back streets were full of grubby children and large Cockney mums; and in the midst of it all there was the scandalous spectacle of Society with its season.

It was June. The King and Queen were at the Palace. And everywhere, though it was still so early, there was a beating, a stirring of galloping ponies, tapping of cricket bats; Lords, Ascot, Ranelagh and all the rest of it; wrapped in the soft mesh of the grey-blue morning air, which, as the day wore on, would unwind them, and set down on their lawns and pitches the bouncing ponies, whose forefeet just struck the ground and up they sprang, the whirling young men, and laughing girls in their transparent muslins who, even now, after dancing all night, were taking their absurd woolly dogs for a run.[20]

The abolition of the social extremes was compounded by the loss of so many markets and workshops, so many trades, skills, porters, stevedores, lightermen. But if the saddest thing that happened to the City was the disappearance downriver of its port and all the life that went with it (one must remember that in the thirties ocean-going ships still unloaded opposite St Paul's), the happiest was the Clean Air Act. The City really does, once again, as for Wordsworth, 'like a garment wear the beauty of the morning ... all bright and glittering in the smokeless air'. Now buildings were worth cleaning, and all sorts of humble Victoriana and Edwardiana from individual terrace

houses to pubs and public buildings were washed and brightly painted. What came up best were the great historical fantasies – Street's
Gothic Law Courts, Waterhouse's Romanesque Natural History
Museum and Caroe's Elizabethan Church Commissioners' Building in
Millbank, with the V & A and St Pancras still to come. Romantics may
mourn the sooty shades and shadows, but for the majority in the
inner city the whole visual tone has been lightened.

This much, neo-technics could do. But with the dirt the drama had
silently departed. Neither the splendours nor the miseries – the
chiaroscuro of cities since their first emergence – any longer marked
the life of London. Society could no longer flaunt its beautiful riders
in Hyde Park or its jewels at the Opera because it no longer existed.
The Parks themselves were threadbare relics of their bosomy Victorian prime. Derby Day and the Boat Race had ceased to draw the
greatest crowds of any popular festivals in the world. Above all, the
fabulous wealth, the consciousness of power and the brutal energy of
the world's commercial capital had fled across the Atlantic. The
crowds had gone home.

CHAPTER 4

Newcastle-upon-Tyne

Hadrian's Wall was a fall-back position. The Romans at their most expansive had picked on the natural neck of the island, the 30-mile isthmus between the Firths of Forth and Clyde, as the most economical line to hold against the barbarians; and after the withdrawal of the legions it still seemed good sense to the invading Anglo-Saxons to colonize the east coast right up to the Forth. The New Castle by the Wall's End was thereafter central in the kingdoms of Bernicia and Northumbria, and Henry II's immensely powerful keep was significantly built, like the Roman fort before it, not defensively on the south bank of the Tyne, but on the far bridgehead – a sally port into the debatable land between the Tyne and Tweed. In this region of castles it was the only royal one, and lay between the Percys' at Alnwick and the Bishop Palatine's fortress at Durham, though to the monarchy they were all outposts of varying reliability: the Court never ventured beyond its northern capital of York. But Newcastle, at the crossroads of the only all-weather north–south and east–west highways in the north, had the better site for growth.

Thus guarded, the navigable Tyne was never a barrier, and could develop in some security as a port. Already in the thirteenth century it was exporting sea-coals to London, and until the eighteenth century it had a virtual monopoly of this increasingly lucrative trade. There was no other way of moving the stuff. For those five centuries, as London grew Newcastle coastal traffic grew with it, and the monopoly only ended when first the canals and then the railways opened up a national network of coal transportation. Export to north-west Europe then rapidly took up the slack. By then the plateau north of the Tyne was a cat's cradle of little lines and sidings, and when the coast wind blew the sheep as far as Hexham were grey with coal dust.

The site on the north bank was not an easy one. Scored by ravines running south into the river, it was well chosen for a fort but not for a city, and all development, not least the two-mile square of the thirteenth-century walls, needed a lot of cut and fill. Consequently, after the Union in 1603, when the walls could be dispensed with, there was a tendency to build on easier ground outside them. As late as 1740 Sir William Blackett still had twenty rolling acres of orchards and paddocks surrounding his substantial manor house *within* the walls. Heavy coaches and packhorse trains struggling through the mud of the wide Great North Road passed his front gate and farm buildings as in any country town. The population of 20,000-odd was sharply divided between the tradesmen of the spacious market town on the plateau and the teeming inhabitants of the congested quayside.

Then in the early nineteenth century the economy of the region was transformed. From a means of keeping Londoners warm, coal became the prime energy-source of modern industry. Diversification into glass manufacture, chemicals and heavy engineering was rapid, but for Tyneside, once Brunel had developed his iron ship, the obvious future must be ship-building: and as the Royal Navy and the merchant fleet grew phenomenally in the second half of the century, Newcastle grew with them, from a town of under 30,000 at the beginning of the century to the capital of a conurbation of 750,000 at the end.

All ancient English cities subjected to expansion of this order suffered fairly early on from strangulation of the heart. Gentry and prosperous tradesmen would sell up their Georgian-fronted houses and move to more salubrious suburbs, and back gardens and paddocks would be turned over to workshops, front parlours to shops. Many of our county towns, even though not subjected to a major population explosion, have remained in this state of cardiac arrest ever since. But Newcastle was uniquely fortunate that John Dobson, one of only two architects working in the north of England, had set

65. Grey Street, 1980

66. Surrealist Newcastle, 1979

up practice in the city in 1810. Dobson was a practical man with some engineering knowledge; he was also a romantic with a sure sense of composition, and he adhered to a severe and sober Roman style, avoiding the Grecian straitjacket. What he lacked was push, and by great good fortune this was made good by Richard Grainger, a South Shields speculative builder of vision and energy. Between them these two, with the support of a progressive town clerk, gave the city exactly what it needed: new middle-class housing outside the walls and then a splendid commercial centre, opening up in the modern manner back-land between the two main streets of the medieval town to provide the largest covered shopping centre in England. Grey Street did for Newcastle what Regent Street had done for London, but its gentle curve and slope, its masculine and unaffected architecture and the tawny stone of which it was built made Nash's work look cheap. Dobson went on to complete in 1850 one of the most spectacular of Victorian railway stations.

For the railway was the other main agent in the transformation of the city centre. Robert Stephenson leaps the river and as at Conway makes a dead set at the Castle, blithely smashes through between keep and gatehouse, bends sharply back, strides high across the old port on its steep slope and then like some mad futurist completes a round-

67. Quayside, regatta time

about in the sky 95 feet above the water. Piranesi never conceived anything to touch it. Add two elegant skyline silhouettes, one Gothic (the model for St Giles Cathedral in Edinburgh), the other Classic (an impeccable essay in the manner of James Gibbs), and you have within the space of a few hundred yards one of the world's most dramatic townscapes.

After all these excitements absolutely nothing of architectural value happened for a hundred years. The High Victorians, perhaps sobered by the prevailing classicism, contributed none of their Gothic monsters. Even William Armstrong, second only to Krupp among armament manufacturers, though a benefactor of the city in other ways, confined his architectural adventures to his wild Shavian eyrie at Cragside. Nor can one except the New Tyne Bridge of 1926, because although it climaxes the riverine drama it was built too soon for its planners to realize that to carry it through on the line of the Great North Road and deliver its traffic straight into Pilgrim Street would set insoluble problems to road planners of the next generation. Ten years later, in the by-pass era, they would probably have got it right.

Newcastle's housing followed the pattern of that distressful century. Shipyards and engineering works naturally hugged the river bank and the workers' terraces climbed the steep slopes behind them, generally taking the form of 2-storey flats. Your height and distance from the river soon became a status symbol. First Jesmond and then Gosforth, on the airy plateau beyond the Town Moor, were the garden suburbs of the middle classes. Byker and then Walker to the east, Elswick and then Scotswood to the west, were the close-knit communities of the artisans, first in their blackened terraces, then in interwar red-brick estates laid out in the usual manner. It was notable that Newcastle's East End tended to be more highly-skilled and stable, its West End more casual, unskilled and poverty-stricken. By 1939, low-density estates spread in a wide arc from Leyburn round to Wallsend and a small amount of slum clearance had been done; but slums on the scale of the Black Country and the north-west were never a characteristic of Newcastle.

Lacking the geographical advantages of the western ship-building ports, Newcastle missed the worst of the population explosion and consequently the worst of the slums. Conversely, it missed the grand High Victorian architecture of its great rival Glasgow. What was disastrously characteristic, as the heavy industries declined, was unemployment. Across the river, Gateshead had 44 per cent unemployed in 1934 and Jarrow (whose march to London made it a national symbol) 68 per cent. The Special Areas Act of 1935 and the new 'trading estates' like Team Valley helped only marginally, until the war abolished the problem.

The city emerged shabby and even blacker but almost unscathed by the blitz, so that for some years the national priorities for reconstruction seemed to be elsewhere. A Conservative Council got out a perfunctory Development Plan to meet Whitehall requirements in 1951, and large areas of windy farmland around the northern and western fringes were eaten up by run-of-the-mill council housing, mainly low-rise but including (by 1978) 44 tower blocks of over 8 storeys. T. Dan Smith in his autobiography describes these estates as 'an indictment of the Council which allowed them to be built, and of the professionals who were prepared to design them. People ought to undertake penitential pilgrimages to look at the houses that were built in 1951 in Denton, and later in Noble Street and Kenton.'

This remarkable man, a miner's son from Holly Avenue in Wallsend, was to dominate the Newcastle Labour Party for a decade from 1953, until his ambition led him to wider horizons. A powerful speaker and a formidable negotiator, he was also a visionary with a romantic *penchant* for artists and intellectuals. 'So far as the north was concerned in 1950, we had to try to get people to understand that it was not just a question of pulling down houses and rebuilding, but of entering into a dialogue on the enrichment of life.' His teacher in the early days was the gentle and enlightened J. S. Allen, the first professor of town and country planning in the university – a relationship not unlike that of Dobson and Grainger. Achieving power in 1958, Smith rapidly established himself as one of a select circle of northern Labour bosses that included Sefton of Liverpool and Meldrum of Glasgow, and invited them to Newcastle to discuss how to promote regional development. On a visit to Coventry he had been impressed by a young planner in Gibson's team, Wilfred Burns, and engaged him to come up to Newcastle and set up a new City Planning Department the moment the City Engineer retired in 1960. Most important of all in those early days, he established a relationship of mutual regard with Lord Hailsham, sent up to the north by Macmillan in 1963 for reasons which wisely combined enlightened policy with party politics. Hailsham paid a series of visits – not the first southerner to fall in love with the region and its people – and, according to Dan Smith, 'made an impact which was quite fundamental'. Investment discrimination in favour of the north, in terms of industrial development and a major highway network, followed forthwith and was maintained and increased by Wilson's Government after 1964. And Hailsham enthusiastically supported Smith's cultural enterprises and the development of every kind of sport and leisure facility. The Northern Arts Association, under the leadership of the energetic Sandy Dunbar, rapidly established itself as the most effective public sponsor of the arts in the kingdom. Smith made no bones about it: Newcastle was to be transformed into 'the Brasilia of the north'.

The new City Planning Officer had no time to lose. He had to build a new department from scratch, 'fired with a great urge not only to give of their best in making the city physically as efficient and beautiful as possible, with an inbuilt local character and a firm belief in the good life of the city, but also to understand human beings in their personal moods and social aspirations'. The still-operative 1951 plan now looked absurdly thin and amateurish in the light of two unforeseen phenomena: the explosion of road traffic and 'the prosperity of the nation which, because of changing demands and higher standards, reflects itself the need for the possibilities of redevelopment and environmental improvement not contemplated in earlier days'. Within four months of appointment, taking advantage of recent traffic surveys, the tiny skeleton staff of the new department was able to put out a 'first report' on the city centre which anticipated Buchanan in its concern for 'environmental areas', pedestrianization, conservation and the securing of all this by a system of urban motorways and distributors giving access to 17,000 parking spaces. Cheaply and urgently cobbled together to hold the situation, this document shows how strong a counter a first hunch can be. Two years later, as the formal 1963 Development Plan Review, it emerged filled out in detail but in essentials unaltered. Consequently, late starter though it was, the Council was in full control when development pressures duly materialized, though whether the concept was right or wrong is still debatable. For at its heart lay a conflict between the Planning Officer's sincerely felt admiration for the powerful character of the old city now in his hands and an equally sincere determination to transform it. Love, in other words, slides easily into domination.

Burns was a 'big city' man and there was to be no truck with mini-Abercrombie satellite development. 'It is argued in some quarters that peripheral expansion of a conurbation is a bad thing. The City Council reject this generalization in the case of Tyneside, which is extremely compact [and] abuts immediately on to vast tracts of open country.' On the latest reckoning, 40 per cent of the city's 88,000 dwellings were without proper plumbing, and of these 25,000 were unfit by civilized criteria for long-term rehabilitation and would have to be cleared or replaced. Moreover, there was still a good deal of overcrowding in the inner city, and it was disquieting that the highest occupancy rates (168 p.p.a.) were to be found not only in the old terraces of Byker but also in the Council's post-war flats in Noble Street. But the Review, in this also ahead of its time, set great store by 'revitalization', and urged the Government to give it financial support. 30,000 of Newcastle's houses were pre-1914, and it was correctly foreseen that for the rest of the century the main task was going to be the rehabilitation of great tracts of these houses as well as their environment. Unfortunately for the pilot project of this programme, a carefully worked-out mix of selective demolition, infill and landscaping, the Council chose a down-at-heel inner suburb called Rye Hill where the old rooming-houses were a little too spacious and high-ceilinged for working people to be able to afford to heat in the straitened circumstances of the late seventies; so it went downhill again. But by the late seventies 20,000 old houses had been improved, the great majority of them by the City Council.

It was consistent with the big-city philosophy that people should be encouraged to come back and live in the city centre itself. This 'area of classical splendour, so powerful with its wide streets and solid buildings, its great stores and banks and commercial buildings, is in its unified conception a striking contrast to the medieval winding streets in the older part of the town. Power and contrast are the crucial factors in the city's character.' Newcastle was and remains privileged among Tyneside towns in being undisputed capital of an isolated but populous region containing nearly 3 million people, and consequently in having a large proportion of white-collar employ-ment and of the prestigious consumer-durable trade. The big stores, which had started life in Grainger Street, had spread northwards up Northumberland Street since the Tyne Bridge traffic had discharged into it in the twenties, and created a congested corridor like London's Oxford Street in miniature. The problem was to pedestrianize it and expand it, and in so doing to make the walk a circuit. This was to be done by westward extension which would wrap new covered shop-ping and parking round Grainger Market (1834), all within a stone's throw of Grey's Monument, the navel of the city. Time was to show that this was a correct and commercially rewarding decision; but after all the appreciative references to classical Newcastle, it seemed disin-genuous that it involved the total destruction of Dobson's even earlier Eldon Square. This was the kind of modest late-Georgian survival, with some regrettable attic additions, that is occupied by solicitors and architects in so many British provincial cities. Dan Smith sought to expiate the felony by engaging the Danish maestro Arne Jacobsen to design the skyscraper hotel that was to be the showpiece of the new square. In the event the hotel project was abandoned when the ad-venturous Forte teamed up with the more conservative Trust Houses, but on the other hand the eastern and most altered limb of Dobson's square was allowed precariously to survive. By the late seventies the square had given its name, its green lawn and its St George War Memorial to one of the largest, most glamorous and most elegantly designed covered shopping and sports centres in Europe, the work of the Capital and Counties Property Co. with Chapman Taylor as archi-tects. For a city two thirds of whose workers were now in 'service' employment and nearly a half of whom were women, this environ-mental transformation was a calculable commercial success and an incalculable morale-booster.

In the thinking of 1963, Eldon Square was only a fraction of the planned rebuilding of the city centre, which it was hoped would replace all those dingy quarters that spoil even the best of northern cities, both within and without the central Conservation Area, amounting to about a half of the existing fabric. On its northern fringes, close to the vast and featureless Town Moor, large reservations were made on each side of the City Architect's elegant white stone Civic Centre for the expansion of the University and the new Polytechnic. To the south, overlooking the decayed, dramatic quayside, the black silhouette of Stephenson's All Saints Church was seen as centrepiece of a group of office buildings by Ravenseft, another London developer, for which Basil Spence had been appointed consultant. This would match Eldon Square's 600,000 square feet with a similar amount of office floor-space, exploiting, it was hoped, the Government's new policy of office decentralization from the southeast. And to the east and west 'traffic architecture', as visualized by

68. The 1963 model: all the white buildings were to be new

the Buchanan Report, would 'integrate' the ring of great urban motorways with the city's reconstituted heart. It would consist, inevitably, very largely of multi-storey car parks and the backsides of warehouses or other introverted buildings.

The north–south perimeter motorways, in line with the Buchanan consensus, would as far as possible exploit the 'cracks' partly created by the railway between the old centre and the twilight areas beyond, though even so they must inevitably destroy pleasant Victorian residential areas. For the east–west alignments no such cracks offered themselves, and an expensive breakthrough was envisaged along the Tyne escarpment and an even more expensive tunnel further north. Traffic would weave its way into the heart of things off an elaborate interchange on the eastern perimeter. Finally it appeared (though in 1963 it was still left uncertainly dependent on traffic projections) that this whole inner ring of motorways would need to be by-passed by an expressway, tunnelling below the Tyne, for north–south through-traffic. All this, it was hoped, would cater for about half the twenty-year private car demand. The balance would be handled by a greatly improved surface transport system.

But the road plan, like the shopping plan, ran headlong into a conservation controversy. We now know that if you point a modern main road at anything, be it the Chiltern escarpment or the central axis of a medieval city, you are as certain as a man who fires a machine-gun into a crowd to hurt somebody. Had the Tyne Bridge planners skirted the line of the medieval wall, there would have been no problem, but the railway planners had scarcely set a good example, having plunged for the heart. So what the quayside had gained in drama the east side must lose in architectural integrity. Smith resorted to his usual *deus ex machina*, a world-class consultant this time in the person of Robert Matthew; but it was obvious that there was no way by which the volume of traffic for which the bridge was built, once funnelled into Pilgrim Street, could be distributed east and west even if the listed buildings mainly concerned (the Royal Arcade and the Jesus Hospital) were not actually demolished, because their environment would be wrecked. It was true that John Dobson's solemn and vaulted arcade of 1826 never had led anywhere and consequently never had prospered commercially, but it could have been made to, and its frontispiece closing Mosley Street was in his best Roman manner. In the event it found itself undermined by a subway and stranded on a traffic island of which the raised roundabout road missed the corner of Jesus Hospital by only a few feet. After much argument and anger, it was decided that to rebuild the frontispiece would be a solecism, but the arcade was reconstructed and embalmed inside Matthew's Swan House, and the Jesus Hospital was painstakingly restored, in the usual gesture of contrition, to become the Joicey Museum. The device of importing a famous name failed most miserably here. Swan House, an office block of minimal architectural

69. The Swan House débâcle: the Great North Road viaduct of 1926 plunges under Stephenson's of 1846, then vanishes below Matthew's building, which buries the Royal Arcade. The Jesus Hospital is nearly strangled on the right

interest, need not have loomed up at the end of Mosley Street: Dobson's terminal feature could have been saved.

But could the whole dilemma have been by-passed? Undoubtedly Newcastle had fallen into the theoretical error of forcing cross-city motorways[1] to do double duty as distributors to city-centre car parks, for which latter role it was necessary to bring them in too close. This same tight squeeze on the heart was already under construction at Birmingham, and was on the drawing boards for other cities, including exceptionally sensitive ones like York and Oxford. Theoretically again, the great Tyne Bridge could have been downgraded to carry city-centre traffic only, with no northward issue for through- or cross-city traffic. The latter would then have to be carried by a replacement bridge and motorway downstream, or another upstream west of the centre, or both. It could not have been expected that the immense extra cost and community disruption would have been borne. Not only listed buildings but good environments like Victoria Square and Windsor Crescent had to be sacrificed as it was. The official handout made no bones about it: 'The motorway will slice through building blocks, cut off existing streets and will intensify noise and fumes in an already deteriorating environment.' So it must be lined by warehouses et cetera. But, some day, the passenger 'looking at the surrounding development as he travels smoothly along, and the viewer who sees the structure from some vantage point, will both enjoy the experience'.

In 1968, having got everything moving, Wilfred Burns resigned to become Chief Planner in Whitehall, leaving his deputy Kenneth Galley to oversee the implementation, first as City Planning Officer and later as Chief Executive. And in the landslide of 1968 the Labour Party lost power. Dan Smith himself, at the behest of George Brown, had illadvisedly moved out of local government to chair the new Regional Economic Council in 1964. But there was no loss of momentum. As late as 1973, the year of the oil crisis, Galley was able to publish a progress report which still stands up as one of the most attractive and convincing statements of policy put out by any middle-sized industrial city in the world.[2] By then the regional policies of successive Tory and Labour Governments had borne fruit and the report could note that 'in the Tyne and Wear area the excellent main road network is nearly complete'. South of the Tyne, on the recommendation of the Regional Economic Council, Washington New Town had been designated not, like Aycliffe and Peterlee, to 'relieve' the conurbation but to enrich it; and to the north the City and the County had jointly promoted little New Towns of their own at Cramlington and Killingworth, in the second of which an outstanding local architectural partnership, Ryder and Yates, was engaged on a brilliant group of buildings for (of

70. Norgas House, Killingworth, by Ryder and Yates

all people) the Gas Board. In a Tyne and Wear Transport Plan private consultants had proposed a Metro system for the conurbation (the writing on the wall for urban motorways) which, it could be claimed, was strictly in line with Burns's policies on public transport. As for housing, 11,000 slum dwellings had been cleared and replaced, and a 500-acre extension of the city to the north-west was under way, a good deal of it by private builders. And the Housing Act of 1969 had at last given the city the powers it had long sought to promote the rehabilitation of whole areas. Consequently, a 'Revitalization Agency' had been set up in 1970 and it was hoped that a thousand dwellings a year would be tackled.

'Cleared ... replaced ... tackled' – these words can imply human misery or human joy, depending on how you do it. Increasingly in the seventies, housing management became more significant than house building, and in this field the city's record was excellent. It needed to be, for by now it owned over half the housing stock. This was because the policy was not (as in Tory London and Liberal Liverpool) to sell out but to buy in, since this was seen as the only way to step up the pace of revitalization. So it was essential that the process be as humane as possible.³ On the modern estates, pre-war or post-war, it was not the Council's policy to juggle 'problem' families about in a fruitless attempt to distribute them evenly. Given the self-protectiveness of English communities, both working-class and middle-class, this would have been a hopeless undertaking. The aim was rather, by employing young people close to the ground and by patient talk with individual families, 'to stabilize each community, to make people less dissatisfied and more willing to make it their home'.⁴ Inevitably there were failures: the post-war Noble Street flats had to be demolished amid nation-wide publicity, and the too-sophisticated centre of Ryder and Yates's smart Kenton Bar neighbourhood succumbed to vandalism. But good management and caretaking ensured that the tower blocks (quite contrary to southern stereotypes) were almost universally popular: in the areas of stress it was the back gardens, which everybody is supposed to love, that were widely neglected and overrun by packs of dogs. Where these Garden City estates went downhill, the Council sent in 'action squads' for physical and social rescue, put in new heating systems, repaired garden fences, laid on daily cleaning, planted and replanted trees. 'We have housed our people; now we have to help them', is how the Director of Housing puts it. And the director of the local Housing Aid Centre, well placed to know of the failures, considers Newcastle 'a very open authority'.

Of all this the outstanding example is Byker. This compact artisan community of 13,000 had long lived in its tightly packed terraces of Tyneside flats sloping steeply down to the shipyards, many families undisturbed since it was built in the 1870s. Now it demanded new houses; but just as firmly it demanded not to be broken up. The inspired choice of Ralph Erskine, the eccentric British architect who had made his name in Sweden, was in fact made in 1969 not by T. Dan Smith but by his Conservative successor Arthur Grey. His brief, however, had emanated from the previous administration and it had had two main features: first, the survival of the existing Byker community and, second, its protection from the cold north and east and from a proposed new motorway on those sides by some kind of south- and west-facing wall of flats – that same 'traffic architecture' as Burns, following Buchanan, had visualized for the city-centre motorways. The Byker Wall was to be 'outside the scope of participation', but in all else the desires of the people affected were to be paramount. What followed is well known. Erskine's first move was to establish his drawing-office in an undertaker's premises in the heart of Byker, with his young site architect, Vernon Gracie, and his wife living over the

71. North side of the Byker Wall

shop; his second was to look for volunteers to inhabit a pilot project. It was not easy. 'Janet Square' was at the foot of the hill, literally a come-down for the potential guinea-pigs; and now and all through the early days at Byker the ingrained dread of British working people of getting roped in by 'them' was an obstacle: they were especially suspicious of councillors. However, eventually they inched forward and Janet Square produced its invaluable feedback. Thereafter the ice seemed to melt. Three things were decisive: the fact that you could watch your own house go up just round the corner, the fact that the Gracies stayed on in Byker – architects transmuted into community leaders – and the fact that all the old community meeting places, the churches, the pubs, the schools, the corner shops, were preserved or, if rebuilt at higher rents, subsidized. In the end, the quantity and quality of social activity in Byker became a by-word – a local joke – but a triumph.

The architecture is, of course, eccentric. The secretive nooks and alleys, all richly planted, the wooden seats and pergolas and porches, the rather Japanese flimsiness of everything, the naive colours – it was all a hemisphere away from the black northern brickscape then so fashionable in the south. And the great Wall itself, tall, austere and abstract on the cold side, bending, rising, falling, projecting, receding

72 and 73. Two views of the south side of the Byker Wall

for a full mile and a half, has on its seemingly lower sunny side the intricate, shabby, makeshift, intensively humanized quality of a shantytown in Hong Kong. It is inhabited mainly by old people, who say, 'It's like the Costa Brava. Whoever would have dreamt that *Byker* could look like this?' The analogy is fortunately inaccurate, but it speaks for the happiness.

But to believers in the conflict theory of urban society the 'participation' achieved at Byker was a triumph for Authority only. The Skeffington Report of 1969 had had no illusions about the limits of participation: 'Responsibility for preparing the plan is, and must remain, that of the local planning authority.' One should listen to people and then at the end of the day one should do what one thought right. It was easy for the radical critic to see this as nothing better than manipulation. 'Participation has become merely an aspect of urban management rather than a means of giving people a decisive voice . . .

the irony is that whereas participation should normally be about uncovering conflict it has been used in Byker to prevent conflict.'[5] What a disgrace! But in fact Byker is no Garden of Eden and residents have made plenty of noise about the delays and discomforts that have dogged the initial decision to rehouse them *in situ*, which inevitably condemned them to many years of life on a building site.

But having willed the end, which was that Byker should be rebuilt, local people had the sense not to want to determine the means: they saw it as their job not to run the operation, but to make a fuss if it went wrong. In this they differed from the Covent Garden community, whose participation amounted to a veto on intervention of any kind. Both places illuminate the central dilemma that for the extremely complex processes of urban renewal cooperatives are grossly inefficient, yet mere participation is liable to be seen as manipulation. The planner has to find his way between these horns.

Galley's 1973 progress report was, consciously, a swan song. The proud County and City of Newcastle-upon-Tyne was about to become a Metropolitan District in the County of Tyne and Wear. And the national economy was already on the skids. But on the whole, Newcastle managed the retreat from the great expectations of the Smith/Burns era with some panache. It soon became plain that the first arc of the projected circle of inner motorways would be the only one. When the new County produced its Structure Plan in 1978 the reign of the private car was long since over, and the building of the Metro was well advanced. The Plan supported the long-standing proposal for a rebuilt Redheugh Bridge just upstream of the city centre, but strictly to carry a local distributor road. Apart from this, only the outer perimeter by-passes are now to be completed. East–west traffic will be carried south of the river through Gateshead, missing central Newcastle altogether. This Structure Plan is an admirable example of late-seventies professionalism sobered by hard-won experience. New house building, for example, is 'to meet only those needs that cannot be satisfactorily met by the existing stock of housing, improved or adapted as necessary'. Only those houses whose improvement is a poor long-term investment are to be cleared. On these criteria the city is not expected to expand by more than 70 hectares, at the most, by 1991. As for the great new centre, shopping expansion must now stop, though new office development in this regional capital (if the developers come back) is encouraged – no mention of microchips.

In that same year the City Council embarked on a carefully thought-out campaign of public consultation on the future of the

much-ravaged city centre, the results of which were published in
1980.[6] It is of course disingenuous to ask ordinary people to take a
view on alternative development or transportation or parking
problems which interlock in complex ways: one is apt to get incom-
patible answers which cannot be assembled into a package, and of
course one only gets answers at all from the tiny interested minority
– some two thousand in this case, despite strenuous efforts including
household surveys, public meetings, leaflets and the use of all the
media. In the absence of a social breakdown of the respondents, one
must assume that apart from named organizations this was the business world and the educated elite, centred in the University and the
Polytechnic – the vocal minority whose support would ease the
passage of the eventual plan. Anyhow the message comes through
with crushing unanimity:

> The city centre must be made a more pleasant place. It must be made easier
> to move around as a pedestrian, there must be less conflict with vehicles,
> character must be retained and enhanced, new development must be on a
> scale that 'fits in'. Respondents want a familiar, pleasant, congenial place in
> which to work, shop, live and find recreation.
>
> The city centre's character and environment is highly valued. Modern
> development is seen as having caused extensive damage and added little of
> value. Older buildings and areas must be retained and where necessary res-
> tored.

If a 'Brasilia of the north' had ever been wanted, it is not wanted now.
Eldon Square, for all its inner glamour, is seen as having sucked all the
life and prosperity out of the medieval core round the Cathedral and
the quayside. 'No more northward extension of the shopping centre'
is the cry. It is suggestive of the social composition of the respondents
that the shortage of 'operational' (i.e. business) parking comes third
in order of interest, the improvement of public transport tenth.

In his draft City Centre Plan of 1980 Roy Angell, who had succeeded Galley as City Planning Officer, was able to accommodate
these interests in a report which, characteristically of its moment, is
long on care and concern for the heritage and the nurturing of all
uses, new and old, that will tend towards its revitalization, short on
imaginative or aesthetic notions of any kind. 'Not too much of anything' is the classic formula – a little housing in converted upper
floors, in the snug medieval village around the restored Blackfriars
and on the derelict slopes around All Saints; a little inner ring road to
relieve the hideous and congested Percy Street; a little more
pedestrianization around the Grey Monument; a little more office

development, since it is all taken up and has been found, surprisingly, to encourage the re-use of the Dobson/Grainger interiors; a very little more shopping to help pull back Eldon Square values southwards into the heart of the old city. The Council's worthy spending record on its surviving historic buildings is to be kept up, though it has still to find a use for the elegant interior of All Saints, whose sharp black silhouette is now regrettably scrubbed to a drab brown.

But the happiest moment of that year was the opening of the first eighteen stations of the Metro, six difficult years after construction began.[7] This inner-circle-type rapid transport system, using wherever possible existing rail track, is the first in Britain in which buses and trains will have coordinated routing and time-tabling. Unlike so much of the London underground, its effect is intended not to extend the conurbation but to concentrate it, and to be the agent of renewal by threading the areas most dingily in need of it; in this it is consistent with the original Smith/Burns philosophy. Unfortunately the most conspicuous single artefact in the system, the new bridge over the Tyne, is a feeble addition to the historic collection because the authorities went about it the wrong way, going out to tender for designers instead of using Newcastle-born Ove Arup as consultant. The weak shape is compounded by being painted the same cissy *eau-de-nil* as was mistakenly used on the great 1926 bridge. But by and large the yellow coaches run through excellently designed stations panelled in vitreous enamel in strong primary colours – vandal-resistant design at last rejecting recourse to the pill-box aesthetic. Atop, where required, are Miesian glass-box stations which are said to be equally resistant.[8] Free rides in the August holidays were just the tonic the city needed.

'The concrete jungle has come to Newcastle and we have wasted our substance.' In these words Bruce Allsopp, architectural historian at the University, sums up the reaction of the seventies. Is it as simple as that? More eggs were undoubtedly broken for this omelette than need have been. Eldon Square façades could have been saved for boutiques with the big malls and big stores hidden behind them. Some quiet Victorian residential enclaves could have been saved if the Central Motorway East had been designed for slower (and safer) speeds, not conceived absurdly as part of the 70 m.p.h. cross-country network. These are lessons perhaps only learnt by the mistakes that were made. But it was the faith of Smith and Burns that the losses would be redeemed by the exciting new city that would rise on the ruins: only the best was to be good enough. It did not work out that way. The great names let them down, and the London speculators with whom they worked claimed that Newcastle rents would not support a high quality of finish; they were in business, after all, not for what they could put into the old city, but for what they could get out of it – 'an extractive industry' as Allsopp not unfairly put it. And of course, like others, the city has had to suffer the failure of that key concept of the sixties, the pedestrian deck. John Dobson Street, created to take the traffic out of the main shopping street, and the environs of the Laing Gallery are a by-word for the chopped-off and the half-baked, made to seem worse by the success, just round the corner, of

74. MEA House by Ryder and Yates is in the Newcastle tradition of astonishing juxtaposition

the brilliant MEA building in Ellison Place, designed by Ryder and Yates as though to say 'Londoners go home'.

It was Newcastle's bad luck that it was virtually impossible to cut out decayed tissue, in an admittedly over-zealous attempt to raise the whole tone to that of the elevated stage-set established in Grey Street, without damaging the souk-like Geordie city of ramifying markets and secret alleys and black chares and steep steps and surrealist juxtapositions. It was these back parts behind the stage-set, loved by the old, which were cut about in the Swinging Sixties in order to attract the young to this cold coast. It was in simple terms a necessary change of user, from industry to business. At any such moment the motion picture of urban change can be stopped and a balance struck. In such a balance, even in the heart of the old city, it seems pretty certain that environmental gains will outweigh losses when the mess

75 and 76. Across the Tyne from the same viewpoint in 1937 and 1980, showing new blocks on the skyline. In 1937 the river is hardly visible and a hoarding in front of the Castle advertises Andrews Liver Salts

of the Metro excavations is cleared away and it delivers its benefits. The new office buildings may be a poor lot, as Newcastle's commercial buildings have tended to be since 1850, but they do little scenic damage. Up north in the civic/academic enclave, Sheppard's and Whitfield's excellent buildings in the University, not to mention the

77. William Whitfield's University Theatre

Civic Centre itself, make handsome amends for the excesses of the motorway. Even in narrowly architectural terms, the city is richer than it was.

But balance sheets drawn at an arbitrary moment are abstractions remote from human sensibility. To most of its own people the city is incomparably improved. As an isolated artisan community it had a long tradition of mutual support and concern. This has developed into the huge network of 'communi-care', of local groups run by working people for their own protection or amusement, which Europe should envy. MEA House alone, for example, houses over thirty such organizations. This is the heart of the city, and despite all vicissitudes it seems to beat strongly in the clearer air. A dustman and his family in Byker, with an income of less than £50 a week, showed a visiting writer 'their pretty little house with its fitted carpets, intelligent open plan and all mod. cons., and the wife said, "We feel reborn." '[9]

CHAPTER 5

Sheffield

'It is in keeping', writes Mary Walton in her delightfully told story of
the city, 'with the whole history of Sheffield, whose people dourly
devoted themselves to the practice of the useful arts in the midst of
such a varied and smiling landscape, that the geological foundation
of the district consists of the most utilitarian elements. The western
hills are of a millstone grit and other sandstones, the subsoil is clay,
and Sheffield itself lies upon the coal measures. Grit for grindstones,
refractory materials for furnaces, coal and water for power.'[1]

The received image of Sheffield Man is of the original *Homo faber* –
a race of Nibelungs in their remote forest clearing, forging the iron-
age sword, grinding out below their water-wheels the tools of
primitive husbandry and housekeeping, while invading armies passed
and repassed unheeding on the plain of York. But Domesday Book
records a normally constituted, if minuscule, Anglo-Saxon hamlet,
and the Company of Cutlers in Hallamshire[2] was in fact slow to
emerge and equally slow to grow. As late as 1615, while the castle of
the Furnevals and the Talbots still stood guard at the confluence of
Don and Sheaf, a survey throws a lurid light on the pre-industrial
economy of a small manufacturing town inaccessible to wheeled
commerce, on the way to nowhere, connected only by packhorse
bridleways to the outside world:

There are in the towne of Sheffeld 2,207 people; of which there are 725
which are not able to live without the charity of their neighbours. These are
all begging poore. 100 householders which relieve others. These (though the
beste sorte) are but poore artificers; among them is not one which can keepe
a teame on his own land, and not above tenn who have grounds of their own
that will keepe a cow. 160 householders, not able to relieve others. These are
such (though they beg not) as are not able to abide the storme of one fort-
night's sickness, but would be thereby driven to beggary. 1,222 children and
servants of the said householders: the greatest part of which are such as live
of small wages, and are constrained to worke sore, to provide them
necessaries.

It was already, and to a remarkable extent was to remain, an
artisan community: the more prosperous citizens and the local gentry
lived well outside. So even in the eighteenth century there was very

little 'improvement'. Fairbank's survey of 1771 shows the sketchy beginnings of some orthogonal streets on the southern fringes and of one miniature Georgian square, but what exists is still pokily 'picturesque', narrow lanes winding along old field boundaries and climbing quite steep slopes up to the steepled parish church. Dun-coloured brick and thatch, roughly cobbled alleys with central sewage gutters flushed down monthly by the simple expedient of pulling the plug of a pond at the top end of town – such was the scene, and cholera epidemics were the inevitable accompaniment. Eotechnic power from over a hundred water-wheels comfortably met the needs of the 'little mesters' – the cutlers and toolsmiths.

Steadily, however, the place grew. Halfway through the century Boulsover and Hancock invented and perfected Sheffield plate and Huntsman developed crucible steel. World markets awaited both, but factors (salesmen) still had to ride to London to exploit them, and communications with Hull, the nearest port, were laborious. By the end of the century, when the turnpike trusts had at last opened up coach and carrier routes to the east and south, there were 45,000 people in the noisy and congested town (one tenth of what it would have a century later), and a third of them were desperately poor. Contemporaries noted the contrast with Leeds, 'a clean and handsome town in course of rapid development, the home of over 1,400 merchants and traders, whose genteel residences are uniform, elegant, and so clean, even externally, that scarcely a speck is to be seen on the broad foot pavement'.[3] Compared with two other towns that manufactured Georgian consumer-durables, Stoke-on-Trent and High Wycombe, Sheffield produced no leaders of the sophistication of Wedgwood, Spode and Minton, and could not, because of its withdrawn location, cash in on the coach and carriage trade as could artisan High Wycombe. No doubt it was the poor representation of the mercantile and banking interests in the town that made its inherited skills so vulnerable to boom and slump, so that while the potteries rode high the cutlers and silversmiths suffered severely in the French wars, and then suffered again when the American trade fell away after 1830. Strikes and sabotage were the result, though the workers in their tiny workshops never achieved the organization of militant Manchester. There was no point in hitting a little mester, as nowadays a small landlord, too hard: he had not the means to do more.

But finally Sheffield took off. Transportation, which had always been the bottleneck, was improved in 1819 by a canal link to the navigable lower Don and thence to the Humber, and finally the railway came through from Rotherham in 1838. Via this rather round-about branch line (the main line did not reach Sheffield till 1870) the steel industry could now interlock with the railway boom, and deliver the larger and larger castings demanded by this second industrial revolution. This transformed the physical and social geography of the town. There was henceforth a gulf of scale between the little work-shops in the old town and the monster steelworks (fortunately down wind) in the valley bottoms. Now the South Yorkshire and Derbyshire coalfield came into its own, and the once wooded banks of the Don and the Sheaf were filled solid with immense faceless mills, smoking chimneys and tightly packed houses of which 38,000 were back-to-back. In the bad times of the early forties the average life expectancy in Sheffield was 24 (a little better than Manchester), one third of children went to school, one twentieth of families to church. Sewage filled the rivers (untreated till 1898) and smoke filled the sky: the city (which it became in 1893) vied with Oldham as paradigm of Thompson's *City of Dreadful Night*.

But then, as a visitor reflected in 1904, 'Why ask Sheffield to be beautiful? Within her bounds she is pledged to other ends, and outside them the morning and the evening are beautiful on her hills ... Sheffield may be likened to an untidy house; it has been enlarged several times, but the entrance is still through the kitchen. You knock at the door and say, ''Will you be good enough to show me over your house, sir?'' and the answer comes, ''Ay, and welcome, lad; come thee out into the garden''.'[4] This, even allowing for the sentimentality of the age, was not the cynical 'where there's muck there's brass' of the Bradford mill-owner. No doubt in 1904 you could still, as has been calculated, have got into the gardens of three prosperous houses on the hilltops two factories, one public house and fifty-four back-to-back houses at the 250 p.p.a. density of the valley bottoms. But densities of this order were quite exceptional. By 1939 over half the population lived at Garden City densities, and only one seventieth at over 150 p.p.a. High Victorian charity and municipal action had gradually disposed of the most scandalous abuses and miseries, while eschewing civic ostentation. It is true that in the early twenties there was a feeling that something ought to be done about the planning of Shef-field, and the city fathers had the good sense to commission the then comparatively unknown Professor Abercrombie. They got excellent value. Like all the inter-war reports, the 1924 Civic Survey and Development Plan was superbly printed on paper of a quality long since lost to public life, and in a style even more conspicuously lost to planning literature. Thus, categorizing Sheffield housing, Abercrombie could write, first, of 'decayed corpses which should not be allowed for a moment longer to pollute the atmosphere', second, of houses 'sunk in senile decay, but which could be allowed thanks to some potent restoratives to totter on for a few more years, and so on up to those whose youth and vigour suggest an almost indefinite existence'. In another section, noting the absence of lunch-hour oases in the city centre, he advocates trees and shrubs in tubs, which, 'after decorating the town gardens all summer, retire to winter quarters outside the smoke zone to recuperate from their spell of dissipated and etiolating town life'.

The writing is not only stylish but refreshingly sensible. Abercrombie is undogmatic about ring roads, pointing out that they are always very unevenly loaded and therefore do not necessarily have to describe a complete circle just to look good on paper. He was writing of course in the tram era, when horse-drawn vehicles still constituted a quarter of the traffic in the Whicker, and most of his road proposals are for inserting missing links to improve cross-town movement. He is equally undogmatic about zoning, supporting the traditional mixing of housing with light industry provided it is decently planned. On densities, he prophetically regards 100 p.p.a. as 'a very reasonable standard' for redevelopment and is worried about the long-term effects of the prevailing Garden City ideal. 'It has not escaped the notice of those who are able to visualize the long-term effects of a certain course of action that the new and widely accepted density of suburban growth is likely to have certain results of doubtful pleasantness' – in fact a 50 per cent expansion of the city for the same population. He goes on to advocate satellite villages, but is aware that they are unlikely to happen because of the cost of buying land at development value – and anyway there was still plenty of pretty country temptingly close at hand. He notes that Sheffield, unlike other northern cities, is fortunate in that the worst slums occupy land badly needed by industry, and does not suffer what was to become the bane of the inner cities later in the century: inadequate commercial demand. Finally, he addresses himself to the old town centre. 'In no sense is it possible or desirable to Haussmannize the centre of Sheffield.' He quite correctly proposes that the central shopping area should extend westwards rather than – as was to occur – sprawl southwards along the Moor, and he suggests a far better site for the City Library than was later adopted. But this was a period of elegant thinking aborted by the inability to act. Virtually nothing came of

Abercrombie's ideas. Perhaps it was even preferred that the shabby city should continue to fit its people like an old black glove. With 95 per cent of them born in the place, Sheffield had and still has a good deal of social homogeneity. The Council, solidly Labour since it elected the first Labour municipality in England in 1926, was run by working men coming in from council estates. 'Sheffield people's comfortable,' a lady on a bus told a modern writer.[5]

But on the night of the 12th December 1940 the old glove was torn to shreds. For nine hours, and then on the 15th for another three, large parts of the city centre (including its two best shopping streets) were pulverized, 80,000 houses destroyed or damaged, and 700 men, women and children killed. For the first time, it became necessary for Sheffielders to forswear patchwork and to think in terms of 'a replanned city of which we may be justly proud. The reshaping and rebuilding of the great city of Sheffield [the City Engineer went on] is a vast undertaking; but, as a consequence of the war, it is one we must engage in, whether we like it or not.'

All the same, the City Engineer and the over-age staff he had been able to hold on to went at it with a will, and the document they produced (*Sheffield Replanned*, 1945) and were able to put on the market at the splendid value of five shillings is a delightful period piece, done with love, charmingly illustrated with lots of colour, and above all comprehensible – and consequently far more useful than the abstract diagrams or the patronizing style adopted for 'participation' a generation later. Of course, it was naive. Advice from Herbert Manzoni, the powerful City Engineer of Birmingham, had resulted in a tight inner, or inmost, ring road, even tighter than Birmingham's, to be called the Civic Circle and to embrace a grandiose symmetrical Civic Square of which Mountford's romantically Elizabethan Town Hall of the nineties made a most awkward component. This was the era of the Architectural Roundabout of Parisian origin, and those planned for Sheffield were only that little bit more absurd than other people's because the natural character and contours of this overgrown village lent themselves so ungratefully to such treatment.

Sheffield Replanned was in due course translated into officialese to meet the requirements of the 1947 Act and, as far as the central area was concerned (which had been its main preoccupation), out to and including the inner ring road, the 1952 Development Plan closely followed its wartime predecessor. The main new input concerned housing, now the first priority, and it was an unfortunate one. By the standards of Britain's five other largest cities, the statistics were not horrific – roughly 20,000 unfit houses, with another 15,000 for natural increase, to relieve overcrowding and to clear patches of housing embedded in heavily industrial areas. At pre-war rates of building in the private and the public sectors these houses could have been built in thirteen years, and at the moderate density (70 p.p.a.) that was later to be normal they would have needed 2,700 acres. The City Engineer had some 2,400 available. But while he did not expect anything like the pre-war rate of building, he thought wholly (except for some inner-city sites) in terms of the pre-war semi-detached ideal of 30 p.p.a. The final reckoning showed an overspill of 30,000 houses to go somewhere in the surrounding counties, and the job still uncompleted – the Don Valley polluted sites still occupied by houses – at the end of the 20-year plan. This was manifestly not good enough, as indeed Abercrombie had warned 20 years earlier.

In line with Government policy, nothing but patching was attempted in the ravaged old centre, and all resources poured into housing. And so the slums were indeed cleared, and their inhabitants removed as planned to windy far-flung council estates, whose patterns looked pretty on paper but made no more sense on the steep slopes of Hallamshire than the parallel rows of the old by-law terraces. They were easier to get lost in, costlier to rent, and miles further from work and shops. Complaints ensued, but this was normal form all over Britain, and it is greatly to the credit of the Sheffield Council led by Alderman Jim Sterland that they should have seen at this early date that something different might be possible. When in 1953 a Bill promoted to acquire for the city the boundary extensions it now so urgently needed failed in Parliament, something different seemed not only possible but necessary. The retirement of both the City Treasurer and the City Architect at that moment gave them their chance and they grasped it.

The City Architect they appointed, Lewis Womersley, had made a modest name in the then quiet Midland market town of Northampton, where he had been one of the first to experiment with cottage housing on the Radburn principle – linked by a footpath system separated from roads. He was a no-nonsense Yorkshireman of the West Riding, a man both kind and formidable, with the capacity to express clear thinking in masculine and unaffected English. 'The architect,' he wrote, 'whose fundamental task is to design workable and beautiful buildings, should not endeavour arbitrarily to inflict his personal views on his clients. The fate of large numbers of persons requiring a decent home should not depend solely on the fancies of his profession regarding the ways people ought to live, nor be subject to his desire – however natural – to build a small number of large high buildings instead of a large number of small low ones. This does not mean, however, that he must blindly continue to produce replicas of the sort of buildings which have been deemed to be satisfactory in the past. It is part of his function, as a person with a trained imagination, to portray the sort of buildings people could have.' This was the first and elementary point he had to get over. He then had to plunge into the familiar flats-versus-houses argument and make an equally elementary point. 'Merely to pose the question "do you prefer a house or a flat?" and accept the inevitable majority reply in favour of a house as being the final and conclusive word in the matter grossly oversimplifies the position.' He went on to quote Andor Gomme: 'I am arguing for the closely built town; but if you ask me whether I personally should like a house or garden of my own I should say, "Yes, near the Temple, with a garden sloping down to the river, and my place of work and the theatres and libraries all close at hand, with buses and trains nearby but just far enough away not to be noisy." But what is the value of the question and of the answer to the town planner or to me, unless I am being offered a privilege almost unique to myself?' 'In short,' Womersley goes on, 'on the assumption that urban and city life still suits our industrialized economy and that the bulk of our population is unlikely to leave the factories and offices to go back to the land, it is quite impossible for all of us both to live near our workplace and occupy a house with a garden. For it must be borne in mind that hard physical and economic facts make it impossible to carry out more than a small degree of dispersal from our major industrial centres in this small island.' The third point he had to make is that living high can be pleasurable. He quotes Margaret Willis: 'The idea of living in high flats is often considered with alarm by many people, and frequently when they first move into a flat on an upper floor they say how nervous they are of the height. However, when I went round and interviewed some of these families who had already settled in, I found that not only had they become accustomed to having their homes up in the air but the majority gave positive reasons for liking it that way and did not want to move lower. In fact, out of the 156 families interviewed who were living from six to twelve storeys up, about 90 per cent said that they would choose to live on a high floor rather than go lower if they were given the choice.' Finally it was necessary to establish that the beauty of the whole can transcend personal preferences. A recent Ministry pamphlet had made his point:

'The paradox of inter-war development is that whereas it produced better dwellings it also produced, in many respects, worse towns, and low density lay close to the root of the trouble. It is significant too that the universally admired charm and character of so many old towns is frequently associated with medium or high densities.' 'If we are to design cities and not merely housing,' Womersley concludes, 'we must go beyond the individual dwelling and portray the grand design. This is the challenge, and the opportunity.'

The object, of course, was not to pave the way for any specific solution but to get himself elbow-room. And it has seemed worth while to set out his simple line of argument in sequence because what Womersley was about to achieve in one decade was the first benign urban transformation – a transformation both dramatic and humane – on the scale of a city of over half a million people that we 'had ever seen in this country.

The topography of Sheffield was the first constituent fact. The river Don coming down from the north-west turns north-east at the point where it is joined by the Sheaf, so creating three main land-masses. The northern one, in the bend of the Don, is a steep escarpment rising to a high ridge, then falling away more gently. The eastern is again steep on the city side, then breaks up into a rolling plateau with wooded dells and windy tops. The western, on which the city centre stands, less high at first, climbs steadily in a series of ridges and romantic valleys until it reaches the wild and treeless moorland skyline of the Peak only seven miles from the Town Hall. Over all these hills, excepting only the high western ridges, lay a dark-red carpet of houses: terraced ones stepping steeply up the hillsides above the immense black rectangles of the steel mills; glum groups of 4-storey inter-war flats where slums had been cleared; and conventional council or speculators' estates sprawling over the high land behind. But there was one great asset: it had been council policy to conserve generous stretches of open space, either as public parks or as private farmland. In summer the city was festooned with green, and the prosperous western suburbs vanished into the trees.

The arrival of Lewis Womersley in Sheffield, like the arrival of Robert Matthew in London, signalled to the young that this would now be a good place to work in, and he had no difficulty in enlisting imagination, which he saw as essential if the topographical challenges of the hill-city were to be creatively and economically met. Among the recruits were Ivor Smith and Jack Lynn, fresh from the LCC, whose Ackroyden estate at Wimbledon was nearing com-

pletion when Womersley was appointed. Mixed development on
Swedish lines had made its bow there, with its graceful 11-storey
T-shaped point blocks. But there was to be no provincial time-lag:
from now on London thinking and Sheffield thinking would run
closely parallel.

The first thing for the Council was to reconsider the City Architect's
brief. Ten years of Garden-City estates and of protracted wrangles
with Derbyshire had persuaded them that henceforth housing must
be confined within the city limits and must consequently be built at
higher densities. It was also necessary, and anyhow desirable, to con-
form with Government priorities for slum clearance, and to step up
the provision of small flats to counterbalance the recent concentration on family houses. Applying Abercrombie's London principles,
three density zones emerged – 70 p.p.a. for the virgin sites, 100 – 120
p.p.a. for the major areas of slum clearance and rebuilding in the
inner city, and (on Womersley's advice) one great project, set upon
open space in the heart of the city, at the 200 p.p.a. which was
currently London's highest density (compared with 450 in New
York). Additionally there would need to be a variety of little infill
projects whose character must suit their locality. In 1953 Womersley
took a Council party on a continental tour, from which they returned
much encouraged by the evident popularity of mixed development
(families on the ground, small households without children in the air)
in Holland and Denmark.

And so the adventure began. Straight away, physical problems
arose. The only large site with a gentle south slope left within the city
boundary, Greenhill, could take ten thousand people but could only
be drained by gravity into Derbyshire, and the County, true to form,
refused to play. So the City Engineer was persuaded to pump the
whole lot back over the watershed into the city system. The 70 p.p.a.
density (double the past Sheffield norm) was achieved by long
2-storey terraces with corner flats for larger families, 4-storey
maisonettes for smaller ones, and three rather dull 13-storey towers
of little non-family flats which, being still a novelty, came along a
good deal later and had to be tactfully sited. Planning was Radburn-
style, and twenty-five years later the winding footpaths and the cosily
planted hedgerows and hardwoods have conferred a charming village
atmosphere. Next it was necessary to grasp the nettle of Gleadless.
This was a piece of impeccable English pastoral landscape,
everybody's favourite summer-evening stroll out of south Sheffield,
with fine oaks and steep-sided, richly wooded valleys. It had never

78. Gleadless, an arcadian Womersley suburb of the fifties

been the intention to build on it – it was one of the rural reserves – but
there was now no alternative: it would house 17,000 people. With
slopes averaging 1 in 8 and often steeper, the architects used every
kind of ingenious hill-climbing house or adjustable dwelling capable
of being entered at any level, with results that are both entertaining
and economical. The result is now one of the prettiest suburbs in
England and undoubtedly a powerful agent in the *embourgeoisement*
of the Yorkshire working man – whatever one may think of that. On
the highest crest of the site are three towers, which seen in enfilade
from the city centre look like a castle on the remotest skyline.

   But mixed development already had its critics. It was accused of a
'permissiveness that resulted in schemes of disastrous incoherence.
Anything goes. Point blocks from Sweden, slab blocks from France,
maisonette blocks from Holland, cottages from the Garden Cities;
every material in every colour; flat roofs, pitched roofs; frames, cross-
walls; curtain wall, hole in wall; tall, low; all these, in any desired
combination, may be mixed. In this approach, in default of any in-
herent, structural, organizational relationships between the buildings, aesthetics in the head-on-one-side flower-arrangement sense
come into their own. But a point block lowering over brick cottages
makes one wonder if different kinds of person live in each. One seems
to exist in different worlds built at different times for different people

with different social habits. This coexistence has a surrealist quality. The illusions of each world are shattered by the other. The back gardens are overlooked by a looming tower, the scale of the cottages made absurd.'⁶ The riposte was in fact already under wraps in the City Architect's office.

For the time had now come to attempt the transformation of the inner city itself. 'Flood the valleys, plant the tops' was an axiom of Capability Brown that Womersley was fond of quoting – exaggerate artificially, in other words, England's often too bland relief, a thing which her landscape painters had been doing for a couple of centuries. On each of the three hills of central Sheffield it was now to be done in a different way. The first to be tackled, Netherthorpe, though the last to be finished because of its size and complexity, was the long north-east slope falling away from the University to the south bank of the Don. Packed solid with black housing and factories, it had to be rebuilt piecemeal. The decision was to transform it into a green combe from the Great Dam above the University right down past the old Royal Infirmary, and to shelter it on its north flank by a line of pale-fawn towers marching down the hill, with low-rise terraces on its south flank. This housing is of no great architectural interest (indeed, Womersley towers remained plain box-shapes for his first few years) but the land form is exhilarating – a long ski-run in winter – and from it one looks straight across to the dramatic outline of the second inner-city project, Woodside. This hugs a much steeper escarpment, with radiating terraces below and a group of four towers on the crest, and is conspicuous from all over the city – a kind of man-made rock outcrop. Again, it is clearly intervisible with Park Hill/Hyde Park, the third and much the most remarkable of the central projects.

Park Hill (which has come to denote both the original megastructure opened in 1960 and the crowning edifices of Hyde Park opened six years later) was destined, indeed designed, for international fame, and detailed description is perhaps superfluous. Its great faceted cliffs dominate the central city in rather the same manner as Avignon is dominated by the Palace of the Popes, and against the sunrise its silhouette has the mystery and austerity of a giant crusader castle. It stands on the steepest of the central escarpments and its notorious slums had already between the wars been partially redeveloped with glum walk-up flats; but its people had been attached to it because of its handiness both for the steelworks in the Don Valley immediately below it to the north and for the busy markets in the Sheaf Valley immediately below it to the west. The inter-war tenements had to

79 and 80. Netherthorpe looking downhill in 1951 and uphill in 1979

stay, but below them the scarp was ready to be cleared and greened, and above them the slope rose steeply to a windy plateau. The lower site, a blunted elongated triangle, comes down almost to the floor of

81. Sheffield's Crusader Castle

the valley at its northern and nearest point, then widens as it climbs away to the south.

The young team Womersley put on to the job in 1953 was led by Jack Lynn and Ivor Smith, who had recently left the AA. Le Corbusier's *Unité* at Marseilles had finally opened in 1952, and the 'street deck', the street in the sky, giving access to two-level flats below it and above, was what all the young wanted to do. It had dominated the Smithsons' entries for the Sheffield University competition and for the Golden Lane one in London, and it was the entries of Smith and Lynn (who had teamed up with Ryder in Newcastle) for this latter which brought them to Womersley's notice. You could trace the idea back if you wanted via the Coventry shopping centre to the Rows at Chester, but its new protagonists would have played down this provenance. To them its beauty was social, not architectural: it seemed to promise the rebirth of the Street,[7] of doorstep gossip and children's mysterious games, abolished by the devotees of mixed development, but in its new form safe from road accidents and freed of Victorian claustrophobia. Le Corbusier's deck had been internal and gloomy, but the Sheffield ones would be open to immense panoramas and wide enough for milk floats and tricycles. But best of all, the long slope of the site made it possible for you to walk on to them at the south end and find yourself fourteen floors up at the north, and this in turn meant that the lifts could be 'voluntary' and therefore fewer, their breakdowns less catastrophic, and the ground landscaping less hard, because so much of the circulation would go on up above. This change of scale is even more effective in reverse: the spatial experience of walking out of the cheerful and crowded central markets, crossing the airy bridges over road and rail into the central portal of Park Hill, straight up to the top, then along the highest deck, deflected this way and that with the great building's ramifications, with its scale becoming more intimate and domestic as the ground comes up to meet you, is unique to this particular place. And the architecture, in plain protest against the blandness of Greenhill and Gleadless, is by later standards not affectedly brutalist: it is simply incredibly plain, no doubt reflecting the no-nonsense tradition of artisan Sheffield. Mollified somewhat by the changes of brick colour that denote the different 'Rows' and by variations in weathering, it has not worn badly.

But how has it worn as a social experiment? Mrs Demers, the devoted council officer who moved in ahead of tenants and mothered the infant community in its early years, conducted a social survey in 1962,[8] and the results were highly encouraging. Of course, Park Hill was exceptional in housing more people than the slums it replaced, nearly all of whose inhabitants (like Byker's) had wished to remain there; none were drafted. So it was a stable community (indicated by the seven-year-old girl, met in a lift in 1979, who when asked how long she had lived in Park Hill replied 'sixteen years'). 'You won't find five people in a hundred who don't like it,' a resident told another reporter in 1965. 92 per cent in Mrs Demers's survey felt no loss of privacy, and only 13 per cent complained of the lack of yard or garden; only 2 per cent would have preferred to live further out, only 7 per cent did not care for the look of the building. Of course the high density produced problems for children (said 21 per cent), with boredom leading to casual damage and rowdyism which in 1979 caused a tragic but exemplary accident when a little girl was killed by a television set hurled from one of the decks. The Garchey refuse disposal system was inadequate; the noise of footsteps on the decks could be irritating in the rooms below; the lifts, as so often, were insufficient in size and distribution, and the stupendous view you got out of the lift window as it climbed the highest tower in Hyde Park scarcely compensated for the biting wind as you waited too long on an exposed landing. Indeed in Hyde Park, the central and highest

82. Central parts of Park Hill, with Hyde Park behind

'keep' of this superhuman castle, Womersley had overreached himself: the hill-crest topography did not allow the decks to emerge on to
the ground, and the building was altogether too exposed and too
remote. Time showed it to be the most unloved of Sheffield's high-rise
projects, and it was decided in 1976 to thin out its large proportion
of big families, with their 1,132 children of 18 and under, and gradually to replace them with University and Polytechnic students. But in
the late seventies the original Park Hill could still be officially
described as 'something approaching a model in terms of community
interest and pride'. The ratio of transfers to total tenancies was lower
than in the Council's suburban estates, and the community's stability
was such that there was a desire to reserve flats as they fell vacant for
the married children of the original population. 'There can alas be no
doubt', wrote Pevsner in his West Riding guide, 'that such a vast
scheme of closely set high blocks will be a slum in half a century or
less, but hopefully a cosy slum.' There seems to be some determination
in Park Hill to prove him wrong.

The rest of the story of Sheffield housing can be briefly told. Inevitably, under the population pressures of the sixties, the city continued to build high. A repeat of Park Hill was tried up-valley at Kelvin as a Byker-type wall to shelter low-rise housing from industry to the north of it, and a group of tall towers, now more sophisticated in design, rose on the high ground of the beautiful Norfolk estate south of Park Hill. Simultaneously, with Whitehall encouragement and even participation,[9] three kinds of prefabricated housing were tried, some of them depressingly shoddy and ill-built. Nearing the end of his time, Womersley persuaded the Council to set up, with Leeds, Nottingham and Hull, the Yorkshire Development Group, in hopes that the successes of the CLASP consortium could be repeated in the field of housing. A young ex-LCC architect, Martin Richardson, disenchanted with towers, using a domino-like concrete slab system, designed one rather sombre group of collegiate-scale flats near the University, redeemed by lavish landscaping. This flexible, low-rise version of Park Hill was capable of considerable development, but by the time it was finished (1968) Womersley had gone, Ronan Point had collapsed, the Labour Party had collapsed too all over the north and the era of mass housing, of prefabrication and of high densities had gone for good.

Ten years later, the wheel had just about completed its circle. The city had at last acquired its new territories in the south, and little brick cottages on winding lanes, substandard as to space and minimal as to cost, were being built to a Harlow-type master plan in the rolling fields of the new Mosborough neighbourhoods, previously in Derbyshire. To ex-urban residents the nice landscaping scarcely compensates for their remoteness from the city, not to mention their total lack of cupboard space. But their low density was no longer seen as reprehensible: there was now more housing land than housing demand, the main applicants being pensioners, and even in the inner city vacant sites were being turned over to semi-detached houses and bungalows. Even so, three compact urban projects of the late seventies showed that good men were still at work: the first a tight little group of terraces by Jefferson and Sheard in the tough Housing Action Area of Darnall; the second, an immensely long crescent of houses by Ivor Smith and Hutton crouching on a gale-swept crest properly called Sky Edge; the third, a sheltered and sunny deck-access scheme at Stannington by the City Architect, mainly for old people. But by the time they were finished they already seemed the last of their kind.

For by the late seventies, the problem in Sheffield as in most cities outside London was no longer a housing problem but an environmental one. The slums had been disposed of, and so had the crude

83 and 84. The view across the Don valley, before and after

shortage of dwellings in relation to households. But there were still depressing districts like Darnall and Pitsmoor overlooking the steelworks of the lower Don, ravaged by clearances, unappealing to private enterprise and yet slow to respond to Council action because of the complexity of the interests involved, not least the hostility of community associations to any further clearances. Compared with the Newcastle Council, Sheffield's had done virtually no house improvement before 1975 and housing associations had been a good deal less active – a symptom no doubt of the lack of middle-class leadership that had long characterized the city. So there was leeway to make up in the remaining twilight areas. But by the same token the legacy of the years of the great projects was a great deal happier than most. Of the city's 90,000 council houses and flats of all ages, only 900 (one in a hundred) were vacant in 1979, and the one in thirty of the population (compared with one in forty in Newcastle) who lived in high flats were, as far as was humanly possible, people who had no desire to move.

In all the new neighbourhoods many excellent schools and one or two good churches were commissioned from first-rate architects, but

the city centre was another matter. While Burns in Newcastle got to work on his ambitious three-dimensional plan for a city that was already splendid and little damaged, nothing of the kind emerged for Sheffield which was neither. Formally, there had been Abercrombie in 1924 and *Sheffield Replanned* in 1947 but both were in architectural terms obsolete, and the statutory plans of 1952 and 1957, like so many others, failed abjectly to provide any graphic image of what the centre might become, or any three-dimensional guidelines for developers. Womersley, well aware of the deficiency, hopefully put another highly talented young West Riding architect, Andrew Derbyshire, in charge of the centre, and they devised an exciting multi-level structure that would fly over the gloomy trench of the Sheaf and make the arrival from St Pancras less dispiriting than it was (and is), as well as wafting the Park Hill people straight into the heart of things. As a foretaste, Derbyshire was able to build on the site of the vanished castle a brilliant three-dimensional market structure of many levels and surprises, in the same plain language as Park Hill, which makes all our later musak-conditioned paradises seem vulgar and rapacious, and remains immensely popular. But he was not the

Planning Officer, and without that authority there was no point in staying for long. Sheffield therefore continued to bumble along, fortunate accidents alternating with errors. Of the latter, the most inexcusable (since Abercrombie had advised against it) was to encourage the bombed-out multiple stores to ribbon-develop the Moor, a radial road too far from the centre of things, with pallid Portland stone fronts quite out of key with Sheffield, and then to compound the error (as was common in the fifties) by widening it. It is now, needless to say, pedestrianized. It only needs a new-style air-conditioned shopping centre closer to the central markets (as was recently proposed) to kill the poor Moor stone dead.

Like Birmingham's used to be, Sheffield's centre is hemmed in by tiny industries, even though the 'little mesters' have diminished in numbers since the war from 630 to 150. But their sheds and shacks remain, among them every now and then a good classical chapel, and a certain sentiment attaches to this twilight area. Of course it would be felled overnight if the big developers were interested, but, unlike Birmingham, central Sheffield suffers from inadequate commercial demand, and while the obvious change of use must be to housing, this too no longer has its old urgency and is deterred by its new costs. However, one or two housing associations are at work in this area. Meanwhile, the western half of the so-called Civic Circle has been built. Its architecturally miserable Birmingham-style roundabouts are known as Squares, perhaps in affectionate reference to Sheffield's only Georgian example, the tiny Paradise Square (which is characteristically built on a slope, unfortunately a north one). One of these roundabouts, officially Castle Square but unofficially the Hole in the Road, has pedestrians circulating below the gyrating traffic, daylit by this great hole in the middle – a solution disapproved by Womersley who preferred to put people on top. It too is on a slope. Fortunately, these rather ill-coordinated road widenings and roundabouts and fragmentary rings have sufficed, for a variety of reasons. The city is on the way to nowhere, so it has no through-traffic; the centre is underdeveloped; traffic peaks are mitigated by off-peak shift-working in the steelworks; and last but not least, Labour Councils continue to subsidize bus fares to an extent unique in England. Even the much criticized shortage of parking space can nowadays be counted a virtue.

No doubt Sheffield's failure to achieve in its civic and commercial centre what used to be called Civic Design would nowadays be counted a virtue too. Scattered about in no relationship with one another

are individual buildings of character – the Cutlers' Hall, the Town
Hall, the workmanlike series of buildings lining the west bank of the
Sheaf and dominated by the Polytechnic, one or two modest office
blocks (but not the most conspicuous) and, best of our own age, the
attractive and well-liked Crucible Theatre, situated in a characteristically disorderly space. The most popular feature of the city centre is not,
needless to say, a building at all, but the cheerful green 'square' on the
warm side of the Town Hall, achieved by the scandalous demolition

85. Town Hall in winter, with the new annexe on the right

in the thirties of a Georgian church and festooned over summer
lunch-hours with half-naked office workers. It is now overlooked by
the 1978 Town Hall extension, a clumsy butter-yellow block which
has belatedly gone overboard for that cliché of the sixties, the bellows-
camera window. Its one virtue is that it is only 3 storeys high.
Another large and recent disappointment is the ponderous red-brick
office block built by the PSA to house (great scoop for Sheffield employment) a couple of thousand civil servants of the Manpower Services Commission – if this survives. Axially placed like London's Bush
House at the bottom end of the dead-straight Moor, it fashionably
refuses to acknowledge the fact. In the end, the most moving architectural experience in the heart of the city is the interior of the Cathedral,
a monument (once again) to changes of mind, yet finally as a result
of Ansell and Bailey's additions of the sixties a marvellously complex
and colourful interior space, as columnated as a beech-wood.

Recounting this rather downbeat story, it is easy to understand
how important it was to Womersley to achieve by some means that

architectural overview of the commercial and civic centre which he had so vividly exercised elsewhere. In their respective spheres the City Engineer and the Estates Surveyor were powerful and effective figures, the former having won for Sheffield a route for the M1 with its spur into the very heart of the city, which made the journey by car from London faster than by high-speed train, the latter having handled office developers with considerable panache and secured for Sheffield (against the competition of Leeds as natural regional capital) an impressive total of new floor-space and new white-collar jobs. But the architectural input into all this was minimal, and the opportunity for a combination of the offices of City Architect and City Planning Officer, the stock solutions of the sixties in all enlightened cities, would obviously arrive when the City Engineer (and Planning Officer) came to retire in 1964. In fact an adverse report from this latter postponed the change, and Womersley inevitably treated the matter as one of confidence and withdrew, like too many of the best people in public architecture, into private practice.

But if the post-war city centre is a missed opportunity, the post-war University area is a triumphant success. The old red-brick (literally) University buildings were by chance situated just the right distance out on the ridge where a well-wooded Victorian inner suburb meets a large working-class area. When the time came to implement the Robbins Report and quadruple their output, the University authorities organized in 1953 a well-timed competition which attracted a glamorous entry and resulted in the appointment of Gollins, Melvin and Ward, who were to retain the confidence of their clients for a generation. The Library and the Arts Tower were classics of the late fifties, and later additions by the same architects like the Students' Union and the red-brick additions to the old building, linked by Ove Arup's exciting underpass/concourse, have enlarged their vocabulary and enhanced the scene. Other good architects like Tom Mellor and William Whitfield have contributed. On a late May morning when every tree and shrub is in fresh leaf and flower, there is no more life-enhancing experience than to perambulate this now rather Ivy-League University quarter. William Flockton and his son, one of those sound Victorian firms wholly dedicated to their native city, and contemporary Edmund Ward marvellously complement one another over a gap of a century. Flockton's masterly terrace of 1832 (The Mount, now HQ of British Steel), his sonorously classical King Edward VII School (1840), his son's elegant Mappin Gallery (1884) and soaring spire of St John's (1888) are the star performers, with a great

86. The University: Ward's red-brick extension, Arup's flyover

Paxton orangery in the nearby Botanic Gardens. To all these and to the north-Oxford residential ambience in which they are set, Ward's stylish modernism is a perfect foil and tribute, and Womersley has

87. Sheffield's red-brick Edwardian building with its 1960 additions. The Arts Tower is the centrepiece

wisely irrupted into this superior scene with a group of his workers' flats. But his intention was that the glass Arts Tower should preside unchallenged over the University ridge, and this has recently been fatally compromised by the monstrous slab of the Hallamshire Hospital: so hard is it to achieve a unity and hold to it.

The loss of Womersley was to be followed a decade later by the loss of several of the leading people in the city administration who had been responsible for the post-war transformation. Some of these losses were a direct consequence of the Walker 'reform' of local government. It was bad enough that the new and artificial Metropolitan County of South Yorkshire was to be run not from its natural capital but from Barnsley. It was worse when the County's Structure Plan belatedly appeared in 1978. It turned out to be based on the well-known left-wing principle of clobbering success. Under a photograph of a bent old miner in a scene of industrial dereliction, 'The Structure Plan is aimed towards helping the have-nots' it piously announced. It was galling for old Labour stalwarts in Sheffield to find that their prolonged efforts to attract and diversify employment in the city, which had resulted in its having (at 4·5 per cent) an unemployment rate well below the national average, were now to disadvantage it: it was not henceforth to be a 'job priority area', and new industry was to be steered to the mining areas north of Rotherham. Knowing the precarious fortune of steel and the secure future of coal, this did not look objectively wise. The city also strongly objected, in a document of remarkable bitterness, to the 'fine detail' in the plan devoted to matters such as shopping and parking which it did not think concerned the higher authority, and to meaninglessly precise target figures rather than the range now generally considered more realistic. Conflict of this kind is of course now normal form under the new dispensation, but it is inevitably worse when a city of 555,000 people is no longer master in its own house.

But nothing can detract from the triumph that clean air and brave architecture have wrought in Sheffield, so that what was a generation ago a blackened and impenetrable urban wilderness is now, with Edinburgh, Bristol and Bath, one of the small company of British cities which can be seen in its totality, in its uniqueness, and taken pride in.

CHAPTER 6

Liverpool

Medieval kings in western Europe were never better than *primus inter pares* in their uneasy relations with the great territorial magnates, and none more uneasy than King John. With the loss of his Angevin inheritance and the breaking of traditional continental ties, his attention turned west and north to the untamed Celts, best approached across the Irish Sea. But the only port in those parts, Roman Chester, lay under the domination of the quasi-independent marcher Earls of Chester. For a safe royal base, the Mersey suggested itself, and in 1207 the King's surveyors recommended a little inlet on the east bank, a mere pool a few feet deep, where some fishermen kept boats, three miles from the parish church at Walton-on-the-Hill. Their plan for the new port, an H of streets oriented east–west with the crossbar pointing south to a castle site overlooking the pool, met the needs of the little town for five centuries and survives to this day. In due course a royal castle, a grim Bastille lacking the elegance of Edward I's Welsh designs, glared down on the town on one side (to the discomfort of its citizens) and surveyed on the other the wide hunting grounds of Toxteth, artificially laid waste for the purpose.

Continually resented by the merchants of Chester, who as late as 1565 described it as 'a creek of the port of Chester', Liverpool prospered in the otherwise miserable fourteenth century, then decayed with the Wars of the Roses in the fifteenth – its activity much dependent on whether some new Welsh or Irish campaign was in hand. But even in Tudor times, with the Royal Navy transformed and trade opening up across the Atlantic, the place was tiny: in 1565 it had 185 cottages and a dozen ships, the largest the *Eagle* of 40 tons with twelve men and a boy, plus a bunch of casual waterfront workers adept at pilfering from ships.

One should not suppose from its early charters and its royal castle that Liverpool was any freer than other English towns from the grip (which could vary in character from charitable patronage to extortion) of the local aristocracy. The Molyneux of Sefton, the Stanleys of Knowsley and (later and by marriage) the Salisburys had important and subsequently valuable estates surrounding the town. Of the three, the Stanleys were paramount. From their keep at the water's edge they sailed to their private kingdom of the Isle of Man, and after Bosworth in 1485, as Earls of Derby, they predominated in local life well into the twentieth century. The 16th Earl was the first Lord Mayor in 1895, and the 17th was Lord Mayor, President of the Chamber of Commerce for thirty-two years and Chancellor of the University. But they saw no need to risk their large resources in 'trade', or in the civic improvements that flowed from it, such as the building of the first dock in the old pool in 1715, the levelling at the same time of the ruinous castle, or the building of a new church on its site. Georgian Liverpool, unlike Georgian London, was the creation of merchants, not of landowners. In that age, the town's first great period of expansion and prosperity derived from the plantation economies of the American east coast and the Caribbean. This Atlantic trade was triangular – down to west Africa to unload textiles and pick up slaves, across the tropical Atlantic with the trade winds, then back with the Gulf Stream carrying raw cotton, sugar and tobacco. The unlimited scope for dock expansion north and south along Merseyside gave Liverpool first an edge over Bristol, which had pioneered this trade, and then an overwhelming advantage. The Georgian town, which by the end of the century had reached a population of 80,000 (a tenth of London's), was much like other red-brick provincial towns of its day. One can judge only from old prints, because like the post-Fire City of London it was completely replaced by the Victorians, and only two buildings of significance, the elegant Bluecoat School of 1716 and John Wood's mid-century Town Hall, have survived. All four of the town's Georgian churches have gone. Among Liverpool's many demolitions the most regrettable was the rapid removal after the last war of Foster's grand Ionic Customs House, bombed but repairable, at a time when such removals could be effected without fuss.

Around the turn of the century the components of Liverpool's trade began to change, and with them the character of the town. The moving spirit in this transformation was the liberal intellectual William Roscoe. As MP he took a leading part in the abolition of the slave trade in 1807[1] (while the Town Council commissioned a local clergyman to write a pamphlet in its support). Three other factors combined to set the pattern of Liverpool's nineteenth-century expansion: first and foremost, the industrial revolution in the Lancashire cotton mills; second, the end of the East India Company's monopoly of trade to the Far East; and third, the opening up of the American West and the consequent surge of European emigration.

The port now grew with the Empire, importing raw materials from the Americas and the East, exporting the phenomenal output of west Yorkshire and south Lancashire to the entire world, and exporting people in their millions. Of the 5·5 million emigrants who crossed the Atlantic between 1860 and 1900, 4·75 million, many of them Scandinavians landed at Hull, sailed from Liverpool. The flood was by no means one-way. In 1847, the worst year of the Irish famine, when there were already, according to Liverpool's (and England's) first Medical Officer of Health, 40,000 people living in the 8,000 cellars of Liverpool, no less than 300,000 starving people came ashore. Between 1801 and 1841 the population of the city had already quadrupled. By 1884 the housing density in parts of the dockside was 1,200 p.p.a.

Against this brutal background the city's Grecian civic buildings may now appear the blandest hypocrisy. But it was Roscoe's belief (and he died in 1831 before the worst happened) that ever since classical Athens Art had flowered on the proceeds of Trade. The following is an early specimen of an art-form to which he became increasingly addicted:

> From climes where Slavery's iron chain
> Has bound to earth the soaring mind,
> Where GRECIA mourns her blasted plain
> To want and indolence resigned;
> From fair ITALIA's once-loved shore,
> (The land of Freedom now no more)
> Disdainful of each former seat,
> The Arts, a lovely train, retreat:
> Still prospering under FREEDOM's eye,
> With her they bloom, with her they fly;
> And when the Power transferred her smile
> To ALBION's ever-grateful isle,
> The lovely fugitives forgot to roam,
> But raised their altars here, and fixed their happier home.[2]

The first monument of neo-classic Liverpool is of course the Lyceum Club in Bold Street (1801), but for many years the *literati* of Liverpool concentrated on the founding of cultural institutions, on the principle that education was the best antidote to crime. It was an uphill fight. 'There are too many boys belonging to the schools, and the savage brutality behind is dreadful: no attention or common civility,' complained a visiting lecturer.[3] It was not till the forties that the great masterpiece of Grecian Liverpool, St George's Hall, rose on a spur of the low crescent-shaped ridge that overlooked the Mersey and the spreading slums behind the new docks. As with most Victorian monuments, it had a purely picturesque and not a formal relationship with the layout of the town, and though a backcloth of appropriately columnated edifices was later contrived for it, Liverpool (despite the firm conviction that it is the greatest neo-classic building in Europe) has never been able to manage its environment. This is mainly because it immediately became the hub of the transportation network. The railway was first brought right up to its flank and later (1870) proclaimed by Waterhouse's towering, and needless to say non-axial, Gothic hotel (now empty). Fifty years after that the Mersey Tunnel emerged on its other flank. This was fatal. In due course, traffic volumes produced their inevitable coils of spaghetti and gantry signs blocked every view of the main portico. Of course the building

88. St George's Hall: 'suicide to look at it'

had always been seen kinetically, not frontally: now it was suicide to look at it at all. To add insult to injury, an ill-sited and ill-fated commercial complex with unnecessarily heavy pedestrian bridges, supposed to represent the Swinging Liverpool of the nineteen-sixties, was placed immediately in front of it. Finally the pediment sculpture was declared unsafe, removed and never replaced.

While Grecian Liverpool rose on its plateau, Cyclopean Liverpool emerged on the banks below. Jesse Hartley's materials were granite, hard brick and cast iron, used with a logical severity that makes Georgian and later Victorian warehouses look pretty or pretentious. The culmination was Albert Dock, completed after much argument in mid career (1845), but the whole thirty-six years of Hartley's career as Dock Engineer witnessed the reflection in architecture of oceanic forces on a scale which the more sheltered and scattered docks of London never emulated. Ferociously bombed and fortuitously demolished, its remains survive precariously.

Over this first half of the century the 'two nations' of Liverpool grew apart, and as usual the rich moved up to higher ground, leaving the poor below. Most of 'Georgian' Liverpool, like 'Georgian' Newcastle, is early Victorian, and none the worse for that. But, unlike Newcastle, it was built strictly for residence, and then, like the similar parts of

89. 'Georgian' Liverpool

other provincial cities, its terraces and squares were taken over for professional chambers and consulting rooms. Late-Victorian institutions, university colleges and teaching hospitals, were naturally sited close by – cuckoos in the nest of any pleasant residential district. So inexorably the fate of Bloomsbury overtook its Liverpool equivalent, but with the difference that what was torn apart in Liverpool was the only decently laid-out urban housing the city possessed. The university explosion of the nineteen-sixties, so impressively coped with in Newcastle and Sheffield, has ironically been a visual disaster in the city that possessed the first and best University Schools of Architecture and of Planning in the United Kingdom, and under the professional eye of the country's most distinguished line of urbanist professors – Reilly, Abercrombie and Holford. Pevsner ascribes this sad outcome to 'a nimiety of architects', and one can only concur, noting that the last injury, the brutal new hospital, is perhaps the worst.

Of course the really rich moved further out. In the 1820s Everton, so soon to be swamped in a sea of black slums and then in our own day in a forest of grim towers, 'may be said to have reached the height of its beauty and attraction … From the umbrageous foliage of the gardens noble mansions in tier above tier looked out on a lovely landscape.' But the best move was south. Paxton laid out Prince's Park for a private client in 1843 and girdled it with curving roads in the manner of Nash, with villas whose sales paid for its upkeep. A ring of larger municipal parks followed in the sixties, laid out to provide not only privileged building sites but also environments where 'the most obdurate heart may be softened and gently led to pursuits which refine, purify and alleviate the humblest of the toil-worn'. Sefton Park, largest and grandest of them all, is surrounded by more opulent houses embosomed in a rich variety of trees, now mature, dark and immense. The romantic groves of Allerton, with stone-walled lanes over-arched by great trees, fittingly commemorate Roscoe's pastoral view of Nature, and seem all the richer and greener now that the farmed landscape of England is so tragically denuded. Virtually under siege in all these suburbs are the locked churches, which include in their intriguing variety Rickman's lacy experiment in cast iron, Pearson's most beautiful chancel, and a church in Allerton glazed entirely by Burne-Jones.

Meanwhile the slums spread, engulfing earlier suburbs. Mrs Gaskell, whose *Mary Barton* directly confronts the theme of the 'two nations', set her novel in Manchester because she lived there, and her picture of Liverpool is a breezy and lively one:

And Mary did look, and saw down an opening made in the forest of masts belonging to the vessels in dock, the glorious river, along which white-sailed ships were gliding with the ensigns of all nations not 'braving the battle', but telling of the distant lands, spicy or frozen, that sent to that mighty mart for their comforts or their luxuries; she saw small boats passing to and fro on that glittering highway, but she also saw such puffs and clouds of smoke from the countless steamers, that she wondered at Charley's intolerance of the smoke of Manchester.

In fact, in the years in which she wrote (1846–8) Liverpool's slums were notoriously the worst in England, because of the general use of cellars, the tidal wave of Irish immigration and the lack of local industry to absorb it. A century later, after generations of pioneer municipal housing, Charles Reilly noted that Everton 'has for several years held the record in the country for the tonnage of soot per acre deposited as a sort of sewage on people's heads, their buildings, their clothes and all they possess ... In the Liverpool slums which get the full density of the smoke from the river, the gloom of the black joints is enhanced by the coating of soot on the dark bricks which the rain, itself sticky with smoke, is unable to wash from the crevices. Miles of narrow streets of such buildings, with separate families living in the basements and in each room of the three or four floors above, with every other window, it seemed, broken and stuffed up with sacking, every doorway worn shiny and darker still with the grease and dirt of the inhabitants and their clothes, every other child with bare feet – that was what this dockline of slums was like nearly as far as the docks extended.'

The second half of the century and the Edwardian summer saw the port reach its apogee and with it the commercial centre behind it.

90. The silhouette from the Mersey

Both basked in the sunshine of the great American boom that followed the victory of the North and the exploitation of the West. The age that began with the *Great Britain* and ended with the *Titanic* (which, ominously, sailed from Southampton) saw the size and speed of liners expand with the expansion of European emigration and American tourism. Downtown Liverpool on its gridiron plan transformed itself into a miniature New York, architecturally innovative and even eccentric, and is still second only to Glasgow in the quality of its surviving High Victorian commercial palaces. The Athenian model was soon jettisoned in favour of the Florentine one, with the office building as *palazzo*, the period that had begun with C. R. Cockerell's classic Bank of England ending with Aubrey Thomas's *Art Nouveau* Liver Building. In this progression, the scintillating Oriel Chambers of 1864 by the unknown genius Peter Ellis is the central masterpiece and an epitome of the verve and originality always characteristic of the city.

But the Great War, the beginning of the end of the British Empire, was the beginning of the end of its great trading port. Liverpool's shipping companies lost one and a half million tons of shipping to enemy action and now had to face unprecedented competition from countries that had stayed neutral. The decline of the Lancashire textile industries and the cost of transportation from the Midlands and the south where the growth industries had established themselves scaled down demand for the port, so that while London retained its 40 per cent of UK trade Merseyside's contracted from a third to a fifth. And of course the great liners on the New York run, soon to reach their peak of glamour, had left Liverpool for ever. However, the Addison Act now made housing a charge on the Exchequer, and the long effort to civilize the brutal old port and to give a decent environment to its three-quarter million inhabitants[4] could be tackled in earnest.

The only way to do this seemed to be to extend the city all round its semicircular perimeter in the prevailing Garden City manner, so as to thin out the worst of the overcrowding in the inner core; then one could get busy on the slums. It meant long tram-rides to ever remoter suburbs, but to Liverpool's lasting benefit Brodie, the City Engineer, laid out the new axial roads in generous American parkway style and linked them by an equally umbrageous ring road, Queen's Drive. Here L. H. Keay, first of City Architects, deployed his handsome neo-Georgian houses and well-grouped flats, very much in current LCC style but more generously and substantially built. These are still the

91. Housing by L. H. Keay, now listed

city's most popular council estates, are now 'listed', and are rapidly
being sold off. Keay's most ambitious undertaking, the 'new town' for
20,000 at Speke, was overtaken by World War II and lapsed in quality
thereafter. But between the wars some 65,000 families were re-
housed, 38,611 by the Council (compared with 2,895 in all the years
that ended in 1914). And the city acquired, almost behind its back,
another masterpiece in Scott's Cathedral, won in competition back in
1903, like St George's Hall, by an unknown architect in his twenties.

92. Scott's Cathedral in characteristically Liverpudlian environment

But the slums were only nibbled at, and the depression of the thirties hit Merseyside as hard as it hit New York. To mitigate unemployment the stock solutions in the cities of the north were public works and 'trading estates' offering cheap out-of-town sites to 'footloose light industries'. The Council pursued both energetically, the great achievement in the former being the first Mersey Tunnel, with its tasteful ventilation towers. Industrial estates at Speke, Aintree and Kirkby offered work to the new suburbanites, and contributed to the diversification and de-casualization of Merseyside labour; but in the black Victorian terraces life remained grim, and it took another war to dispose of unemployment. After the bombing there could no longer be any question that most of the inner city was a wreck, not fit to live in. If there was one thing on which opinion was unanimous, it was that the slums must go. Keay retired in 1948 to be succeeded by his deputy, Ronald Bradbury, who was in many respects the man for the hour, with a punching committee-manner and the capacity, once pointed in a certain direction, to drive on relentlessly. That his architecture was consistently mediocre no longer seems relevant, experience showing conclusively that in housing there is no correlation between originality and success. Regional policy was a scaled-down version of London's – Green Belt and satellites, with two New Towns, Skelmersdale and Runcorn, earmarked mainly for Liverpool. Additionally, on a disused army ordnance site beyond the city boundary at Kirkby, the plan was to develop a 750-acre industrial estate and a 'complete community', four times the size of Speke. Reviewing progress in 1965, by which time 50,000 people had moved in, Bradbury could claim that it had achieved the fastest growth in the UK and that it was 'not possible to convey in print the spirit of Kirkby or the enthusiasm which has gone into its creation'. This was perfectly true of the time. The first generation at Kirkby, mainly families with young children, were happy: they had a job and a home. Those were the children who were to transform Kirkby into a by-word for alienation and vandalism. For the industrial estate, unable to compete with the glamorous and geographically better-placed facilities offered by Runcorn New Town, flopped. The place was remote from the County's base and interests, and the split of responsibility between three authorities – City, County and District – meant uncoordinated and inadequate services. Neglect lapsed into dereliction. The Corporation, at its wits' end for resources to cope, even appealed for EEC regional funds. A visiting Commission could see nothing wrong with the housing: 'Our people would be delighted with it.' In 1974 the

Corporation was clever enough to unload the whole place on to the new Metropolitan Borough of Knowsley.

Now it was at last possible to tear down the inner-city slums on the scale that had been dreamt of for half a century. And of course, at this scale, a great many habitable houses went down with them. As in London, high densities were called for on the cleared sites so as to minimize overspill while still making land available for schools and playing fields and parks (and above all, as would soon appear, for roads). So, again as in London, slabs of maisonettes and towers of flats were the answer. Even so, in the twenty years since 1945 the city gained only 56,400 new dwellings from all sources, which compared poorly with the twenty years after 1918, when it had gained 65,000.[5] So, as enjoined by Whitehall, the Council turned to system building, and following an expedition to Paris in 1962 ordered twenty-two Camus towers, six of them of 22 storeys. By 1965 Bradbury was able to report that 110 tower blocks were built or building.

93. Everton landscape, with five of Bradbury's 110 towers

With all this effort going into 'social' building, with Gibberd's elegant Catholic Cathedral rising on the site where Lutyens had fortunately been denied his last and vastest monument, precious little had been done about the black and bomb-scarred business centre; and the little

94. Gibberd's 1960 Roman Catholic Cathedral

that was done, like the replacement of the blitzed shops in Lord Street, was the usual third-rate Portland stone commercial frontages. Local government was bipartisan and conservative; there was full employment and the workers had 'never had it so good'. In 1957 a local historian could describe Liverpool as a 'boom-town'.[6] Inevitably if gradually, the failure to do anything about its image was becoming an embarrassment. In 1960 a new generation of Tory councillors, led by Stewart and Entwhistle, took over. For the first time, an input came from the University's prestigious Chair of Town and Country Planning, when Holford with the strong support of Dame Evelyn Sharp persuaded the new regime that a consultant for the renewal of the city centre should be appointed. The choice fell on Graeme Shankland, one of Percy Johnson-Marshall's three chief planners at the LCC, who had been in charge of the planning for the South Bank and the Elephant and Castle, already being sadly compromised. The retirement in that same year (1962) of the City Engineer (and Planning Officer) at last made it possible, as in Newcastle, to set up an independent City Planning Officer,[7] and the appointment went to another leading LCC figure, Walter Bor. For the three years of Shankland's appointment two of the brightest stars in the high planning firmament of the sixties were in conjunction in Liverpool, and much was expected of them.

The mood was highly positive. 1962, the year of the start on the new Cathedral, was the year of the Beatles' 'Love Me Do', and the cellars – nearly a hundred of them – that had so recently housed huge families of Irish or coloured immigrants now housed the Liverpool Sound. Characteristically, it was Littlewoods that set the pace with the first large modern office slab in Old Hall Street and John Moores's sophisticated and generous art patronage (the first *Biennale* at the Walker Art Gallery was in 1957). Native painters like Arthur Ballard, Sam Walsh and Adrian Henri brought a breath of fresh air to the Liverpool Academy, while in pubs in the city centre poets like Brian Patten and Roger McGough set up jazz-and-poetry sessions. Even the declining cinemas were doing more business: 'With the passing of the craze for television and bingo and with improvements in the quality of films, attendance figures are beginning to level out.' In the prevailing euphoria, Shankland could write:

In the next fifteen years, the country will undergo changes that will have considerable effect on entertainment and recreation. People will have more free time as a result of the working week dropping from its present average of forty-six hours to a probable thirty hours by 1980. The population of the city region is expected to increase by 400,000 by 1981. Rising incomes will give most people greater spending power and the growth of education could well lead to increases in intellectual and artistic pursuits. The number of cars is expected to triple by 1981 and this will enable more people to come into Liverpool and also to go to other towns and to the countryside.

It is likely that the use of pubs will increase in intensity as some of the existing ones are demolished or moved in the course of redevelopment. Clubs of all kinds can be expected to increase in number as well as in quality.

Walter Bor, on his broader canvas, paints an equally expansive picture:[8]

While the extensive slums and largely obsolete Central Area are Liverpool's most glaring shortcomings, these defects also represent the city's unique redevelopment possibilities. The whole of the inner crescent of 'twilight' areas and two thirds of the Central Area are due to be rebuilt by the turn of the century.

Compared with other war-damaged English cities which have been rebuilt since the war, Liverpool's post-war development, particularly in the Central

Area, has been slow. However, this slow start may yet prove a blessing in disguise since town-planning ideas and techniques have advanced dramatically only in recent years, culminating in the publication of *Traffic in Towns* by the Buchanan team. Liverpool's vast urban renewal programme, coupled with the city's extensive land ownership, provides the unique opportunity to incorporate most of the Buchanan principles into the redevelopment; the comprehensive reshaping of the city can now be based upon the most recent techniques of integrated traffic/land use planning and the most advanced design ideas in traffic architecture and in urban development and redevelopment.

It was reckoned that the city's population would be close to a million by 1981, a quarter of whom would have to be housed outside its boundaries. The region's present programme for New Towns and overspill estates fell short by 100,000, so new ones must be started. The port is described as 'Merseyside's greatest single commercial asset ... and a marked expansion of its activities is predicted'. And 1,000 or even 2,000 acres must be reserved for new industries, which 'in the national context of steady economic growth from year to year' are expected to flock to Merseyside. For all this growth, a 'comprehensive regional transport system, integrated into the national network' and preferably run by a single authority, is plainly essential. Brodie's Queen's Drive is dwarfed by inner, middle and orbital motorways and by inner and outer rail loops.

The inner motorway defines the central area of Shankland's remit. Trenched in front of the Anglican Cathedral, elevated elsewhere, its line was suggested by the areas of maximum dereliction and minimum architectural value. So as to avoid the University quarter, it had to cut off both Cathedrals from the city centre. Apart from this it was easy, hugging the dockside on the line vacated by the old elevated railway, and turning inland through some of the worst parts of the inner city. Bor had after all laid down that 'the whole of the inner crescent of twilight areas and two thirds of the central area' were due to be rebuilt. Land availability presented no problem: two thirds of Shankland's area already belonged to the Corporation (though over half of it was under lease).

The philosophy was simple. The inner city was obsolete and needed to be replaced, and at current economic growth projections we could afford to do it. As Le Corbusier had said: 'What gives our dreams their daring is that they can be realized.' The only parts which should be retained were those of architectural value or recent construction. Anticipating the 1967 Civic Amenities Act, Shankland delimited Conservation Areas, but more narrowly than was later to be the fashion: the Victorian 'downtown' on both sides of Castle Street and up to Chapel Street, the St George's Hall plateau, Bold Street, Rodney Street – that was all, apart from individual landmarks. But to these he attached great importance and genuine affection. On either side of the conserved Victorian core there could be groups of new towers, offices to the north, middle-income flats to the south. For a great deal of new office space would be needed:

Our studies have shown that over the next twenty years Liverpool could be faced with the need to accommodate a minimum increase of 3·5 million square feet of office floor-space. In addition to this growth, a further 4 million square feet of new space will be needed to replace obsolete buildings.

Of the increase, over half will be derived from the expansion of existing firms; the remainder will result from the growth of new firms, from increases in the standard of floor-space per worker and the immigration of firms from elsewhere. Growth on this scale presupposes that Liverpool will enjoy its share of rising national prosperity, that the city region will largely accommodate its own population increases and that the city will, by determined effort, meet the demands of the region's growing population for jobs. These three conditions underlie the whole Liverpool City Centre Plan.

The physical concept was simple too, and under the heading Urban Form he was able to express it succinctly:

The new central area will have a clear and memorable form. This will be achieved by a well-defined system of linked open spaces and precincts, and by the careful placing of tall buildings. A new square, with grass and trees, will mark the still centre of the city and the focal point of its pedestrian routes. Around this square and amongst the traditional core of the city, buildings will be kept low. But tall towers will be encouraged at the northern end of Old Hall Street so that, together with the five towers of Strand/ Paradise, the edge of the core will be dramatically marked. The Cathedrals will remain dominant on the ridge, separated from the towers of the office area by a wide swathe of medium-height building.

As to the flats, Shankland points out that whereas 130,000 people commuted daily into the centre, the 21,000 people who actually lived there were mainly large working-class families with a more than average (even for Liverpool) number of young children, whose breadwinners travelled to remote docks and factories. So it seemed sensible to do something to reduce all this travel.

The 'still centre' was to be the heart of a new group of public buildings, complementary to St George's Hall, mainly in order to bring

95. Shankland's three-dimensional concept for the city centre

LIVER BUILDING

233

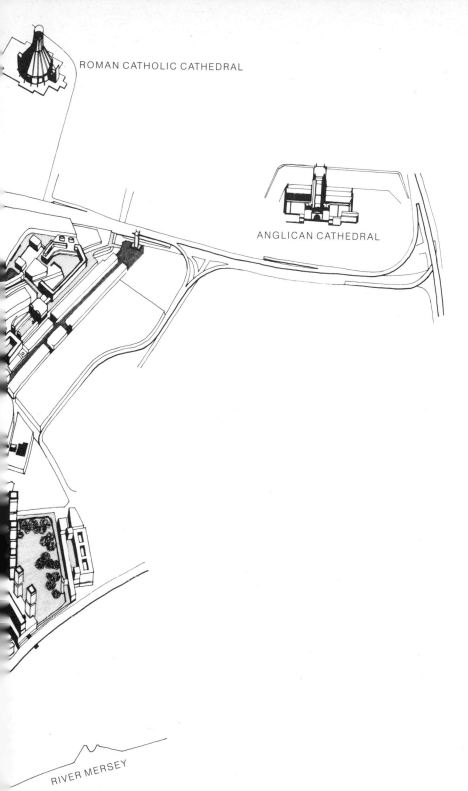

ROMAN CATHOLIC CATHEDRAL

ANGLICAN CATHEDRAL

RIVER MERSEY

together scattered council offices and law courts. Much was hoped of this central project, which would clean up the visual squalor to the south-west of the great portico. Distinguished architects from Britain, Italy and Holland were interviewed, and Colin St John Wilson, who had for many years worked with Leslie Martin at Cambridge and would later succeed him in the Chair, was appointed. It turned out an unhappy story. Wilson, whose first design for the new British Library in Bloomsbury had been so grandly related to another great neo-classic portico, that of the British Museum, seemed to be defeated by the much more complex visual relationships of St George's Hall and produced an insensitive solution, which, to everyone's relief and em-barrassment, was rejected by the Minister after a public inquiry in 1973. This was pure bad luck for the city which had tried to do the right thing.

Half way through Shankland's triennium the Conservatives lost power, and the colourful Labour husband-and-wife team, Tom (Leader of the Council) and Bessie (MP) Braddock, gained it. They were, like many northern city bosses, not enamoured of clever planners from London; but after an internal power struggle in the course of which Tom Braddock dropped dead in the street the Labour leadership passed to the formidable W. H. Sefton, who gave (and still gives) the Plan unqualified support. 'Its publication is a call for action – NOW!' he prefaced it in 1965. Alas, it was too late. For already the storm clouds were gathering. The new Wilson Government, com-mitted to the defence of the pound, had been 'blown off course', and it would never, in our time, be glad confident morning again. So the programming of the City Centre Plan was its first casualty and, as the deferments accumulated, the concept of an urban transformation, which it represented, became increasingly unappealing as well as unaffordable. Shankland and Bor incurred the odium of the vast clearances of derelict property which had in fact been a policy decision that had provided the occasion for, and not been the consequence of, their plans. It was easy to denigrate Shankland's urban form as sim-plistic and brutal, but it was unfair, because it failed to recognize the urbanist's dilemma. Experience had already taught Shankland and Bor that three-dimensional planning can look naive when ravaged by time and poor architecture; but they also knew that the city needed a tangible, dramatic goal, and the crowds that stared down on the great model in the Walker Art Gallery seemed to confirm it. The role had to be played.

In fact the concept has stood up as well as any. The office towers
to the north, and the highly sculptural Law Courts that do duty in lieu
of the five Strand/Paradise towers to the south, together frame the
conserved Victorian core just as intended, and greatly enrich the city's
silhouette from the Mersey. The two Cathedrals on their ridge, and the
St John's Beacon symbolizing more mundane pleasures, further diversify a skyline which is wholly the creation of our century. Inside, the
picture remains patchy. Close-up, the new office buildings are at best
conventional and at worst bizarre, and as in London the deck systems,
isolated from one another, are inevitably under-used and therefore
dangerous, whereas pedestrianized Church Street seems to contain all
of Merseyside on any fine Saturday or weekday lunch hour; and even

96. Lunch hour in Church Street

makeshift Williamson Square, with the gaily extended Playhouse, stands up to the oppressive St John's precinct and the ramshackle site for the 'green heart' with intriguing (unintended) changes of scale.

97. The Playhouse and its extension, facing Williamson Square

Buildings of such character stand about in the background that the foreground muddle is in a Liverpudlian way acceptable. But traffic-free Bold Street is not the smart street it was, and fussy municipal planting now obstructs the vista to St Luke's that the traffic used to hide. By the standards of the past, when architects of the first rank were employed, post-war infill in the business centre, starting in the cissy style of the fifties, then catching the brutalist bug of the sixties, is only now beginning to be acceptable. Too many second-rate minds have relied on the fact that Victorian Liverpool, like Victorian London, has the guts to swallow a good deal of vulgarity.

In 1966 Walter Bor, with an eye on wider horizons, left to set up an international planning consultancy with Richard Llewelyn-Davies, and was succeeded by F. J. C. Amos, who was to see Liverpool through its traumas of the next seven years before going to Birmingham as Chief Executive. The descent from euphoria to cynicism was of course a national experience, heightened on Merseyside by the local

98. The Town Hall at bottom right surrounded by inter-war office blocks
with post-war offices beyond

temperament, as mercurial as the weather, by special factors such as
the symbolic collapse in 1970 of the historic Docks and Harbour
Board, and by the spectacular nature of the planners' mistakes. There
were two sides to them. The first was the gross overestimation of what
the national and local economy could bear. In a chastened policy
statement of 1971, Amos puts it with disarming simplicity: 'The
overriding problem, in terms of implementation, has been the
discrepancy between the resources available and those desirable at
any one point in time.' Surveying the four zones into which he divides
the city, he notes in the city centre 'an inability of public investment
to keep pace with private' (i.e. the speculative office blocks got built
but not the roads or the car parks); in the Redevelopment Zone – the
desert where the old slums were – the failure to provide buildings for
social purposes so that this zone of wholly new housing 'suffers more
than any other from the effects of a poor environment'; in the Improvement Zone the plain shortage of cash for rehabilitation, on ac-

count of the intense concentration on slum clearance; and in the
Outer Zone, which ought to have no problems, the same failure to
build anything but housing, without even the Victorian institutions
to fall back on.

The second count of the indictment was that the resources there
were had been misapplied. Obviously the motorway network was a
glaring instance: the scaled-down version showed Queen's Drive restored and only the inner ring, soon to be reduced in standard, the
orbital M57 and the M62 spur retained. But it was the 'clearances'
(now taken into Irish/Scottish mythology) that horrified: it was now
said that only half the slum-dwellers had ever wanted to move.
Television soap operas like 'The Liver Birds' showed slum families
heroically fighting off the bulldozers and making rings round
ludicrous council officials, while passengers in a passing bus sing
'Land of Hope and Glory'. Then the 140 p.p.a. density of the new
housing, when at last it occupied some of the cleared sites, was seen
to be excessive: the city had by 1970 put a ban on multi-storey
development and brought average densities down to 95 p.p.a. Before
long, even this looked unnecessarily high as the land shortage was
transformed into a surplus. For the last and gravest count in the
indictment was the policy of decentralization. Whether by organized
or voluntary migration, the New Towns and the peripheral estates
had, as in London, drawn the best of the young out of town, sterilizing
farmland at a time when the whole vast acreage of the South Docks,
with its marvellous views, had been evacuated. It could be said that
the old city had been systematically eviscerated and left half dead.

Not all of this was fair. Most of Merseyside's troubles were due to
bad luck rather than bad management. Given the economic and
population forecasts, Bor's report of 1964 still makes good sense, and
his pleas for housing rehabilitation, described at the time as 'fobbing
us off with old houses', and against high-rise flats were ahead of local
opinion. So, properly, was the University School of Architecture
under Robert Gardner-Medwin, which in the later sixties developed
a radicalism it had hitherto lacked, with graduates like John Ritchie,
John Turner and Des McConaghy (later of SNAP) working on the
social problems of housing rehabilitation. The trouble was that in
contrast to Newcastle and Sheffield, both of which poured investment
into the city they had and resisted decentralization, Liverpool like
Glasgow tended to accept the popular image of the inner city as a
slummy place, best escaped from. Instead of reinforcing success, it had
grown used to failure, and relapsed into it almost overnight and to

excess. Politically, both the big parties had to carry the can, particularly Sefton's Labour group, the party of big government, which was in power through the years of disillusion. The beneficiaries were the Liberals, political guerillas, who had the wit to develop the techniques of community activism and to exploit the reaction towards conservation. With the reorganization of local government in 1974, which made the city one of the five metropolitan districts in the county of Merseyside, they took power, though without an absolute majority.

By now, local analyses of the 1971 census gave all too solid statistical evidence for what all could see had happened. Comparing Liverpool with five other English provincial cities,[9] the City Planning Officer was able to demonstrate that whereas Sheffield had none of the lowest grade of housing, Liverpool had most of all, with over a third of its population living in 'low status areas' – mostly Keay's inner-city tenements, but also Bradbury's 3-storey walk-up flats, and many of the tower blocks, of which the three 'Piggeries' became national symbols. The fact was that people had become choosy because there were fewer of them. In the decade 1961–71 the city had lost 135,000 people and a similar number of jobs, despite the 100,000 new jobs that governments had brought to Merseyside. By 1976 a quarter of the 1961 population had gone. In this accelerating decline the city centre had suffered worst of all, losing 65,000 of the 75,000 jobs lost in the last five years, despite the new office buildings. For Manchester as regional capital had scooped the office boom of the late sixties, and Liverpool had been left comparatively out in the cold. In the worst wards of the inner city there was 40 per cent unemployment (including the unregistered) and over the city as a whole, at 22 per cent, the rate was three times the national average. And these 'worst wards', containing 'a proportion of vulnerable and low-skill groups unparalleled in Britain outside Glasgow', containing also a large proportion of young children, where 90 per cent of the housing was council-owned, were the very wards which had been almost totally rebuilt since the war. In ironic contrast, those Victorian terraced housing areas that had survived the clearances were said to be 'relatively stable in terms of social and economic problems'. In all these ways, Liverpool by the mid seventies provided the *locus classicus* of the collapse of the inner city: the loss of the go-ahead young; the consequent shrinking of the tax base, yet no diminution in the number of underprivileged needing multiple support, of young children, of the impoverished old; the loss of jobs within reach of the centre; and

99 and 100. The two sides of Liverpool

above all the failed, frightening environment. With power, in such circumstances, came not only responsibility but odium amounting to contempt, which the locals were adept at putting into words for the benefit of the media.

It was inevitable, and consistent with current Liberal philosophy, that the rescue operation should be mounted from the two ends of the power spectrum – government money and community politics – since the local authorities in between seemed to have failed in their task. Of course they would be the main executive arm, but policy was now a matter of national concern. It had become plain that local government reform and planning machinery, our great expertise, on which so much thought and re-thought continued to be expended,[10] were irrelevant in this context. The first move, made by Peter Walker in 1972, was to appoint consultants to study the problem and for Liverpool, inevitably one of the three inner areas chosen,[11] Hugh Wilson and Lewis Womersley were appointed. The 'total approach' they advocated was designed to bridge the historic gulf between socio-economic and physical planning, but bitter experience made this an unfortunate choice of words (it would later be called a 'systems' approach, if that is any better); and Wilson and Womersley were equally unable to resolve the contradiction, which they recognized, that positive discrimination in favour of the inner city required strong centralized control, whereas the crisis of alienation and poverty required extreme sensitivity to local needs and opinions. In the end the Secretary of State for the Environment, by then (1976) Peter Shore, resolved it after a fashion by personally taking the chair of a Partnership Committee consisting of the appropriate Ministers, County and City Councillors and the Chairman of the Area Health Authority, serviced by a network of working parties with some citizen participation, and with £48 million to spend in inner Liverpool over the three years 1979–82. In its first report, the Committee recognized the 'rich diversity of voluntary and non-statutory organizations in Liverpool', but there was a dispiriting tone about the City Council's statement that its 'community development policy is to promote activities and procedures which will enable the authority to mount a dialogue with, or respond to, community groups in a coordinated way ... ' Nothing isolated Authority more from the young that it needed to work with than its incurably 'square' use of language.

The Partnership Area was the whole city as it had existed in 1921. It had then contained 725,000 people, now shrunk to 300,000 – just under half the extended city's present population. Well over 1,000

acres were unused and derelict. And to this the Government added a
decayed district near the airport, recognizing the awkward fact that
the problems were by no means confined to the inner city. (Kirkby, as
we have seen, was someone else's problem.) The list of promised
remedies, starting with industrial regeneration and ending with
refuse collection and the Arts, is inevitably long, given the 'total
approach', and at risk of excessive diffusion. A good deal of cynicism,
the fruit of experience, seemed in order: people had seen it all before.
On the bookstalls with the first Partnership report was a hilarious
report in the *Architects' Journal* of a well-meant attempt to sell Oscar
Newman's concept of Defensible Space to the tenants of Angela Street,
a group of Bradbury's walk-up flats. Newman's dogma required the
substitution of private yards (to be taken pride in) for public space, and
the package was to include new front doors, 'Guardiphones', colour
schemes chosen by tenants and tree-planting. The doors were
'nicked', the phones ripped off, the colour schemes used for new
graffiti, the trees chopped off and the shrubs removed to private gardens. Tenants, the report concluded, were 'extremely embittered and
antagonistic towards the local authority, and were prepared to be
against anything remotely connected with Liverpool Corporation'. As
Colin Watts, the leader of the Wilson/Womersley team, bitterly
admits: 'Whole neighbourhoods are classed as apathetic and then
have to have their communities developed by outsiders. The truth is
hard to take by those who are doing their best to engender change.
Most people see them as having little to offer. Promises have been
made and palliatives offered for too long. People do not want to take
part in these things. They want decent, secure jobs and houses like
anyone else. Then they will decide whether or not to "participate" in
other things.'[12]

But one could not sit back and wait for a British *Wirkschaftswunder*
to bring about this change of heart. One had to get on with the job.
To Trevor Jones, Liberal Chairman of the Housing Committee in 1975,
it was apparent that all the landmarks had changed. There was now
a gross surplus of housing, and analysing the lists he found that of
27,000 applicants only 595 had 'any real claim'. On the other hand
Keay's tenement blocks of the thirties and forties, on modernizing
which £11 million had lately been spent, were intensely disliked, and
Bradbury's little less so. It was reckoned that for 4,500 of them
demolition was now the only answer, so a substantial rehousing effort
was still necessary and the plan was that for these and other special
needs 20,000 new 2-storey houses should be built by 1986, half by

the Council, the rest by private builders and the excellent local housing associations, which had already provided over 12,000. But the
Liberals, anticipating Tory attitudes of 1979, were committed to the
retreat from paternalism and the dissolution of the Council's housing
empire, the main cause in their view of dependence, cynicism and
vandalism. So the majority of the new housing would be for sale, and
to encourage house-builders the planners were instructed not to be
difficult about looks or landscape. When Wimpeys got busy in Everton
it was seen as a historic watershed – 'the first private houses built in
the inner city for a century', according to Trevor Jones's successor as
Chairman of Housing, the young MP David Alton. Architectural
criticism of the commonplace results was muted; it was in no position
not to be. Housing policy for the eighties now had four components:
little houses only, as much house ownership as the market would
bear, the rapid improvement of the remaining 27,000 old private
terrace houses and of the 18,000 difficult-to-let council ones, and the
much more intensive and participative management of the surviving
council estates.

It was here that the 'dialogue' with community groups was so
critically important. As in Newcastle, this was a subtle exercise, given
the long history of suspicion. For example, in 1969 Shelter, the high-
minded and well-endowed London pressure group for the homeless,
decided to set up its first provincial project – the Shelter Neighbourhood Action Project (SNAP) – and settled with the Corporation
(above the heads of the locals) that this should be located in the
Granby area near Prince's Park and become the country's first
General Improvement Area. But despite strong left-wing student participation it took many months to live down the 'patronizing' image
it was inevitably saddled with. Eventually, its three-year assignment
completed, SNAP was succeeded at Granby by NHS (Neighbourhood Housing Services), a consultancy for new-born housing
cooperatives. Others, such as the 1969 COMTECHSA, were officially nurtured as recipients of Partnership funds. One could feel the
immense power for good of these alliances between working people
and young professionals. By 1975 amazed radicals could write that
'the massive financing of radical projects makes it difficult to decide
just what is Alternative'.[13] With these funds, with experience and
with dedicated leadership, the city's Community Development Section slowly began to be trusted in varying degrees by the two hundred
or so local groups it endeavoured to help, and the same could be said
of the many housing associations, of which the Liverpool Housing

101. Alternative Liverpool

Trust, Merseyside Improved Houses and the younger Cooperative Development Services were the most highly regarded. Official policy was now to give the voluntary movement all the rope it could use, coming in only where the market in old houses dried up to ensure by compulsory purchase that the total programme of regeneration hit its target dates. When in 1979 Michael Heseltine took over the chair of the Partnership Committee from Peter Shore, he announced that this programme at least would be protected from the prevailing cut-backs.

You could now take two views of the prospect for Liverpool. In the first, the anarchist view, this was the first great post-industrial city, leading the rest into the era of 'the informal economy'. Anthropologists had noted that (for example) in Bogota 'there seems to be no economic base to sustain the exploding population ... but no one looked ill-nourished, and everyone was shod ... [for] besides the official economy that figured in the statistics, there was an unofficial, invisible economy of tiny enterprises and service occupations'. And in Nairobi 'the self-help city is now building more houses, creating more jobs, absorbing more people and growing faster than the modern city'.[14] Liverpool, by force of circumstance and by force of character, might be well placed to demonstrate that the First World could do likewise. In the Merseyside Draft County Structure Plan of 1979, the most attractively presented sub-regional planning report since the days of Abercrombie, optimism, despite all the statistics, keeps breaking through, perhaps through the personality of its main author, Audrey Lees, with her long experience of Liverpool.[15]

Merseyside can now benefit from its fall in population over the past 30 years. Given the right policies and resources, the county now has enough houses to accommodate its population with ease. Past policies have reduced overcrowding both inside people's homes and in their surroundings. Future policies must build on that achievement.

For example, when all the clearances have been completed and all the spare sites thickly planted with trees, the housing land in Liverpool will be exactly right for half a million people at the 70 p.p.a. average density we now see as civilized. Of course this Structure Plan can be seen as a set of platitudes, the problem now being no longer what to do, but whether we can do it.

For the second view is more straightforward. It is that now, as in the past, Liverpool is a microcosm of the state of England, and can never recover until England does.

CHAPTER 7

Milton Keynes

The eight 'first-generation' London New Towns were seen by Abercrombie as very much a part of his Greater London, and Peter Shepheard's sketches in the Greater London Plan pictured them in the same style as West Ham – an integral component of the Third Rebuild. But they were inescapably a chapter in an older story, indeed a Movement, which was nearly half a century old when the Plan was published. Its only begetter, the social idealist Ebenezer Howard, published his immensely influential *Tomorrow: a Peaceful Path to Land Reform* in 1898. Because he later changed its title to *Garden Cities of Tomorrow* his concept has been misunderstood ever since. He was not, for one thing, particularly interested in housing layout,[1] and still less in architecture. His concern was to rejuvenate the depopulated countryside as much as to loosen the bonds of the congested city, and he pictured a symbiosis between town and country taking the form of a constellation of small towns, each limited to a population of 30,000, each with its own industrial, commercial, educational and social facilities and each with its own farming hinterland. This medieval symbiosis turned out a fallacy in terms of modern marketing, but in his exploitation of fast transportation to break down Megalopolis into intelligible units, in his insistence on public ownership and planning, and in his firm limits to growth, Howard anticipated the thinking of the 1940s. On the other hand he was very much a late Victorian in his pious hopes of 'a new civilization based on service to the community', his prudish aversion to the 'gin palaces' and other indecencies of urban life, and the high moral tone of his prototypes at Letchworth and Welwyn, into which the brewers were denied entry.[2] With no pubs, no television, no youth clubs, there was, in our terms, 'nothing to do in the evenings'. It has taken the post-war New Towns a whole generation to live down this rather smug and high-minded inheritance. The voluminous literature of the movement is suffused with it still.

It fell to the architects Barry Parker and Raymond Unwin to put flesh on Howard's abstract skeleton, and Unwin's *Town Planning in Practice* of 1909 at once became the bible of the movement. This was a document of very English eclecticism, not to say schizophrenia. After a brief Grecian excursion, Germany rather than Italy or France is the source of most of the examples, but Unwin seems uncertain whether he most admires classical Karlsruhe or romantic Rothenburg. One feels that he would have wished to emulate the subtleties of Camillo Sitte, but those soft curves only work with hard and continuous frontages, and Unwin had no blitzed inner cities to re-plan. In the end the Arts-and-Crafts *Zeitgeist* takes over the book, Wade's gingerbread cottages decorate the pages, and all is domesticated and suburban. In Hampstead Garden Suburb, his masterpiece, designed in 1907, Unwin with Lutyens at his elbow produced the perfect middle-class middle way, bounded by a medieval wall like Rothenburg, but laid out classically like Karlsruhe, since he saw that the only way of disciplining such a mass of little houses was to assemble them with formality.

For half a century English town planning theory remained stuck in this groove. At Welwyn in 1920 Louis de Soissons, with his *Beaux Arts* background, expanded the Hampstead concept only to dilute it, so that it was said that the Garden had taken over the City; and lacking the Lutyens touch the neo-Georgian central buildings were merely insipid. By the thirties it had become fashionable to poke fun at the Garden Cities in particular and at suburbia (built in their image) in general. For some it was not funny. For Thomas Sharp, 'Howard's new hope, new life, new civilization, Town-Country is a hermaphrodite; sterile, imbecile, a monster; abhorrent and loathsome to the Nature which he worships'. For D. H. Lawrence, 'the English may be mentally or spiritually developed, but as citizens of splendid cities they are more ignominious than rabbits'. But no alternative image was forthcoming. In his *Town Design* (1953), a useful manual incorporating the best English thinking of the day, Frederick Gibberd, like Unwin, provides sensitive analyses of historic urban spaces, in this case mainly Italian, but here too the jump from these splendid cities to their successors, the New Towns, is a visual shock and come-down on which the author makes no comment. He does not notice that his own low-rise housing in Hackney has a truly urban intimacy he was never to achieve on the broad acres of Harlow, just as Hampstead was never to be recreated at Welwyn.

The best thing about Harlow is the earlier housing. It has chimneys, and after thirty years the planting is in beautiful order. In June, vast lawns spread in all directions and scented footpaths wind secretly

102. Harlow in 1980 is a foretaste of the look of Milton Keynes in 2000

through the may and alder. Houses peep out as in picture-book villages. In the early sixties, unlike most other London New Town planners, Gibberd was persuaded to countenance some system-built and even brutalist imports, but they were not a success. The best-known, the 'casbah' project Bishopsfield, won in a competition in 1960, is a fish out of water in the arcadian scene. This higher-density Great Parndon neighbourhood, described by the *Architectural Review* in 1966 as a '*locus classicus* of the most imaginative ideas in recent housing', now seems a *locus classicus* of what went wrong. Harlow's other disappointment is its Civic Centre, nicely landscaped and furnished with sculpture but built in a bad period for monumental architecture. Its crowning 'vertical feature' has been crowded out, like so many others, by commercial competitors. None of the early New Towns had a central armature powerful or spacious enough to absorb the new scale of shopping, parking and recreation without the totality coming to resemble too closely any run-of-the-mill modernized commercial centre.

In every other respect the first-generation New Towns were a success story. The machinery set up by Silkin's New Towns Act of 1946, which had closely followed the recommendations of the Reith Committee, had worked like a charm. Of course rural interests made a fight of it in the designated areas, particularly at pioneering Stevenage; of course the county and district authorities were jealous of the un-democratic Development Corporations, Quangos with an apparently unlimited call on the public purse, and asserted themselves by insist-ing on conventional spaces between buildings and on other suburban standards which blocked or watered down any experimental notions the planning consultants had hoped to try out; of course life on the duckboards and among the concrete-mixers was a trial for the first families, though it was better than the war. But by the late fifties, halfway through their construction period, all the indicators showed that the strategy was going to work, that the tenants thought them-selves lucky, as did the rest of the world, and that this first batch, built with what now seems incredibly cheap money, were going to be, in the words of Sir Henry Wells of Crawley, 'the gold mines of the future'.

The six non-metropolitan New Towns of the first batch were never so golden. Conceived more in terms of regional development and the reversing of industrial decline, they were very largely working-class communities and the Garden City tradition hovered over them to less effect: indeed, gardens as such were little cultivated in the mining regions of Scotland and the north-east. Not swimming, as the London eight were, with the exurbanite tide, they had a tougher time getting started and a bleaker character, in landscapes where trees too grew less luxuriantly. Consequently there was little enthusiasm in Conser-vative political circles in the fifties to add to their number, which would only divert into infrastructures a building industry fully stretched to achieve Macmillan's housing targets. So between 1951 and 1960 only one New Town was designated. But this, Cumber-nauld, fifteen miles east of Glasgow, was of seminal importance. By 1955 the reaction among architects against 'prairie planning' was in full swing. Compactness was now the aim and, since the site was (unwisely) a cold and windy hilltop, functional as well as aesthetic (Italian hill-town) considerations supported the new fashion. More-over, a sufficiently compact town could dispense with the 'neighbour-hood' concept, which had never registered visually where densities within the housing areas were so low and was now thought to be a piece of sentimentality in a car-borne generation. The right answer for Cumbernauld, it was felt, was tightly planned housing linked by footways to a single multi-purpose centre and girdled by an urban motorway system. In 1960 Hugh Wilson, the Corporation's architect/planner, entrusted the design of this centre to a young brutalist architect on his staff, Geoffrey Copcutt. It emerged five years later a classic[3] megastructure – a massive extensible framework capable of carrying whatever assortment of central buildings (principally, of course, shopping floor-space) the town might need over the years, threaded by tunnelled service roads and swallowing its daily diet of parked cars, though many had to be spewed out over the windy spaces surrounding the monster. It was complained in later years that only a state monopoly would have dared assault a female clientele with so much raw concrete. In fact the sixties saw commercial developers doing it too (as, for instance, at Portsmouth's Tricorn centre). It invariably failed. But the concept of the town and its centrepiece as a single community exploiting the new mobility did have a future.

The classic presentation of the concept, alas, had no future at all. This was the fully worked-out scheme for an LCC New Town for 100,000 people at Hook in Hampshire, whose abandonment in 1960 demonstrated (which was obvious) that lacking the powers of the New Towns Act no city, however powerful, could hope to secure legislation that would enable it to override local opposition. The comparison with Harlow shows that the second-generation New Towns have arrived with a vengeance. Housing densities now climb from 40 p.p.a. round the fringes to 70 within the bent rectangle of the inner motorway (regarded at the time as the 'ideal' density) to 100 in the central core, the town thus thickening and rising higher towards its centre as cities have traditionally done. The centre itself, poised like Cumbernauld's above axial service lanes, but sensibly located in a sheltered valley, is not a single megastructure but an assemblage of courts and towers in the Barbican manner, rising off a mile-long platform, so that the city has a diversified (San Gimignano) silhouette. With the exception of many small urban squares and a single green boulevard running due west to the stadium, all the town's open spaces are gathered round its perimeter, including a string of lakes reflecting the central silhouette and flecked with sailboats. The vision of the medieval city, rising white above its common fields and their dark encircling forests, which Unwin had seen but lost his way to, seems now within reach. But the reach exceeded the grasp.

The expansion of Basingstoke and Andover, imposed by the Government on the LCC in preference to Hook, signalled the end of the concept of the town-sized satellite on a virgin site. Hook would have been the size of Oxford and had an equally vivid (if not equally graceful) urban identity. There was no hope now of finding such sites in the numbers[4] that would have been required to match the population projections of the early sixties. In an urbanized country like England, we were bound to reach the realization that all the best sites for new towns had old ones on them. And in any case it seemed better economics, and better geography, to enlarge the policy of expansion to transform thriving towns like Peterborough and Northampton, sited on high-speed rail and road routes, into new cities of a quarter of a million, or to achieve similar populations by knitting into cities groups of scattered townships in appropriately sited semi-urbanized regions. The extreme case was Central Lancashire, which already had a population of 225,000. This was soon after scaled down when the drain on the economy of Merseyside began to register. But the West Midlands equivalent, Telford, with an initial population of 70,000 and a target of 220,000, went ahead. It seemed unlikely that there would be another chance to create a city that would be better than patchwork, that would express the life-style of the twentieth century as memorably as Bath had expressed the eighteenth.

But one last chance there was. Early in 1962 Buckinghamshire County Council, contemplating the quinquennial review of its Development Plan in the light of these same population pressures, decided on a new and simple strategy. It would of course have to allow for the expansion of all its main towns and particularly of Aylesbury, the county capital. But beyond this it would dedicate the whole of its segment of the Chilterns to the metropolitan Green Belt and in exchange would offer to build, in the rather dull and quite empty rolling country between Bletchley and Wolverton, on land of mediocre agricultural quality, a new city of a quarter of a million. Halfway between London and Birmingham and on the main rail line between the two, and alongside the M1 motorway, the site seemed a natural magnet both for industry and for overspill populations. It was intriguing to note that the County Architect and Planner, Frederick Pooley, a brick-and-tile man who had had the courage to turn his back on prefabrication, had gone overboard for high technology. The widely disliked council monolith that now dominated Aylesbury had perhaps gone to his head. He now offered two alternative structures: a grid of urban motorways, multi-level intersections and all; or a necklace of high-density townships, each for 5,000 people, 'beads on a string', linked to a single Hook-type centre by a monorail circuit. Scoring the two, the second won hands down, particularly on the last criterion of all – New Image.

If it is possible to allow people to have their cars and yet save money by offering a much cheaper and convenient alternative for in-city travel, if it is possible to make industrialized building produce less monotonous and cheaper housing accommodation, if it is possible to produce a plan where schools and similar buildings, which will be erected anyway, can be made to do the job of other expensive buildings, and if it is possible by whole-city heating to cut fuel costs, then in the long run these features will add up to economies.

Not all of these prescient conditions were to be given as much weight as they might have been among the goals adopted by the eventual planners, the last and most prescient being lost sight of entirely.

Certainly the proposed location was a winner. In its own *South-East Study* of 1964 the Government took it on board, at the same population, and the County felt justified in publicizing it nationally and marshalling the support of the district and parish councils affected. But just as a Conservative Government had refused to delegate its New Town powers to the socialist LCC, so a Labour one refused them to Tory Buckinghamshire. In 1966 the Minister adopted the infant himself and issued a Draft Designation Order covering no less than 25,000 acres and embracing the towns of Bletchley (already being expanded under the Town Development Act), Wolverton and Stony Stratford. After a public inquiry this was reduced to 22,000 and in 1967 a Development Corporation was nominated for the job, with the socialist businessman Lord Campbell of Eskan as its Chairman. The Minister announced that the new city would be known as Milton Keynes (a neat marriage of two impeccable personalities) after a tiny village on its eastern marches.

Four firms of planning consultants were interviewed. That appointed was the high-powered group of Llewelyn-Davies, Weeks, Forestier-Walker and Bor, which had only come together three years before. The first two had met in the forties as research workers on modular building systems in Leslie Martin's department of the old LMS railway, and had gone on to research hospital design for the Nuffield Foundation. Both were scientist-architects of high intellectual calibre and both were by temperament and training suspicious of the preconceptions that had determined English town design hitherto, whether these were 'traditional' or 'modern'. To Richard Llewelyn-Davies, a veteran of the A A *événements* of 1938, the formalist and brutalist excitements of the last decade had prevented true functionalism, the subordination of the architect's ego to human needs and desires, from ever being tried. John Weeks, as a hospital architect, was well aware of 'the problem of sheltering an organization which has a rate of growth and change which is so great that it makes its buildings obsolescent before they decay naturally'. He noticed that a century earlier Paxton had solved this problem in one way, by building the great glass tent of the Crystal Palace – a loose fit if ever there was one – and Brunel in another, by shipping out to the Dardanelles a prefabricated hospital consisting of pavilions clipped to a spine corridor which could be infinitely extended. The result was a new version of the functionalist philosophy:

> I see no absolute value in shape control by sets of formal conventions. I am prepared to take the deformations of the site, the contractor's available techniques, the poverty of the clients and the principle of indeterminacy itself as shape-making forces and to derive systems which will allow them to operate as shape-makers. I see no more value in one force than in another. Nor can I see that to aim at completeness in an indeterminate situation is to aim high. It is simply to aim badly.

Both partners could see the relevance of this philosophy to urban design and planning. If 'a building for an indeterminate brief cannot adhere to a finite geometrical control system', still less could a city. When Walter Bor, with his years of experience and expertise in the problems of London and Liverpool behind him, joined the firm in 1964, their conquest of this new territory was assured.

In their submission for the appointment the firm had expressed their vision of the role of the new city in these terms:

> The new city at Milton Keynes offers an opportunity for imaginative study, invention and experiment and could lead to a new model for urban life for Britain a quarter of a century ahead.
>
> The new city will be reaching maturity at about the turn of the century, when patterns of life, work and recreation will be far different from what they are today. Most of our existing cities have a form derived from the manufacturing patterns of the industrial revolution. In the advanced nations of the western world this pattern is rapidly changing, as human effort switches from the heavy work of nineteenth-century manufacturing to the information-based technology of today and tomorrow.
>
> This new pattern puts education and learning in the forefront of our concern in human society. In a rapidly advancing nation such as Britain, we have to recognize that the educational patterns of today will not produce sufficient people ready to face the challenge of the immediate future. One of the main tasks of urban society, therefore, is to provide a setting for a vastly richer and fuller education for our children. It is no exaggeration to say that whereas the historic purpose of our older cities was largely to concentrate a labour force for manual tasks, the purpose of our future cities, for which Milton Keynes could be the prototype, must be to provide a setting for learn-

ing, for the development of imagination, and for the interchange of information. This would also mean orientation towards youth.

With masterly opportunism, Lord Campbell was able to meet this last aspiration by capturing the Open University with its 400 teaching staff but (alas) no resident students.

The brief received from the Corporation was a conventional one in New Town terms – a 'socially balanced' population, as close as possible to the national average, a diversified pattern of employment, the integrity of existing communities to be respected etc., etc. But two items, both aspects of the current consensus that economic growth would go on for ever, were significant: at least half the housing was to be by private enterprise for owner-occupiers, and 1·5 cars per household were to be accommodated. The new city, in other words, whatever the Minister's socialist convictions, was to be market-orientated. But at the same time the Corporation, notably, wished it to be 'readily recognizable as a cohesive entity, both as a community and as a structure, and having a strong urban character and well-defined boundaries to separate it from the rural area around it'. In a series of seminars in the early months of 1968 the planners translated the brief into their own 'goal-orientated' terminology. They identified six goals:

1.   Freedom of choice
2.   Easy movement
3.   Balance and variety
4.   Attractiveness
5.   Public participation
6.   Efficient and imaginative use of resources

Obviously they all reacted on one another, but the *sine qua non* was mobility. Here the influence of the Californian planner Melvin Webber was paramount, and the concept of the highly mobile urban region, by now a vain hope for London as a whole, seemed manageable here. Freedom to choose your school or work-place or sports club or supermarket city-wide must mean an equivalent freedom of movement for the private car, and alongside this (unlike the Californian model) a public transport system equally accessible wherever you lived, so that the average journey to work of 15 minutes by car could be done in 24 minutes by bus. The object, in line with the Llewelyn-Davies philosophy, was to give people the way of life they wanted. The visual consequences would emerge through the passage of time and the ingenuity of architects.[5]

The way of life the southern English wanted was in no doubt. 90 per cent, for a start, wanted a garden and so must have it, and a similar majority wanted a garage attached to their house. Housing densities therefore must revert to Garden City standards, averaging 8 houses (or 30 people) to the acre, and the overall urban density, given modern needs for road space and open space and parking, must be lower still – lower than that of any existing English city. This in turn ruled out any other form of public transport than the bus, and ideally for frequency of service the minibus even if it cost more per passenger than the double-decker. With 50,000 people going to work every morning and schoolchildren being shuttled all over the city, it was essential to avoid tidal flows of traffic; so work-places needed to be dispersed rather than concentrated, even though modern weekly shopping patterns indicated only one major commercial centre (the whole city, after all, was to be no bigger than Lambeth). The road pattern that rapidly emerged was a surface-level grid, strengthened by a motorway by-passing the old A5. In little over a year (February 1969) and halfway through the planning, the Corporation was able to put out a sketch scheme sufficient to put farmers in the picture, to get infrastructure contracts under way, and to enable the now elaborate process of public consultation to be put in hand. Like most such sketches, like Burns's for Newcastle and Bor's for Liverpool, it emerged from the process little altered.[6]

This net of roads, thrown casually like a fish-net across the gently rolling landscape, has a 1-kilometre mesh. Compared with a 1-mile mesh, this was found to have the great advantage of avoiding two-level interchanges at each crossroads. Synchronized traffic lights would save not only money but also space, which mattered equally if the miles of low-rise housing were not to be dominated by road structures. A second advantage was the shorter walk from the middle of each 'square' to the bus stop, a meeting-point of footpaths where it would be natural to site (at what were called 'activity centres') the first schools and pubs and social centres and local shops. The hope was that these local centres, each with their own name and character, would help identify the main roads alongside which they would lie, so that the stranger would not lose himself in an anonymous network of standardized twin-carriageways, bending about the landscape like main roads anywhere. And of course a strong point of orientation would be the city centre, with its towers of offices and so on, situated on a high point and occupying eventually two of the kilometre squares at the centre of gravity of the grid. For the more low-key and

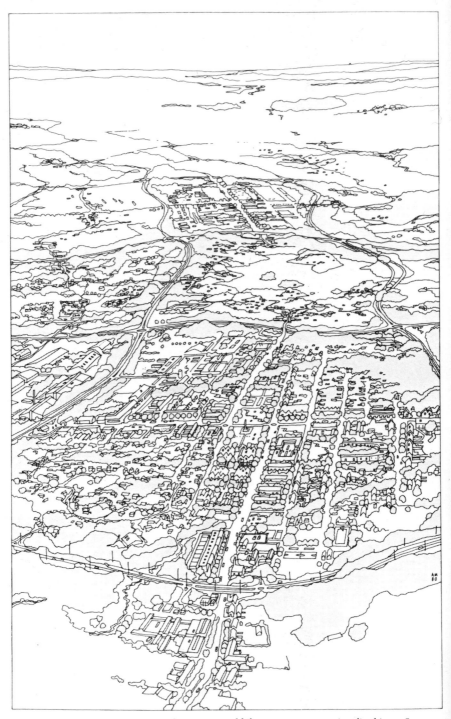

103. Sketch by Andrew Mahaddie shows a typical kilometre square as visualized in 1980

modest the private realm the more crucial the role of the public, cities in any case having always depended on their hearts to impress their identities.

The first necessity was to build a Corporation team that would carry forward the community of ideas between Campbell and Llewelyn-Davies that had smoothed the planning stage. Two strong characters, both architects, were to be the dominant figures of the first years of building. Fred Lloyd Roche, the General Manager, had made a name for himself as Chief Architect of Runcorn, a New Town for 100,000 whose intimate housing and highly successful centre were in fact a distinct advance on Cumbernauld's. A man of restless energy, he was inevitably attracted to this larger canvas. Derek Walker, Chief Architect, also from the north, was an individualist and perhaps the most sophisticated modern architect to commit himself full time to any of the New Towns. A born impresario, he could be guaranteed to attract a brilliant team and to ensure that the Corporation's own buildings, and the private architects commissioned for individual projects, were of high quality. But he was no easy colleague, no organization man. After six years the inevitable breach occurred, and Walker returned to private practice, now within Milton Keynes itself.[7]

An early decision was to endorse the consultants' proposal that for the first decade or so development should be concentrated in a wide crescent linking Stony Stratford and Wolverton with Bletchley, east of the old A5. New commercial centres would be fitted into all three towns and would have to carry the main shopping load until the great new City Centre opened towards the end of the decade. They would also, as it turned out, help to mollify the always sensitive feelings of the existing local authorities. Exploiting the last flicker of the pre-1973 boom, land purchase and infrastructure works were pushed forward on a scale that frightened the accountants (but later justified itself), and for some years, as with the earlier New Towns, vast engineering works savaged the modest, low-key landscape – all the vaster and more costly because of the policies of low density and universal car-ownership. Several lakes, eventually to be windy amenities, were excavated to handle the formidable run-off from the acres of roof and tarmac, necessity now justifying what in Lancelot Brown's day had been pure extravagance. Each year some 100,000 saplings were lavishly dispersed in the linear park along the Grand Union Canal, and packed into the embarrassingly wide open spaces that had to be reserved for road widening and into all the other SLOIPs[8] inseparable from modern planning. Hedgerow elms were safeguarded, in all innocence of what was to hit them, and a beautiful Miesian sewage works signposted the main entrance from the M1. Meanwhile the Corporation's first housing projects, reassuringly bricky, were slotted into the existing towns alongside conventional local council estates and, in Bletchley, the better-designed but somewhat more austere expanses laid out by the GLC. Characteristically of the early seventies, bricks and bricklayers soon vanished over the horizon, and Walker found himself forced (not wholly against his inclinations) into system building and alternative materials, examples of which were still *sub judice* in 1980. At Coffee Hall, concrete-box houses are having to be pitch-roofed a few years after completion. Accidents were no doubt inevitable in the rush to have enough housing, schools and other necessities available to support the vital desire to attract industrialists large and small (as well as bricklayers). Elegantly designed speculative factories and office buildings were an additional bait.

The trick worked, as in the exceptionally favourable planning context it was bound to do, but better than anyone in those difficult years could have counted on. Ten years from the effective start of building, 26,000 new jobs, half of them industrial, had been created; and of this half, two thirds were in new or comparatively small firms renting the Corporation's handsome Advance Factories, already a welcome relief of scale and colour amid the acres of brown roof. The fact that half of

104. An Advance Factory Unit of 1976

these new jobs were filled by commuters from outside was untidy, but not unpredictable from the experience of earlier New Towns. 'Advanced' technology featured strongly, and international companies which would never, they asserted, have gone to London found Milton Keynes ideally placed for their British and/or European operations. The GLC, enviously watching all this, was so informed, and was also reminded that of these new arrivals only one in ten were companies previously in London. The policy, in contrast to the Abercrombie era, was to work in close contact with the hard-pressed inner-London boroughs to ease their housing load, and particularly to take a fair share of handicapped or other disadvantaged *people*, but not to encourage *jobs* to move out of the capital. In other words, it was to match ex-London workers with new employment opportunities.

But housing, dogged by its customary vicissitudes, consistently failed to keep pace. By 1980, against master plan projections of between 20,000 and 26,000 new dwellings, about 15,000 had been built on MKDC land (5,000 elsewhere) and the recent rate of completions had fallen to little better than half of what had been hoped. Consequently the population, which should have reached 125,000 by 1980, had only just passed 90,000, a gain of 50,000 in this first decade. At this rate (which it was still confidently hoped to better) the reduced ultimate target of 200,000 would not be hit till the late nineties, and this depended on market conditions which were increasingly unpredictable. The Corporation had originally seen a population gain of 70,000 in the first ten years as not only feasible but desirable 'because of the early benefits in terms of better social facilities and because of the wide and expanding range of opportunities that will come with a rapid rate of growth'. In the event, the lower growth rate does not seem to have been as damaging as was feared, because of the deliberate and energetic social, educational and cultural provision pursued from the start. At all costs, the planners were determined that the young population of MK should not suffer from the much advertised New Town Blues of the fifties. With the aid of pump-priming grants from the Corporation, Artist in Residence bursaries from the Arts Council and Crafts Council, and above all the dedicated leadership of artists such as John Dankworth and Cleo Laine, every conceivable voluntary organization, club, society, community centre, refuge, workshop, news-sheet, play-scheme and sports facility could be promoted or accommodated. Of course, even a paternalist Corporation neither could nor wished to do it all. The notion, often propagated outside, that in a New Town everything was their responsibility was hotly denied. External authorities with statutory responsibilities much wider than Milton Keynes itself, as well as the new Borough Council that came into existence in 1975, had to be consulted or cajoled as the case might be. The town, like any other, was a resultant of converging or even conflicting forces. Thus the Area Health Authority for frustrating years was unable to achieve a start on the new hospital ('Milton Keynes is dying for a hospital'). Conversely the County Council played up superbly over schools, and in the Buckinghamshire tradition these were barn-like deep-roofed affairs that married happily with the new orthodoxy of brick-and-tile housing. Outstanding among the successes of the first decade were the three new district shopping centres. Bletchley, a sprawl of commonplace, mainly inter-war, commuters' estates, acquired a chic new black-glass group of shops and offices which was neatly slotted into its dim Edwardian core, and supplemented this with an appropriately vulgar sports centre paid for by the old Urban District Council out of its own resources which (like other small towns similarly placed) it was determined should not fall into the hands of the successor authority in 1975. Wolverton, the red-brick Victorian railway town, gained the Agora, a combined shopping centre and covered piazza for events of all kinds, which turned out an entrepreneurial success. And Stony Stratford, the dear little roadside town with its coaching inns long assaulted by the lorry traffic of the A5, did best of all with Cofferidge Close, designed by Wayland Tunnley in Nigel Lane's department in a sympathetically homespun style which met all the psychological needs of the battered seventies.

If the social and commercial development of the new city was the happiest story it had to tell at the end of its first decade, the public transport story was the most depressing. The population was not as rich as had been so confidently forecast: only a quarter of it – instead of the half that had been anticipated and was still desired – could afford to own its own home. And the policy of housing a proper proportion of elderly and disadvantaged people exacerbated the problem. After a half-hour wait at a windy bus stop in the denuded landscape for a bus that failed to arrive at the advertised time, those who had heard of Pooley's high-speed monorail must have sighed for it. The planners had not foreseen the frustration of dependence on a 'country' bus company which it could not control or even subsidize and which, with the best will in the world, could find no way of making an adequate service for the widely scattered housing estates economic.

105 and 106. Two district shopping centres, bronze glass at Bletchley and red brick at Stony Stratford

'If public transport in the growing city is to offer an efficient service which the citizens are attracted to take advantage of rather than condemned to use,' wrote the Chairman in his 1973 Report to the Minister, 'we are convinced that a more fundamental approach must be made to change the whole performance, image and therefore the economics of public transport. We hope to put proposals to you for this new fundamental approach during the coming year.' No such proposals were ever made. A limited 'dial-a-bus' experiment was tried and abandoned as uneconomic. It was apparent that only by running its own service at whatever loss seemed socially necessary could this fatal flaw be overcome, and in the economic climate of 1980 this was not on the agenda. Yet some day it would have to happen.

The lonely bus stop felt all the lonelier because the local 'activity centre' which it was supposed to have signposted was, by and large, not there. In one of those decisions which seem insignificant at the time they are made, these little centres – a first school, a meeting-place, a workshop, a pub, a supermarket – had mostly been placed not where the master plan had recommended but at the centre, or any-way deep in the interior, of each kilometre-square village. Walter Bor, revisiting the scene after ten years, heavily criticizes this main depar-ture from the spirit of the Plan. A contrite Corporation report, *Places of Connection in Milton Keynes* (1979), issues an equally urgent *rappel à l'ordre* (in itself evidence of the high regard in which the Plan is still held). Both documents are concerned that the popular image of MK as 'fifty villages in search of a city' can only be reinforced if each one turns inward on itself. It was crucial to the original mobility concept that this is a single town formed by a limitlessly complex pattern of intersecting circles of interest. The neighbourhood in any shape or size was anathema. We must also take into account the planners' sensitivity about the huge scale and uniformity of the main-road grid (made worse by their acceptance of the engineer's recom-mendation that the kilometre crossroads should be roundabouts and not traffic lights) which these local centres, no two alike, were to have mitigated. But would they have or, where they are in the right place, do they? Experience suggests not. These single-storey buildings make little impact wherever you put them and least of all beyond the wide verges of a divided highway. Where (as at Neath Hill) they are expen-sively dug in so that they connect two 'villages' via a pedestrian underpass, the road strides over the top regardless.

For the fact is that the roads dwarf the city, as the car does the house, for perfectly respectable reasons. The sort of buildings that would have put such roads in their place would have been the sort that none or few would have chosen to live in. The policy of putting known contemporary desires ahead of architectural preconceptions and protecting people from traffic noise produces Milton Keynes as naturally as Victorian society produced Kensington and Camden Town. If the private car disappears the way the servants did, similar adaptations to the unpredictable will have to be made. Meanwhile the roads are lavishly planted out. Having subscribed enthusiastically to

Alexander's philosophy that 'a city is not a tree'[9] the Corporation proceeded to make it into a forest, and we can only pray that our world will survive in recognizable form long enough for the forest to reach maturity. For only then will retreat from townscape justify itself by becoming landscape.

As for the embarrassment about the islanded villages, those who live in them take a relaxed view. They know two or three immediate neighbours, but their friends, their school friends, their workmates, are scattered about the city and the surrounding countryside in the usual way, and they really do not know what the planners are upset about. They just want a better bus service. Where the villages through the accident of leadership do acquire a strong identity and field their own teams, why not? They are linked by a footpath-cum-bicycle-track system known as Redways from their pink concrete surface, ideal for school children, circuitous and exhausting for shoppers, even quite tiring for cyclists since the city seems to consist of a hundred little hills, and in places rather scary for younger children. The original planners, in accordance with the fashion of the time, concentrated their thoughts on unimpeded vehicular mobility at one extreme and segregated pedestrian routes at the other, and forgot that the familiar multi-purpose 'estate road', with footways alongside as in any old-fashioned American suburb, is really the safest for all concerned provided cars are physically constrained from going too fast. If this intermediate network had been seen as a totality and sensibly inter-woven with the kilometre-square highways, the whole town would have been more intelligible to the visitor and easier to live in.

Inside the villages all the styles of the last forty years are on offer, the policy once again having been never to plunge too heavily for any one. Rental and mortgage housing mix happily together, confound-ing time-honoured English custom – a product of the policy that all rental housing must be marketable. The private builders still churn out condensed versions of the New Town house-types of the fifties as well as the so-called Georgian of the seventies, and no hands are held up in horror. As for the public sector, there are square buff-brick boxes that might date from 1936 symmetrically disposed along straight tree-lined boulevards (Fishermead), there are concrete block-houses reminiscent of wartime austerity (Coffee Hall), endlessly long system-built terraces faced with silvery corrugated aluminium panels charac-teristic of the late sixties (Netherfield), elegant black high-tech bungalows in ribbed GRP by Norman Foster (Beanhill), a beautiful deep-eaved housing association project by MacCormac and Jamieson

(Chapter House), innocent red-brick cottages by a regenerate Martin Richardson (Great Linford) that recapture the bland dullness of the streets near the station in any provincial town, and (most recently) elaborate compositions by Wayland Tunnley with half-timbered oriels and pergolas that recall the 1890s of Wright and Mackintosh (Neath Hill). Like several of the London boroughs, Milton Keynes can show splendid examples of the great leap of policy and imagination

107 and 108. Housing of 1974 (Netherfield) and 1978 (Neath Hill) show change of taste as well as technology

that took place in the seventies. Netherfield is a monument of rational-
ism and glitter; Chapter House (significantly a housing scheme for
single people) with its red brick and black timbers and its deep
shadows a reversion to the mysterious. There is also of course a great
deal of decent brick housing that might be in any of the New Towns.
Layouts vary from the severely orthogonal to the wavy picturesque,
but everywhere the planting is generous and tirelessly maintained,

109. Terraces by Martin Richardson at Great Linford

the cars are mostly on the premises or (now that garages are excluded
by cost limits) on screened standings out in front, the street furniture
is smart and there is no sign of vandalism. This wild variety, more
striking than in towns that have been building for centuries, can be
taken as you choose to illustrate the eclecticism, or the new-found
tolerance, or the loss of nerve of the seventies. What posterity will find
it hard to believe is that it was all going on virtually at the same
moment.

But the real test of the claim of Milton Keynes to be a city at all
would be, as all concerned had known from the start, its new centre.

What, after all, is a city? The possession of a cathedral seems to be the best claim, but not the only one, since Cambridge is a city and Ely is not. Nor is it mere size, since Bath (pop. 85,000) is a city and Brighton (pop.160,290 without Hove) is not. Partly, it was the staking of a claim: Milton Keynes did not want to be just another New Town, and no doubt, knowing itself headed for the same population league as Plymouth, Portsmouth and Newcastle, it wished its place in their company to be recognized from the start. The risk of the slightly comic associations of the Garden City had to be taken, increased though it was by the unprecedentedly low density and the aspiration (in the annual report of 1971) to be known as a 'city of trees'. The one thing on which all were agreed was that it was the centre which would make Milton Keynes the 'alive, rich, busy place' that would best promote it from town to city status on a par with its older sisters. It was decided to entrust the realization to a young architect called Stuart Mosscrop, who had Walker's confidence from the start and when the latter left assumed direct responsibility.

The 1970 Plan had put the social objective in these terms:

> But beyond the nature of a new city centre as a central place for exchange of the widest range of goods and services, a variety of social expectations about the city centre must also be satisfied. Indeed, commercial success is to a certain degree dependent upon the extent to which these expectations can be fulfilled above merely economic parameters. These social factors include:-
>
> (i) Identity with a place felt to be the heart of the city to which all other specific places can be related. It will be the place to which people from each part of the city can go to see people from all other parts of the city on common territory.
>
> (ii) Identity with respect to the outside world, of a place that residents and visitors can recognize as the primary face of the city, and where they feel they can meet the people of the city. A visitor can thus 'know' the city even if not familiar with every part, and a native of the city can relate the image of his city to others he may visit.
>
> (iii) A place simply to go to be in, to be anonymous or to dress up for; to be able to watch the world go by; to see and be seen; a place to find out what is going on and to participate in events.

Reserving two kilometre squares (470 acres) on the flat windswept top of Bradwell Common which, they pointed out, would in London cover all of Mayfair and Soho – the whole length of Oxford Street – the planners envisaged no less than 4 million square feet of retail space, 3 million square feet of offices, 16,000 car spaces and 5,000 residents, together with 50 to 60 acres of public buildings and facilities of all kinds for entertainment and recreation. They asserted strongly the principle of keeping all traffic movement and parking and pedestrian access on the ground (with basement truck-servicing) so as at last to avoid the horrific concrete stairs and smelly approaches of earlier centres; and finally they illustrated their concept by means of a rough plaster maquette of masterly and, as it turned out, beneficent vagueness even by English standards. All one could make out was that the central axis bent about for picturesque effect, and that the taller buildings were to be out on the edges of the bent rectangle where they would best show up from afar.

The hollow crown atop the domed head harks back, of course, to the German concept of the *Stadtkrone*, so named by Bruno Taut half a century earlier to describe the sentimental image of the medieval city crowned by its turreted fairy castle – now available to all at Disneyland. This was one unconscious source, explicitly acknowledged by Gibberd at Harlow and implicitly present in the megastructure at Cumbernauld. The other inescapable source is English nostalgia for the piazza, the theatre of urban life, so easily managed it seems by Mediterranean peoples, so hard to bring to life in Atlantic climates. With no great church to crown its holy mountain, no castle to command its radiating streets, no actors for its theatre of life, this was a pretty bankrupt set of symbols.

Stuart Mosscrop turned out to be wonderfully free of these besetting associations. His own allegiance, a clean break from those of all the earlier designers of Garden Cities and New Towns, was classically Vitruvian. The great Roman codifier, writing in the first century AD, laid down principles universally adopted by the world's most prolific builders of new towns. Unseen forces and practical good sense were given equal weight. The priest guided the plough in cutting the initial boundary furrow, and the dead-straight cross of main streets was oriented north–south to harmonize with cosmic order. Above all, geometry, the sign of human uniqueness, regulated the whole, and Vitruvius illustrates it by a characteristically Platonic anecdote. 'It is related of the Socratic philosopher Aristippus that, being shipwrecked and cast ashore on the coast of the Rhodians, he observed geometrical figures drawn thereon, and cried out to his companions: "Let us be of good cheer, for I see the traces of Man." '

As we decelerate to Junction 14 on the M1, the centre on its skyline makes scarcely any impact. This can be corrected, and no doubt will be by some signpost in the sky close to the new central railway station at the far end, which closes (very traditionally) the central axis. But

110. Central Milton Keynes under construction

we must also hope that the present circuitous and tedious approach from the M1 will be superseded by a more vivid and purposeful arrival, bridging Willen Lake as close as possible to the water and then plunging into a deep cutting pregnant with anticipation (like the railway entry into Lime Street, Liverpool); Stowe, after all, is only a few miles away. But breasting the slope, we become aware that the easy-going utilitarianism that dominated the original Plan and properly characterizes the residential areas has been gripped by a firmer hand. The two kilometre squares bounding the centre are real squares at last, with straight sides, and the housing on either hand is truly urban, coming to proper right-angles at the many crossroads of a gridiron of tree-lined avenues. There being no ley-lines discernible, Mosscrop was nevertheless able, in the Vitruvian spirit, to align his long axis on the sunrise at the summer solstice, and the great avenues of London planes that vanish into the afternoon sun are named Midsummer and Silbury Boulevards – the second for a new Silbury Hill not so far achieved.

The scale of the land-take is vast, and the Corporation seems to glory in the fact, having put out a diagram that shows the Palace of Westminster (inter alia) tucked into one block out of twenty. It is probably too vast – an outcome of the Plan's determination to be ready for all eventualities that will be regretted, though obviously it can be filled in with housing some day. Perhaps already embarrassed by the length of the central feature – the great million square feet of shopping centre – the architects talk of putting the next phase alongside instead of (as was originally intended) end on to what exists. Be that as it may, what exists is a triumph: it has to be seen to be believed. One notes at once the benefit of the linear form in being able to park so near an entrance, and the parking neatly avoids both multi-storey purgatory and ground-level desert of pressed steel: it hardly shows at all. Similarly the servicing circuit (at high instead of basement level for economy) is invisible. The building seems to be all front – a white steel and plain or mirror-glass front, the graph-paper aesthetic *in excelsis*. Inside, the two tall arcades that run the full length of the huge building – glasshouses displaying the now conventional tropical exotica, with polished travertine floors – are flooded with changeable English light. This is no commercial Aladdin's cave of pop-art wonders: the cool and rational architecture requires and reflects the light of common day, in which it is no doubt that bit harder for the seller's

111. Inside one of the long arcades

con-trick to come off. In the midst is a vast central covered square equipped and much used for every kind of event, sporting or cultural, and further on a too quiet 'garden court' with a wild fountain and a sundial open to the sky. The lavish familiar stores, souk-like and open to the passer-by, do best business on Saturdays and Tuesdays when the open-air market alongside is thronged. Crowds are still somewhat bemused by the glamour of it all. 'PICK THAT UP [father to small son dropping sweet wrapper]; you'll lower the tone.'

Nothing else in Central MK can as yet rival the impact of this great building. Tower blocks in the post-war English manner have been eschewed as otiose in the mood of 1980. Instead, ranged alongside are some extremely elegant low-rise glass office blocks, some bachelor flats, a chunky red-brick Public Library, and symbolically sited where it is guessed the Saxons held their councils, a rather heavily designed Town Hall – first swallows of what will need to be a blazing summer if the power of his geometry is to evoke the human energy Mosscrop believes it will. At the moment the shopping centre, diffuse by its very nature, has to carry as best it can the whole load of meaning hitherto borne by buildings of deeper significance. One questions whether even at this level these polished spaces will attract the Beaubourg sideshows and the commercial fringe that are so necessary to offset the deadpan service offered by the increasingly standardized chain stores. As with all such enterprises, the third phase will give the answers. Meanwhile one must hope that the national tendency not to complete the sentence – to get bored with the statement before it is intelligible – which we have been prone to ever since the cathedral builders Gothicized the, to them hideous, naves of the Norman cathedrals, will somehow be outmanoeuvred in this place.

How fairly can one judge this self-styled city so early in its young life? On the evidence of its predecessors, scarcely at all. For a whole generation Canberra and Welwyn remained harmless jokes – cities of trees with a vengeance. Clearly at Milton Keynes none of the urban stereotypes are going to apply. Whereas most European cities consist of a snug, organic medieval core wrapped in geometrical modern suburbs, here for reasons sufficiently established it is the other way round. On top of this, like all new towns, MK has to carry the burden of simultaneity, the lack (except in obscure corners conscientiously conserved) of history, of monuments, of social and visual collisions, of creative urban disorder. Then there is the unlucky coincidence of two circumstances, the oil crisis of 1973 and the subsequent collapse of the economy, both unforeseen by economists when the Plan was published in 1970. The timing could not have been worse. Flexible and open-ended though it rightly was, the infrastructure for an affluent car-owning community was irrevocably committed when it obsolesced (apparently) overnight. Five years later, planners would have given absolute priority to public transport, swinging no doubt too far that way. But it is doubtful whether the look of the new city would have been very different. John Weeks's 'principle of indeterminacy' would in any case have debarred the imposition of any dominating architectural image. A new city that genuinely responds to the diverse and centrifugal needs and desires of our age could never have been spectacular. Nevertheless, coming to Milton Keynes after Liverpool, which bears all the scars of all the tribulations of the twentieth century, one can only echo the comment of a French observer of the Munich Agreement: '*Ce n'est pas magnifique, mais ce n'est pas la guerre.*'

CHAPTER 8

At Low Tide

Once cities exist, their renewal is a continuous process: like history itself they are always in transition. To divide either process into 'periods' is therefore misleading, but it is also illuminating, not least in the light it throws on ourselves. Thus the three Rebuilds that have taken place in England were the physical expression of the three cultures we have seen in England since we emerged from the Middle Ages – the Enlightenment, the Industrial Revolution and the Welfare State.

By pure chance the destruction of London by fire in 1666 coincided with the end of 'bigotry', of superstition, of the reign of the instinctive. It could be seen, was seen by contemporaries, as the bonfire of medievalism, of the Anglo-Saxon village that had pillaged the ruins of Roman rationality. But whereas on the Continent, and most conspicuously in the Ile de France, the agent of the new rationality was absolute monarchy, in England (and later in Scotland) it was an intellectual and mercantile elite for which the King provided polarization and patronage but which he had learnt never to dominate. Charles II, having for some reason that remained mysterious to contemporaries preferred Dr Wren of Oxford, was as sceptical as any of the City merchants of his intellectual notions for the replanning of London, and cheerfully let them suffer the same fate as would later befall Professor Martin's scheme for the rebuilding of Whitehall. For the next century and a half, during which all our towns, with one or two sleepy exceptions, acquired their Georgian look, property rights were sacrosanct and the old frontages were either replaced piecemeal or merely given a respectable face-lift. Only the new quarters were laid out in accordance with the best principles of the Enlightenment, and these were applied uniformly all over the English-speaking world from Savannah, Georgia, to Calcutta and eventually to Adelaide, not to mention Edinburgh and Dublin. The scenic formula, rational architecture in a romantic landscape, never varied. But this visual revolution had not yet extended to the technology, which was still blessedly eotechnic. Bricks and tiles came from kilns on the edge of town, roofs from the oak forests of Sussex and Herefordshire, building stones from quarries within easy carting distance with the one exception, for grand buildings, of the Isle of Portland, with its immediate access to the sea. And every tool that one held in the hand, every boat and gate and vehicle, was the product of centuries of refinement and perfectly adapted to its material and its purpose. Whether all this building was done by fashionable architects or serious carpenters or garrison engineers or speculative builders using pattern books did not seem to make a great deal of difference.

English craftsmanship, not having to overreach itself to titillate an idle and luxurious Court, could be widely employed meeting the practical requirements of country gentlemen. So it developed an inventiveness and economy of material that adapted easily to manufacture and burgeoned into an industrial revolution which unlike its political counterparts was not recognized until it had already happened. Well into the nineteenth century the new breed of engineers remained craftsmen by instinct and heredity, and for as long as they did the eotechnic economy retained its eighteenth-century elegance. For a century the two worlds coexisted, but of course palaeotechnic coal-and-iron industrialization had an explosive ferocity that in the end carried all before it, rushing through a thousand channels like a spring tide. Jacquetta Hawkes, in her moving account of the transformation of our island through two thousand millennia, emphasizes the unconscious element in the Industrial Revolution:[1]

To me it seems an upsurge of instinctive forces comparable to the barbarian invasions, a surge that destroyed eighteenth-century civilization much as the Anglo-Saxons destroyed that of Roman Britain. No one planned it, no one foresaw more than a little of the consequences, very few people said that they wanted it, but once begun the impetus was irresistible; more and more individual lives became helplessly involved, drawn into the vortex. It went forward as irresistibly as the evolution of the dinosaurs and in it was included the roaring of Tyrannosaurus. It seems indeed that Tyrannosaurus and Apollo of the Intellect worked together for the Revolution and no combination could be more powerful or more dangerous.

It lent to its instruments an astonishing strength. It enabled this chip of the earth's surface, the small fund of human mind, will and energy that it supported, momentarily to dominate the whole surface of the planet and in so doing, like a gigantic, slow explosion, to disperse fragments of itself all over that surface. It seems possible that had there not been this association of coal and iron, growing population and intellectual ferment within the bounds of a temperate island, the industrialization that in two centuries has totally changed human life might never have assumed its present forms.

In other words, what Patrick Geddes, from his optimistic Edwardian vantage-point, could call the palaeotechnic culture had in it much of the palaeolithic:

> Now those thousands of years of wooing fertility under the sun and rain were to be half forgotten in a third way of living which resembles the first, that of the hunters, in its predatory dependence on the natural resources of the country.

The critical decade was the 1840s when the inevitable decision was taken to abolish the Corn Laws and with them the mercantilist system which had made possible the high farming of the previous century. From that moment the island, which in 1800 had as comfortably supported its 9 million people as France her 27, lost its simplicity and condemned its people to the treadmill of exporting in order to eat – exporting manufactures when it should have exported far more people to colonize the vast empty spaces of the antipodes. For the first time in history a whole region was turned over to the conversion of an imported raw material – cotton. Manchester, the Chicago of the nineteenth century, became the fascinating, horrific symbol of the new age. The 'hands' corralled into the mills had to forget all their inherited skills and all the customary rites and legends that had unified them with their ancestors.

The generations of the Second Rebuild had the colossal task of transforming quiet market towns to accommodate these multitudes. Of course they did not see it in these terms; the only national task they recognized was war. For all else, individual opportunism and self-help were the rule, and to them fell the provision of dwellings for the labouring classes, following the mills and the mines often into wildly inhospitable landscapes. When there was no old nucleus, company towns and mining villages were run up; but it was altogether exceptional for an Owen, a Salt or a Lever to see them as opportunities for philanthropy, and when they did they were apt to impose a collectivism and a high moral tone that were not necessarily popular. The norm were the slum rookeries of east London, the back-to-back cottages of the West Riding, the Tyneside flats and the tenements of Glasgow, through which the rich slept as tight as possible as the Night Scot slipped through on its way to the Highlands. The railways and the steamships now made it cheaper to carry to all quarters machine-made bricks and tiles from the Midlands, joists and boarding from the Baltic and slates from north Wales, often won by quarrymen living in barracks above the tree-line, who saw their women only on Sundays.

Among the rich sleepers were the architects: they did not consider that any of this was their business.

> We were the last romantics – chose for theme
> Traditional sanctity and loveliness.

Yeats's lines, addressed to William Morris near the end of the period, could more appropriately have been applied to the young Goths at its beginning, which we must remember was the age of Telford, the Brunels and the Stephensons. It is customary to attribute to Romanticism the split between the two cultures – the culture of the sciences that dealt in facts and the culture of the arts that dealt in values: the first in what could be done, the second in what ought to be done. In fact the Romantics, from their safe distance, were much excited by the wonders and terrors of palaeotechnic engineering. The schizophrenia that was the undoing of Victorian society was much more than the product of a fashion in the arts. If it derived unconsciously from the loss of the island's economic integrity in the 1840s, it derived institutionally from the rise of the public schools in the same age. There a classically educated elite, contemptuous of facts, was trained in the cultivation of values. Science was only reluctantly admitted to the curriculum towards the end of the century,[2] and by then the split between the two cultures had become total. The little engineer was trained up in the rigours of mathematics and technology, the little architect in the subtleties of the Doric, the Ionic and the Corinthian; snobbery, as much as ideology, split them apart.

Even so, one could have expected the Victorian architect, with his enhanced status, to retain his historic and classic interest in the structure and destiny of cities. But it was here that the Romantic movement affected his eyesight. 'Romantic art,' John Piper has written, 'deals with the particular.' It abhorred the easy generalizations of Augustan art, its conventional imagery, the clockwork universe within which it resided so complacently. The movement's concern was with the truth of the individual Imagination, with a dedicated attention to the detail of Nature, which became obsessive in the case of the Pre-Raphaelites, and with the Past, most of all with the age of chivalry, which it airily sentimentalized. Its attitude to the gross world of business was that of the Flower Children of 1968. Architects, if they were to remain in practice, could not go all the way with this, but they could at any rate avert the eye not only from Coketown and all its problems but also from monstrous London (that the Augustans had so enjoyed) – 'that great foul city of London' as Ruskin now called it, 'rattling, growling, smoking, stinking – a ghastly heap of fermenting brickwork, pouring out poison at every pore'.

So the sense of the whole was utterly lost. Between Dobson's New-castle and the Edwardian return to the principles of the *Beaux Arts* (of which New Delhi is the one great monument) no architect of sig-nificance gave the slightest attention to town planning, or to housing. Victorian 'improvement' was concentrated on two aspects of the urban disaster. The first was public health. The vast modernization and enlargements of London's infrastructure in the sixties and of Birmingham's in the seventies, the water works, sewage works, gas works and slum clearance were public health operations; and when a new main street, like London's Shaftesbury Avenue or Birming-ham's Corporation Street, was driven through, the objects were slum clearance and traffic relief, and architectural considerations were minimal: even Corporation Street was built up slowly and piecemeal so as not to disturb central land values by providing too many sites at once. The second motive was public edification and civic prestige. William Roscoe, last of the provincial Augustans, had died in 1831, but mayors continued to borrow his language for their speeches at the opening of public buildings. When Bradford's own St George's Hall was opened in 1853, Mayor Samuel Smith 'claimed that the hall would meet the needs not only of the "mercantile men" of Bradford but of the operatives, who after attending concerts would go back to their homes "elevated and refreshed, rising in the morning to their daily toil without headache and without regret". There were loud "Hear, hears" at this point. Smith did not need to remind his audience that Bradford, a stronghold of Puritan Nonconformity, had been the first town in England to erect a Temperance Hall in 1837.'[3] And in the discussions on plans for the Leeds Town Hall the local doctor declared that this grandiose project would demonstrate that 'in the ardour of mercantile pursuits the inhabitants of Leeds have not omitted to cultivate the perception of the beautiful and a taste for the fine arts'. Lockwood and Mawson at Bradford and Cuthbert Brodrick at Leeds, the architects concerned, no doubt said a few modest words on these occasions, and of course many others also made their names by the great assemblage of institutional and commercial edifices with which the age ornamented its anthill cities; but they never sought or even imagined the scope that had been claimed by Wren, Wood, Chambers, Adam or Nash. They wished their individual buildings to be substantial, expressive and elevating. As the example of a noble life was, they believed, the most that each man could contribute to the general good, so the influence of a noble building would in due time permeate the mean, dull streets in which it was so often set. The scale of these sermons in stones was formidable, in places even surrealist – a brutal assault on the bland Georgian environment where this existed. But there is no reason to think that Victorian architects were aware of this, and indeed in the northern industrial cities the take-over was complete enough to resolve the conflict.

A similar myopia affected sensibility to local materials. The High Victorians did not hesitate to use blue brick and slate in Cotswold villages or red terracotta in Brighton, and a whole generation passed before the passionate propaganda of William Morris and his followers began to take effect around the turn of the century. So durable was the Victorian fabric that it survived to 1940 virtually intact: apart from their inter-war suburbs the industrial cities and ports when the bombers struck them were wholly Victorian in character.

But if the architects had no vision of the totality, others had, particularly of course the writers and illustrators. The image of the great city had always had its light and its dark sides; but until the mid century the light side predominated, despite sentimental regret for the lost innocence, not to mention the pleasing decay, of the raped countryside and of the last fragments of the Georgian world now to be idealized by generations of novelists from Thackeray down to Georgette Heyer. Cruikshank's cartoon of the March of Bricks and Mortar (1829) is more hilarious than horrific, and a complacent view, not unmixed with commercial promotion, was taken of elegant new squares and salubrious suburbs. It was the phenomenal energy rather than the squalor of the northern cities that first astonished visitors. But with the emergence of mid-Victorian philanthropy and social concern the scale of the human disaster began to register. Thomas Shotter Boys in the early thirties and Gustave Doré in the late sixties represent the change of view as far as London is concerned, the first so bland, the second so crepuscular – both, of course, exaggerated. Finally the crepuscular image, the slimy fog-shrouded wilderness of *Fanny by Gaslight*, the translation into a human artefact of the primitive fear of the forest, becomes the stereotype, and the task of the twentieth century is seen to be to lead us out of it into the sunlight.

As we have noted, the men of the 1940s assembled three weapons with which to attack the myopia, the coal-and-iron technology and the brutality of the Victorian city. These were the Civic Survey, Neo-Technics and Social Justice. The first was the legacy of Patrick Geddes, who in the early years of the century taught the elementary lesson that understanding must come before action and that the key to understanding was the analysis of the morphology and the social geography of the city region. The second was formulated by Lewis Mumford with his vision of a clean, non-exploitative electric world, and by Le Corbusier who translated this vision into the language of architecture. The third was the concept of a Welfare State, fashioned by wartime social democrats in England, which would for the first time in history build cities that were not dramatizations of privilege and poverty. On these three foundations stood the tripod of the Third Rebuild.

Nothing so ambitious – for it amounted to a new society in a new environment – had ever before been seen as the business of architects, and we have watched how Nemesis overtook it. But like most revolutions its work was irreversible before it fell from power, and our urban societies have indeed totally changed. The two extremes of wealth and privilege have been chopped off, so that cities no longer display ladies and gentlemen or barefoot children, though of course gross but more discreet inequalities remain. Their victims are no longer subjects of charity, but claimants of rights, and none can ignore the searchlight the media continuously focus on them. As part of this process, there are no longer any slums. There are 'sink' estates, brutalized environments, design disasters, but they cannot be called slums by anyone who has seen the real thing, yesterday in this country and today in others. The war against the slums, like all wars, was a clumsy, wasteful, here and there even cruel operation, but it still seems against nature for it to have been won in any other way. Its symbols of oppression, the tower blocks, are so conspicuous above our low skylines that they seem more numerous than they are.[4] As we have noted, there are ten times as many childless or single-person households as there are flats in these blocks, so that their social usefulness seems assured once they have been rescued from vandalism by entry-phones, from condensation by double-glazing and heating included in the rent, and from isolation by better management.[5] Aesthetically their eventual approval seems equally assured if we may judge from the Victorian tenements and cut-price terraces that were equally loathed until quite recently. Anathemas pronounced on the tower blocks in 1970 can be compared with late-Victorian descriptions of their newly built tenements. Here is George Gissing in *The Nether World* (1889):

What terrible barracks, those Farrington Road Buildings! Vast sheer walls, unbroken by even an attempt at ornament; row above row of windows in the mud-coloured surface, upwards, upwards, lifeless eyes, mirky openings that tell of bareness, disorder, comfortlessness within . . . Acres of these edifices, the tinge of grime declaring the relative dates of their erection; millions of tons of brute brick and mortar, crushing the spirit as you gaze. Barracks, in truth; housing for the army of industrialism, an army fighting with itself, rank against rank, man against man, that the survivors may have whereon to feed.

History shows that no kind of building, not even gaols, is forever disliked as such.[6]

As unprecedented historically as the disappearance of the slums is the new attitude to the heritage from the past. Until 1940 educated people were extremely choosy about past styles of architecture. The Antique had a century of adulation; Tudor came in and then went out; Louis XV went out and then came in. But outside these decorators' fashions, any new buildings were always thought to be an improvement and in designing them no deference whatever was paid to old environments. Then, perhaps as a result of the uniquely destructive character of World War II, there occurred a change in human sensibility. By 1950 we loved everything, however hideous. Of course this did not immediately prevent an immense amount of destruction for profit or 'planning gain'. But as soon as the intelligentsia could get itself organized and rush through the necessary legislation, it became virtually impossible to demolish a listed building except by the underhand trick, soon acquired from private speculators by philistine public bodies, of encouraging it to fall down. This general benevolence (it stops short of true understanding) towards the past, plus clean air and new techniques for cleaning buildings, has spruced up old towns sometimes to the point of vulgarity. The Victorians would have been shocked by the Australian colour fantasies applied to their decent by-law housing, not to mention the tarting up of medieval streets. But by and large, and conspicuously in the north, the transformation has been miraculous. 'Operation Eyesore', whereby the black cotton towns of Lancashire washed and revealed their tawny Victorian public buildings, their intricate steeples and grand classical porticoes, while every tiny terraced cottage followed suit in its own fashion, has turned out one of the high points of our twentieth-century urban history. The unhappiest aspect of populist preservation is its negativity: 'anything new is worse.' In the extreme forms quoted in earlier chapters this is a national psychosis with obvious political connections. Deeply humiliated by their decline from greatness, the British look around on their society and do not like what they see – and they take it out on what has always been the mirror of society: its architecture. If you are on the political right, tower flats, council estates and prefabricated schools exhibit all the soullessness and inhumanity of penny-pinching officialdom; if you are on the left, speculative office blocks and multi-storey car parks and motorways symbolize gross capitalist materialism. The trouble is that this national loss of confidence in our capacity to innovate only promotes the mediocrity it seeks to protect us from. 'Safe' infill façades inserted into commercial Conservation Areas are depressing examples.

A by-product of the new sensibility is the pedestrianization of shopping streets. In cities of all sizes from Leeds to Hereford this seems the best contribution of twentieth-century planning to the minor pleasures of life. To hear footfalls, laughter, bird-song in the very heart of cities is a real recapture of territory lost to civilization, and the fact that the surrounding architecture is generally mediocre and sometimes absurd does not seem to matter and confirms once again the truth, often proclaimed by architects, that urban design is about the creation of spaces and not about the particular decor of the façades that wall them in. Even the characteristically English fussiness of the floor-space and furnishings is endurable because amendable. It has all been done of course by the diversion of old roads and the building of new ones, and it follows that London of all cities has the least to show – the old radial main roads lined with seedy commercial premises that thicken up every few miles into indistinguishable shopping centres choked with traffic fuming at zebra crossings being by far its most conspicuous failure. Any left turn off these miserable arteries takes one into healthier tissue where the city's cells are being continually replaced.

It has been common in the last twenty years to extend pedestrianized shopping streets into new shopping precincts combined with parking on back land. Some of the earlier efforts got their assessments wrong and were commercial as well as architectural disasters: often the first produced the second. The later and larger ones, more skilfully integrated, wholly under cover and often combined with sports centres, pools and public libraries, deserve to be recorded as another of the great gains of this period, scoring high marks on Wotton's definition for both Commodity and Delight. Here in their different lifestyles working wives, semi-employed moonlighters and jobless teenagers can forget their problems in environments which, undreamt of by the puritanical planners of the forties, combine the delights of the souks of Istanbul and the Baths of Caracalla. Civic spaces of the old kind, like the new square in front of Portsmouth's 1890 Guildhall, may come into their own on great occasions, but unless they are market-places as well can only compete for liveliness on the finest of summer evenings.

Another new pleasure, never alluded to by superior persons, must also be recorded. This is the transformation of the office worker's environment. The granddaughter of the Edwardian stenographer, who rattled her noisy Imperial in a black City lane or glazed-brick light-well, is now, perhaps, over-lit, over-warmed, but from the windows she can look down goddess-like on the neatly weaving, sound-less toy cars far below, watch white airliners glide in across radiant skies and see the whole city light up as the sun goes down. These glass buildings, derided in the daytime by London aesthetes, come together after dark to produce one of the great spectacles of the twentieth-century urban world, which we may as well enjoy while we can. A minority of office workers do better still, when country houses have been taken over by insurance companies or multinationals and glamorously extended by sophisticated architects. Easy parking, cedars and gliding swans framed in great windows, and a swim in the warmed pool before lunch: these are the privileged benefits of decentralization married to intelligent conservation.[7]

112. Powell and Moya's enlargement of Winslade Manor near Exeter for London and Manchester Insurance

All the same, the more we concentrate on this bright side of the coin, the more aware we are that the time comes to turn it over. There is by now a substantial literature on the failure of modernism, most notably in England where failure is in any case a national obsession. The subject is inviting, since it can be put in terms of black comedy as well as high tragedy. But it is too soon to aspire to offer history's verdict on the architecture of the central half of our century, any more than Cromwell's verdict on Charles I is history's. We can be certain that it will be more ironical and therefore more gentle than our own. What follows can be no more than a guess at it.

Perhaps the fundamental cause of unease has been the totalitarian nature of the modernist prescription. In her introduction to Isaiah Berlin's essays, *Russian Thinkers*, Aileen Kelly writes of the nineteenth-century Russian intelligentsia:

> In their fervent moral opposition to the existing order, their single-minded preoccupation with ideas, and their faith in reason and science, they paved the way for the Russian revolution, and thereby achieved major historical significance. But they are all too often treated by English and American historians with a mixture of condescension and moral revulsion; because the theories to which they were so passionately attached were not their own, but borrowed from the west and usually imperfectly understood; and because in their fanatical passion for extreme ideologies they are held to have rushed, like Dostoyevsky's devils, to blind self-destruction, dragging their country, and subsequently most of the rest of the world, after them. The Russian revolution and its aftermath have done much to strengthen the belief, deeply entrenched in the Anglo-Saxon outlook, that a passionate interest in ideas is a symptom of mental and moral disorder.

Berlin himself, whose own standpoint is passionately pluralistic, nevertheless has no use for moral laziness of this order. He shows that we have on the whole found it hard to live without a monistic philosophy of some kind. Art, ever since classical times, has except during brief libertarian revolts been rigidly prescriptive. Our present revolt is therefore not towards the norm, but away from it, and so it will be hard to sustain.

The leading principle of the recent monistic philosophy was of course the application of functionalism to the design of cities. In the past (and to this day in Islamic and colonial Latin American cities) the city block was a little village accommodating every kind and degree of life and work. The form was given and the functions fitted into it. The same applied to the surrounding multi-purpose streets. For the last hundred years or so planners have gone about it the opposite way, analysing the functions of cities including their different kinds of traffic, and then seeking forms and locations that seemed appropriate to them: form followed function. Hans Asplund, son of the father of Scandinavian modernism and needless to say in total reaction against all this stood for, speaking at the RIBA early in 1980, naturally and neatly attributed functionalism to the functionalists and specific-ally to the CIAM Charter of Athens of 1933, which identified the Four Functions of Home, Work, Recreation and Circulation. In fact this rational separating-out of urban functions long predated CIAM. The Circus at Bath was no village and industrial zoning came in when industries became 'noxious' in the nineteenth century. Nor need we romanticize the Neapolitan slum or see anything life-enhancing in putting a factory that produces fish fingers or hair dryers into a housing area. We do not have to react the whole way back to urban anarchy. But we have already seen how even at Milton Keynes, despite the determination not to repeat the mistakes of earlier New Towns and above all to create an exciting, unified and highly mobile city, the separating-out of functions produced, once again, housing areas that feel dead in working hours, commercial areas that are dead after them and main roads that chop the city into pieces. In Asplund's words, 'urban intensity is lost like a fire which dies down when the logs are separated'.

Of course the main agent of disintegration was the motor vehicle. Having cut cities about even more drastically than the railways had done, it additionally, unlike them, crept into every cranny and infes-ted the city like maggots. The visual conflict created by our depen-dence on the private car and our conservation of historic townscapes was worse in English country towns than in any others because of their intimate scale and snugly domestic architecture. In those few courts and alleys and quadrangles into which cars, with their atten-dant tarmac and yellow lines, cannot penetrate, one can recapture the unity of texture of walls and floors and people that a century ago was commonplace, and here and there a few yards are reclaimed and the granite setts go back. But by and large nothing is any longer truthfully picturesque in the proper sense: no village can be photographed. That the absorption of the car would need 'a different sort of city' has been well understood since the 1940s. Its rationale would be the vertical separation of vehicles from pedestrians and the civilized thing seemed to be to put the people on top. But when it came to doing it, three fatal obstacles revealed themselves. The first was a vicious circle. The first instalments of the 'different sort of city' meant a stiff climb or tedious ramp up to a wide deck exposed to the weather. Who wanted that? These foretastes of the hugely expensive system were so unpopular that its completion, on which its success absolutely depended, became impracticable. Moreover, and secondly, the attempt coincided with an unprecedented (and not unconnected) love affair with old buildings and their attendant trees, which persisted in standing about at the old level. And finally it emerged that people preferred the congestion, pollution and din of the multi-purpose street to a regimented environment that would separate them from the cruising taxi, the chaseable bus and the fashionable bike. They preferred to keep the car in or beside the house than to risk its survival, or even their own, in communal garages behind the scenes. In this aspect, they did not take to the modern city.

There were others. The men of the forties had got over what they saw as the naive and socially dubious enthusiasm of modernism, as of all other 'isms. Architecture, they held, would emerge unaffectedly from their crusade against social injustice, hypocrisy and sloppy thinking. They saw these vices as embodied in two physical phenomena: the slums and the suburbs. The worker, the decent, stoical, sociable British worker, must be accorded his Exodus from the first without suffering the Diaspora of the second. This was a tall order. It meant high densities, as Abercrombie was the first to recognize, and it meant a building operation of a scale and complexity that could only be handled, in his opinion, by the kind of large-scale thinking that had won the war. He did not see this as revolutionary, but rather as a belated return from sentimentality to the fine scale of the English urban tradition, born in Bath and developed in Edinburgh and Dublin. The anonymous front door, one of a disciplined row of such, had been the pride of this uniform, whether at the scale of the artisan terraces of Battersea or the mansions of Belgravia. Of course there is no reason to think that the neat terrace, glibly taken by architects to be the 'English tradition', was in fact what the English had wanted, and plenty that it suited the convenience of speculators, large and small. Given their head the rich no doubt preferred villas and the poor their separate cottage, and given their head the middle classes had long since opted for the winding suburban road rather than the corridor street and the square that had provided the armature for the Georgian town. But since the terrace tradition, at all its scales, alone seemed to suit the circumstances, it had to be hoped that it would continue to be acceptable.

We have watched the downfall of this bland utilitarianism of the immediate post-war years, how functionalism dismantled the traditional city block and the multi-purpose street and how the inadequacy of the land-take, the greed of developers, the failure to collect betterment, the inexorable political pressure for numbers, the overstretching of the building industry and the power of Corbusian imagery together produced the draughty new townscape of towers and slabs and podia. Understandably the first shock and criticism was of mere size, as offensive to faint-hearts and moralists as the mills and tenements and commercial palaces of the previous century. It seems unlikely that history will endorse this reaction any more than the earlier one. What had been so depressing about the British industrial cities from London downwards had been their drab horizontal extension to infinity. Setting aside the cases in this book, there seems no question that Birmingham, Manchester and Leeds were more exciting places in 1980 than in 1940, even though by American standards, and even by Parisian ones, they were still nothing like as exciting as they might have been.[8] Constrained by ideology as well as by economics, the British could not emulate the high drama or the glamour that were the great assets of American modernism. Indeed it is the timidity rather than the vulgarity of English 'skyscrapers' that is their most depressing feature. The trivial variations applied to the repetitive multi-storey elevation were insulting to palates that had tasted the rich sauces concocted by the Victorians and the Edwardians (though it is fair to add that those same critics had not approved of Edwardian baroque when it was new, preferring, and in well-known cases moving into, the plainness, indeed the repetitiveness, of Bloomsbury). Monotony was compounded by monochromy. The English reacted against the black-and-white world of modernism exactly as they had reacted against the cream-and-black world of the Regency: they wished to shed stiff shirt and tails and get back into woollens. And when the inevitable entropy overtook the black-and-white world and it all turned grey, reaction turned to revolt.

We can see now that mechanical repetition was the inevitable expression of mass production. The builders could not build cheaply, or fast, any other way. Management and maintenance needed long runs and components that could be replaced from stock. Repetitiveness, in other words, was a design input, a technical input and a management input. So people had to learn to live with an architecture which, for the first time in history, was not malleable, not docile to the human hand. In its place, they were offered paternalism. The word proffers itself, though the abuse, compared with what had gone before, was venial. It is hard to see how the massive demand for rented housing in the cities could have been supplied except by large organizations, whether these were local authorities or housing associations or cooperatives: the little landlord's day was over. All the same, for millions of English people the new dependence, with every tiny repair or improvement having to wait on a low-grade bureaucracy, was a new experience, to which the national temperament was peculiarly ill-adapted. It was crucially important that the protest, however brutal, should be made, endured and met, before the dependence took over and stifled it.

While journalists and critics demonstrated their command of English invective, ordinary people gave expression to their revolt in different ways. The herbivores, if they could afford to buy their council house, proclaimed it by a 'Georgian' front door and coach lamps and inside by miniaturized cornices, coloured bathroom suites and elaborate wallpapers. The carnivores, if articulate, organized guerrilla warfare on council offices, or if inarticulate turned to vandalism. This new phenomenon, humbly accepted by architects as a critique of bad design, was more often a critique of bad management, or of bad upbringing by parents in thrall to television or moonlighting. There was very little correlation with the quality of the architecture. Sociologists, sceptical of what they call 'architectural determinism', tell us that 'the built environment cannot usefully be seen as a major determinant of social behaviour'[9] and that it is the recent and unprecedented concern of architects in social questions, the Corbusian aspiration to transform the life of cities, which have caused them to take on their shoulders the sins of the world.

Housing managers, who certainly were in the front line, responded by recruiting (while they were still allowed to) young jeans-clad social workers capable of bridging the generation gap. Private open spaces, however minuscule, were conjured out of nothing and families with young children were brought down out of the towers as rapidly as possible. And of course such new housing as could be built, in reaction now against high-density/low-rise, was at pre-war densities and almost entirely 2-storey.

Architects in their turn needed no persuading that one of their periodical *bouleversements* was called for. A new generation had taken over from the beneficiaries of the sixties and in the normal course of events it was due. But this time it would not be so easy. Modern architecture was deeply rooted in twentieth-century technology: this was its bedrock philosophy. Buildings and cities, like any other artefact, had no alternative but to say how they were made. It followed that if the technology changed (for example if the energy crisis deepened) architecture would, within the philosophy, change too. But meanwhile to be pernickety about the design of seaside hotels, airports, office buildings, leisure complexes or laboratories seemed as silly as to fuss about the design of jet aircraft, television cameras or taxis. All these high-energy artefacts were offensive or pollutant in one way or another, and all were no doubt on the way out, but not yet, and not for aesthetic reasons.

There was consequently something almost frivolous about the little changes British and American architects now embarked on or advocated. There were three overlapping schools of thought. The first was concerned, fairly enough, with surfaces – with a change of clothing. Some local authorities, led by Essex, decided to chivvy developers into this by issuing Design Guides, the effect of which was to dress new housing and even new commercial areas in a so-called 'vernacular' uniform which soon threatened the one endearing characteristic of suburbia – its dotty variety. Dark brick and dark asbestos slate,

113. Hillingdon Civic Centre - the largest cottage in England

mnemonically introduced by Darbourne and Darke in 1961, rapidly became obsessive and depressing in a new way, so that by 1980 there was a move, under Byker influences, into polychrome brickwork and fancy woodwork. In London even the Camden Borough architects, hitherto whiter than white, switched to yellow brick with red stripes and pretty ironwork. The largest single example of the return to brick-and-tile is the Hillingdon Civic Centre on the western edge of London, completed in 1978 to designs by Robert Matthew, Johnson-Marshall and Partners (after the death of the first and the retirement of the second). Whether this extraordinary building, for whose style its authors were said to have combed the cul-de-sacs of Ruislip and Pinner, will be welcomed to the club of lovable English architectural freaks remains to be seen. From a distance it sprawls like a huge brown marquee, but from close up one misses the fancy with which the Victorians would have ornamented it, and one becomes aware, after the lights go on, that behind its geometrical complexities of brown brickwork is another concrete-framed office building got up in an elaborate, if necessarily cost-conscious, fancy dress.

The second school of thought is the world of whimsy, or more respectably pastiche. Like Gothic in the seventeenth century, neo-Georgian never really surrendered in the twentieth. When the architects abandoned it the builders, in an illiterate version, picked it up and directed it at that intermediate market which was too good for the New Town-type terrace but not quite sophisticated enough for SPAN. One domestic architect of the post-war generation, Raymond Erith, ploughing a lonely furrow through the heyday of modernism, worked unaffectedly in the Georgian tradition, and when in the seventies the nostalgia boom gathered pace his junior partner and successor, Quinlan Terry, found himself (unlike his master) suddenly fashionable among the young. But their work never moved beyond pastiche: it neither transformed an old style as the Gothic and Queen Anne Revivals had done, nor from within the tradition of the new had the wit to parody the old. For this skill the English had, as in the past, to look abroad.

Ever since the war, first in Italy and later in America, modern architects, less puritanically blinkered than the British, had sought to enliven the severities of the modern movement with historical allusions. Often trivial and under attack from the historicist[10] school of critics led by Nikolaus Pevsner, these heretics had over the years consolidated their position, partly through the defection to them of the wittiest of American modernists, Philip Johnson. With the publication in 1977 of Charles Jencks's *The Language of Post-modern Architecture* this third school of thought acquired a necessary label, and a deliberately provocative one. For what was in fact happening was not the displacement of modern architecture by a new style but the emergence within it of mannerist tendencies closely analogous to

114. Mannerist office buildings of 1979 in Westminster

those which emerged within Renaissance architecture in the sixteenth century. In both periods, boredom and impatience with a severely correct architecture led a naughty minority to break the rules, the rules in the case of modernism being, first, that buildings must express the logic of their structures and, second, that historical allusions are nowadays meaningless and subversive. But the essence of 'Post-modernism' is that you have to know the rules to break them: modern mannerism, in other words, can only be pulled off by a modern sensibility.

The relevance to a social history of these aesthetic niceties is that they are yet another symptom of the liberalization and pluralism that characterize the late seventies. The 'anything-goes' philosophy is closely paralleled in, perhaps derives from, the world of Fashion, where the old dictatorship over shape, colours, hemlines, seemed to have gone for ever and Paris itself had become wildly permissive. Widening the field to urban design, the change of view is on similar lines. Old cities had consisted of spaces walled in by buildings, and even the Baroque to Second Empire fire-breaks and vistas aimed at great monuments had still been defined by stage-sets of classical architecture. It all looked splendid as long as you did not go round the back. Modernism, finding this both brutal and bogus, proposed to remove the scenery and set up its monuments – towers and slabs of flats and offices – in limitless space. From too little public space, cities suddenly had too much, and in a wholly unenjoyable form. Ejected from claustrophobia, citizens fell victims to agoraphobia. Some urbanists, overreacting again, wished to climb back into the past – into pastiche. Thus the Krier brothers, young Marxists from Luxemburg much in vogue among students in the late seventies, proposed to slot into the appalling holes left in the urban fabric by slum clearance and road works axial vistas, corridor streets and formal piazzas walled in by neo-classic architecture in the manner of Speer and Mussolini, disinventing, as far as could be judged, the motor vehicle. Others saw that what was called for was mannerism – a casual, witty juxtaposition, collision even, of the two ways of seeing. Colin Rowe, a perceptive critic of modernism ever since the forties, defines his most important book[11] as 'a proposal for constructive dis-illusion, it is simultaneously an appeal for order and disorder, for the simple and the complex, for the joint existence of permanent reference and random happening, of the private and the public, of innovation and tradition, of both the retrospective and the prophetic gesture. To us the occasional virtues of the modern city seem to be patent and the problem remains how, while allowing for the need of a "modern" declamation, to render these virtues responsive to circumstance.' Seeing no reason to throw over either the consolatory or the utopian qualities of architecture, he asks: 'Could not this ideal city, at one and the same time, be both a theatre of prophecy and a theatre of memory?'

The best of the mainstream modern architects, going along with the painter Barnett Newman's view that 'aesthetics is for the artist the way ornithology is for the birds', neither saw the need, nor nowadays had the time, for new theory. English architecture had in any case never conformed for long and the diversity of channels into which the stream flowed in the seventies was characteristic. Some of the leaders who had emerged in the fifties, like Lasdun, Sheppard and Robson, Powell and Moya, YRM, achieved a recognizable and classic consistency. Others, romantics, pushed on to the frontiers either of high technology (Foster, Rogers, Farrell/Grimshaw) or of natural materials and the picturesque (Erskine, Aldington, McCormack/ Jamieson). Two headquarters offices of the late seventies, one in the private sector, one in the public, illustrate the vitality of the tradition: the first at Ipswich by Foster Associates a distillation of the early

115. The Willis Faber building in Ipswich by Foster Associates

dreams of Mies van der Rohe, the second by Philip Dowson of Arup Associates an evolution from the prairie houses of Frank Lloyd Wright. At the same time, just when there was said to be no money to build it any more, English public housing in the hands of subtle

116 and 117. The CEGB building at Bedminster Down, Bristol, by Arup Associates

designers like Darbourne and Darke and Jeremy Dixon re-emerged as the most civilized and classless in the world. Who needed 'post-modernism'?

118. Council housing in North Kensington by Jeremy Dixon

119. Council housing at 100 p.p.a. in Islington by Darbourne and Darke

None of this of course is great architecture in the Ruskinian sense. Time will confer no pathos on it, nor will it fall into evocative ruin. The locked churches symbolize our exclusion from such images of the collective unconscious. But then the modern movement never set out to operate at that level. What it did set out to do, in Mumford's vision, was to build a neotechnic world which would recapture for us the natural balance and therefore the durability of the eotechnic, and so liberate us from the nightmare exponential growth curve of the last century. Regained thus, there might be time for masterpieces to emerge again. But no such relaxation proved possible. Far from flattening, the curve steepened, pushed ever higher by the overriding need of capitalism to promote growth by exciting consumer expectations. Against these pressures, neither the idealism of young conservationists in the West nor the neo-mercantilist controlled economies of the East could make head. Multiplying the cost of oil produced inflation in the rich countries and near-bankruptcy in the poor ones, but the hunger for it persisted. So the world remains hooked on its limited store of fossil fuels while its population continues to explode at a rate which the planet's ecology will not support for long. The sense of failure, even of doom, that haunted the seventies was an epidemic to which the architects of the Third Rebuild were exposed ever since they had made the decision, in all innocence and earnestness, to descend from their ivory towers into the political arena.

Down there, errors of management could by now be inventoried. Planning had adopted a twenty-year time-scale, which might be physically realistic but was financially absurd in an age when Chancellors found it increasingly difficult to look more than a year ahead. Yet the reputations invested in these twenty-year plans made Government slow to change course when they rapidly obsolesced. Disastrously in Northern Ireland and damagingly elsewhere, planners were slow to learn, though they did in the end, that physical and socio-economic planning needed to work side by side. And in Whitehall itself, a consuming interest in machinery, and specifically in a radical and unwise redesign of local government, distracted the higher echelons from concentration on policy. This was odd considering that most of them had been to universities where there was virtually no teaching of how things are done in the world.

Thus over the years when we were being taught the limits of growth we were also painfully learning the limits of power. From the paternalism of the fifties we moved to the 'public participation exercises' of the sixties and the public revolts of the seventies, from which humiliations planning emerged 'indicative', 'flexible', 'broad-brush'. Perceptive architects saw this coming. As early as 1970, reading the signals from Covent Garden, Erskine proposed to push community involvement and Llewelyn-Davies aesthetic pluralism as far as public opinion wished them to go. The Great Concept, the stock-in-trade of the ambitious practitioner since the Renaissance, has been driven underground, or into the Schools, or abroad, where James Stirling works a rich seam of German nostalgia for the neo-classic. No longer the impresario, or the master planner, or the social engineer, no longer the seer, the architect withdraws to his earlier self-effacing role as the servant of society. But the servant is no longer the civil servant, the polite agent of immense power. Mass needs and mass solutions are no longer either identifiable or affordable. In a survey of student attitudes in 1979 the RIBA reported that 'disturbingly few wanted to influence the environment through their work'. Only four per cent wished to work in the public sector: 'Private practice is seen as the glamorous side of the profession.' They were not in the business of finding successor techniques to replace the conventional wisdom handed down through Geddes, Unwin, Mumford, Abercrombie, Le Corbusier and CIAM. No resolution was on offer of the dilemmas that had sunk the great post-war plans, no strategy for the worse dilemmas that an age of shortages was likely to bring. Like barbarian invaders moving into the ruins of Roman cities, the liberators had it easy, exploiting surviving infrastructures and capital accumulations.

This is the opportunity of the 'barefoot architects', whose rejection of Big Government is rooted in the creed long since put in one sentence in George Eliot's *Middlemarch*:

> There is no general doctrine which is not capable of eating out our morality if unchecked by the deep-seated habit of direct fellow-feeling with individual fellow-men.

Fellow-feeling takes the form, such as we have seen at work in inner Liverpool, of direct participation in repair and improvement schemes at street level, with the designer doubling as builder, indistinguishable from other tradesmen and operating wherever possible by bartering services.

One can take a worldly or an unworldly view of this time-honoured Anglo-American way of life. The worldly view is sceptical whether in a developed economy such as ours the road to a new morality lies through the pseudo-medieval exchanges of the Alternative Economy.

We have grown too dependent on the 'social wage' to run away from the high taxes it necessitates and the need for some wealth to levy them on. In fact the Alternative Economy is not alternative at all but parasitic – a product in all societies of taxes deemed too high, bureaucracy too clumsy, work (if available) too monotonous. Whether the parasite, which shows every sign of growing, should be welcomed, legitimized, tolerated or somehow ejected is open to argument, but what it cannot be is paramount. A consumer society could never willingly adjust to the privations such a revolution would entail. Post-industrialism is in other words as naive a notion as post-modernism.

The alternative (but in no sense conflicting) view is that we see in these back streets the fumbling expression of a change of consciousness at work in the world, a change as profound as the one we associate with the Renaissance, but almost its mirror-image. In this view, the retreat from heroic plans, from mass solutions and from self-indulgent architecture, like other British retreats, is not a defeat but a victory. Speaking at the A A as early as 1960, before the age of alienation and mob violence, of vandals and punks, Lewis Mumford had said that 'we have a great deal of moral repair to do before we shall have cities worth living in; and without this our architectural solutions will be empty. We could have a city full of all sorts of elegance and still have an environment like that of Florence in the sixteenth century, when no one's life was safe.' It can now be claimed that short of catastrophe this moral repair can only emerge, is now slowly emerging, from the reassertion of the feminine instincts of protectiveness, conservation and personal concern, after a couple of millennia in which cities have been centres of power and architecture a statement of pride, and that this change of consciousness is the only hope for our survival.

It is in line with this change that we should cease to lay claim to the environment as a primarily visual experience, recognizing that to most of our fellow-beings, who seldom raise their eyes above head-height, it is a great deal more than that; it is apprehended by all the other senses and some we scarcely understand. We no longer expect people to stand back like tourists and gape at our buildings, but simply to use them as they use a pub or a market. We are aware that the people of Bath are no happier than the people of Blackburn, that some of our happiest towns are some of our least designed, and that in these outcomes the architect, with his hypertrophied visual sense, has a part to play among far more other people than he previously supposed

– his role as a scene-shifter in the urban drama a comparatively modest one. Until this century, after all, architects had nothing to do with the common herd, whose crafty dwellings rose and fell, or were swept away by man-made or natural disasters – an obscure tide out of which rose the city's islands of Architecture. Into those deep waters of instinct he can only expect to penetrate a limited distance.

In the end the Third Rebuild turns out to have been as existential, as submissive to political and financial circumstance, as its predecessors. And like them it has no end, dissolving into a new period, taken over by a new generation (not all young, for it includes reformed *dirigistes* well into middle age) which welcomes the unemphatic, the intimate and the affectionate as the creative product of our limitations. Whether this is the swell of a new wave we cannot yet tell. We cannot tell whether from such humble beginnings, such self-denial, architecture as a transforming experience will re-emerge, like Christian cathedrals out of the depths of the Dark Ages. In a statement of defiant romanticism, André Gide indicates the more likely outcome:

> *The thing I am most aware of is my limits. And this is natural, for I never, or almost never, occupy the middle of any cage: my whole being surges towards the bars.*

1

2

APPENDIX A

Early Clients of Maxwell Fry

LETTER FROM MAXWELL FRY, 28 MAY 1979

Dear Lionel,

You ask about the individual clients of the 30s and they are in fact a rum lot, very mixed, some with the light in their eyes but others just trapped.

The house in Kingston happened thus. Our office boy one day produced an unlikely individual with the face of an intelligent pig and the accent of the uninitiated who asked me to design him a modest little house which I did to sketch stage. But one day he came to me saying 'Sorry Mr Fry. It's off. Income tax. Cut me short. Another day. What do I owe you?' After an interval of a year perhaps, he turned up again, very smart, gardenia in his button hole, all smiles and mystery.

''Ave you got them plans, Mr Fry?' He regarded me I would say with something short of veneration. I produced the plans which he regarded dreamily as though discarding them in favour of new visions. 'First,' he said, 'the garridge. Rolls for me and a runabout for Miss Margaret (his pimply daughter), shuffer above. The rest of the 'ouse to scale and don't stint it Mr Fry. The best is good enough for Jerry Brown.'

He had graduated from being a bookie. 'Nasty trade, Mr Fry. Two hundred quid in your pocket on Manchester Races. All gone at Doncaster.' From this he moved to the fur trade, to off licence business and then at last to real estate in NW London buying at £100 an acre agricultural, and coming out at the latter end at £10,000 having bribed the necessary officials on the way and all on the telephone.

He never interfered. He allowed me to furnish his new estate in life like Sancho Panza's island, treating me always with the respect due to my profession and paying up promptly. That was Jerry Brown.

The client for the Sun House was a working sporting tailor with an Italian wife and a shop in Hanover Square. I forget his name. He was that exceptional thing, an architectural addict, and I managed to hook him on a shopping round among the Mars Group architects. He set me a financial target and two pages of typescript saying exactly how they lived, working hard by day and entertaining friends in the evening, the whole outfit centred upon an old Scottish housekeeper. Like Jerry Brown he allowed me to design or choose furniture and fittings, including murals by Hans Feibusch, and was no bother at all.

George Butler who was an art director of J. Walter Thomson's big firm was so faithful that he stood being chased off three possible sites before he built at Chipperfield Common, but there I had to decide between adding a pitched roof if we built in concrete, or using traditional materials if it was a flat roof, and I chose the latter. The local vicar suspected immorality at every move ...

Much love to you both from us both.
Max

APPENDIX B

OBSERVER MAY 1951
The South Bank Style
BY LIONEL BRETT

On a fine May morning the South Bank must be the gayest spot on earth. Approach it, for instance, down the gloomy chasm of Northumberland Avenue, with its peeling black stucco architecture ending in thundering black Victorian engineering. At the end, poised delicately above the Embankment, is a round steel platform in which architecture and engineering are fused. That is the twentieth-century achievement, and it dominates the Exhibition.

Crossing the Bailey Bridge (engineering), with its romantic outlook upon the spires of Westminster (architecture), one sees ahead objects such as the Skylon and the Dome, which are both but neither, because both are transcended. In the misty blue, a series of yellow mobiles make complicated evolutions; ahead, fountains of fire and water add their fantasy. The whole complex of form and colour, with its mysterious depths and transparencies, rests as lightly as a mirage on the water.

This Exhibition is no doubt symptomatic of a great many things, and will be damned with faint praise by all those who are at odds with themselves and the vertiginous world we live in. It will here be examined on its own pretensions as the centenary of 1851, and as the latest variation on the grandiose theme originally propounded by the Prince Consort: the marriage of art and science.

False Starts

Broadly, one can say that from the Great Exhibition of 1851 to the Chicago World's Fair of 1893 science raced ahead; everything memorable in those Exhibitions, from the Crystal Palace to the Eiffel Tower, was engineering. The architects were not interested; their business was 'architecture', if possible in stone. Their come-back was at Chicago in 1893, an overwhelming victory for stone and columns. 'The damage,' prophesied Louis Sullivan, 'will last for half a century,' and it did.

Paris 1900, San Francisco 1915, Gothenburg 1923, Wembley 1924, Paris 1925, demonstrated the wanderings of architects and designers in the wilderness of revivals and false starts. Always (right till New York 1939) the layout was pompously classical, with vast symmetrical vistas so exhausting that eventually toy trains had to be provided for the footsore.

The one miraculous exception was Stockholm 1930, where steel and glass were first exploited by the imaginative genius of a great architect. This was accompanied by so much talk of functionalism and machine aesthetic that there occurred in the thirties a strong Philistine reaction, exploited by the Fascists and Nazis and Communists at the Paris Exhibition of 1937. If the new style was to survive the onslaught of stuffy monumentality, posing as the language of the common man, it clearly needed to be humanized. That was the task of 1951.

Having, with her vast hothouse, initiated the series (and it has been a most valuable hothouse of architectural ideas, even if many have been weeds), Britain lost interest. As far as her Governments were concerned, these were trade shows. As the great Exhibitions, with the entry of the totalitarians, became increasingly bombastic and competitive, we stood on our dignity all the more. A couple of elongated lions at the entrance and a display of tweeds and tennis rackets were felt to be the right note. The first attempt this country made to give any inkling of its national life was at New York in 1939, and this had neither the bravura of the other Great Powers nor the elegant restraint of the lesser democracies.

Vistas

All this lost ground is this summer gracefully and convincingly made good. Not only do we witness here in London the long-awaited opening of the flower of modern architecture. This Exhibition has other virtues which few of its predecessors enjoyed.

This time, enter from the Waterloo end, and look across the great concourse. The vista is closed by no grandiose Palace of this or that, but by the remote and romantic pinnacles of – Whitehall Court. The size of the intervening space is doubled by the invisible Thames, across which all the air in the world seems to flow into what might else seem a pretty constricted site. Advance, and there opens on the left the finest of all prospects of Westminster. Or turn right and pass under the huge leaping arch of Waterloo Bridge, and there is the wide river and the whole City from Somerset House to St Paul's, floodlit by the sun at one's back. The vision of those who chose this dress-circle seat for the Exhibition is triumphantly vindicated. The interplay between past and present, the solid and the evanescent, large spaces and little ones, is a vintage architectural experience.

One Language

This is all done without any pomposity. The layout is an object lesson in asymmetry: the realization in architecture of the English tradition of land-scaping. The story of this country's achievements is told with modesty and charm that keep just clear of smugness and affectation. The result is overwhelming, just because the hand is not overplayed.

Of course, it is on balance an advantage not to have all the nations shouting their wares in discordant accents: but unity might (as at Glasgow 1938) have been bought at the price of variety. The important thing about this Exhibition is that all its designers, young and old, speak the same language, but with a delightful variety of intonation which is the real achievement of the co-ordinating architect, Mr Hugh Casson. He has been able to anchor his deliberately flimsy structures to the fat rectangle of the Festival Hall, which, though not entirely satisfactory as a shape, has the same inevitable relation-ship with the Shot Tower as an Italian Romanesque church with its cam-panile (may they never be divided!).

It seems worth trying to put this visual language of the mid century into words. Its foundation, already mentioned, is engineering touched with magic, or in other words the marriage of science and art. The visual result, given the capabilities of our materials, is as light as thistledown. A puff of wind, one feels, would blow it away. Paper-thin planes of concrete float in the air. Supports are spindly, often attenuated to a point at the base. For contrast, thick slabs of the solidest masonry, even chunks of rock and earth, are introduced with a fine disregard for the impermanence of exhibitions.

This contrast between transparent or opaque *sheets* of glass, canvas, asbes-tos, aluminium, and deliberately heavy *slabs* of wall, is a recurrent theme. Anything intermediate is avoided. The thick slabs are generally isolated and dramatized by adjacent transparencies, as when glass meets rubble, or stretched canvas meets flint, or stair-treads float without risers. Pretty steel balustrades make a lacy edging and a repetitive linear pattern. Sometimes, as inside the Power Production building, the linear pattern becomes fascinating-ly complicated.

Cloud of Doves

This architecture, with its attendant arts, hovers by nature and purpose on the borderline of fantasy. From the Promethean glooms of remote geological epochs or black mines, it soars as lightly as the cloud of doves that spills out from the wicker cage in the roof of the pavilion of the Lion and Unicorn. Nothing could be more arresting than its rather feminine elegance beside the thumping black brick arches that lead up to Hungerford Bridge.

For all their lightness, the Exhibition buildings are tough, and, given more durable finishes and cladding, could be permanent. They must, therefore, be taken seriously, for they undoubtedly foreshadow the public architecture of the fifties. Of course, there is nothing new about it. To people familiar with Scandinavian and Swiss practice, the South Bank style is a summing up rather than a step forward. The great thing is that in a single stride, though working under every possible handicap, our designers have unmistakably taken the lead. And they have put on a show so impossible not to enjoy that there is a real hope that it will mark the beginning of a modern style which will be generally accepted.

APPENDIX C

SPUR 1960 REPORT *

1

SPUR came into existence in 1958 with the objects of:

1. Calling attention to the rapidly approaching crisis of city planning in the UK. This was the purpose of the Exhibition 'Better Towns for Better Living', which is at present on tour.

2. Acting as a clearing house for collecting and disseminating ideas on urban renewal. This has been the aim of the discussion groups which have been meeting regularly through 1959 and 1960.

3. Identifying the problems most urgently needing organized research. This is the object of the present report.

2

SPUR is not the horse, still less the army; but standing outside political or professional allegiances it is perhaps in a position to spot the gaps where attacks ought to go in.

National use of land

3

At the outset we have worked within the principle that urban life and rural life are at opposite poles, and that while interdependent they must not be diluted. We accept the view that in the case of Great Britain variety, economy, the efficient use of existing investment and the preservation of existing beauties will and should perpetuate the present town/country antithesis. We therefore, as stated in our original aims, regard the rebuilding of the obsolete tracts of our towns and cities and the creation of new towns within suburbia not only as social imperatives for their own sake, but also as safeguards against unnecessary inroads into the countryside.

4

It follows that it is impossible to isolate urban studies from the problems of national and even global land-use. But in many decisions on the use of land like is not weighed against like and a value judgment has to be made without the help of any agreed standards (e.g. low grade iron-ore, avoiding imports, versus unspoilt countryside; traffic delays versus the astronomical cost of radical solutions; privacy versus convenience). Even within a single category of land users (e.g. families, sportsmen, farmers) no recognized criteria exist by which one user can be said to be wasteful, another the opposite.

5

We decided that before we could usefully discuss the immediate crisis we ought to consider the basic conditions affecting the present structure of cities, starting from human needs and their expression in building densities and communications. This report therefore follows that sequence.

6

Papers contributed by sociologists have made it clear that in an advanced urban society the study of basic human needs for comfort, privacy, etc. is insufficient by itself. In the search for acceptable standards the useful criteria are not biological but social, e.g. the movement into and out of cities of families at different stages of life, the wish of many young wives to make a home not too far from their parents, the tendency for urban workers to improve their status and be replaced by immigrants at the lower levels. But the translation of such scraps of social analysis as exist into a workable brief for the physical planner remains to be done.

Problems of Density

7

No subject is more beset by loose talk than that of density standards, whether residential or other. None more urgently needs scientific approach. Thus while a variety of residential densities have been discussed and tried, few have appreciated that the significant ratio is not the average number of people on each net acre, but the number of acres developed at each density. What matters is that a town should have a balanced and appropriately related variety of densities rather than any particular maximum or minimum.

8

When it comes to commercial and industrial densities, there has been even less rational analysis. Office zones are redeveloped on the basis of existing plot ratios which came into existence by accident in an age when all the technical factors were different and motor cars had not been invented. Industry, the most wasteful of all contemporary land users, is under no pressure except the general one of land values to compress its processes; on the contrary, local authorities vie with one another in enticing it with generous offers of land.

9

Moreover most density studies assume a homogeneity of land use which is unrealistic, and neglect the substantial economies that can be made by mult-iple use.

10

Very little research has been done on overall town densities, old and new, British and foreign, with a view to discovering within what limits top and bottom a civilized and functional urban environment seems to emerge. The land budget attempted in the Greater London Plan for a population of 100,000 needs to be brought up to date.

11

Without such research, use-zoning and density-zoning will remain as haphazard, and as wasteful of national resources, as they are at present. But research alone will not prevent waste, and the only true guide to the 'land-husbandry' of any urban area is a more constructive analysis of land-use information. By and large, survey data is abundant, but the imaginative interpretation of it is very rare.

12

But whatever steps are taken to minimize waste of land and expedite redevelopment, two factors limit the contribution they can make:

a. The land economies that can be made in housing cannot be made in educational or public buildings or public open space.

b. The space demands for roads and parking in town centres and sub-centres have greatly increased.

It follows that a national policy of decentralization must go hand in hand with urban renewal.

Central Areas

13

In our discussions on central areas and the urban traffic problem we began by rejecting the familiar American combination of suburban sprawl and ruthless superimposition of elevated freeways and, since the problem is one of supply and demand, we advocate the cutting down of demand by two methods:

a. Decentralization to new suburban nuclei of traffic-creating activities such as commerce and industry. The general need is for more homes in the centre, more jobs in the suburbs.

b. Major improvement in the effectiveness of public transport, allied with the development of more compact forms of private vehicle.

14

But the need for a greatly accelerated urban motorway programme remains, and it is vital that all new road works in central areas should be planned on the principle of vertical segregation, the number and use of the various levels depending on the traffic and pedestrian density in each case.

15

In so doing, more thought should be given to the amenities of the pedestrian, to his space and shelter and safety requirements, his maximum reasonable range, his need for somewhere to sit. We have already sought to initiate research into this subject.

16

Whatever the answer, it will ease matters if residential and office densities are allowed to rise to a peak at public transport stations, and to fall away as distance from stations increases.

Smaller Towns

17

These proposals will of course be no help to smaller towns with five-figure populations, many of which are intolerably congested, all of which must face a rapidly increasing influx of private cars, and few of which can command the planning skills to solve their problems. Among them are nearly all our most beautiful cathedral cities and resorts and market towns. We consider that the techniques for dealing with one car per family in old towns of this kind without unbearable expense and destruction have still to be worked out. No realistic traffic planning for such places has yet been done; nor have the economics of single-level and multi-level planning in towns of medium size been fully investigated.

18

It is in relation to these smaller cities in particular that the alternatives of conservation, rehabilitation and renewal have to be carefully balanced finan-cially, socially and aesthetically. We hold no brief for wholesale clearance as a panacea. While there are cases where large-scale public acquisition and rebuilding is the only hope and needs to be facilitated, there are others where a lick of paint and the ingenious intermixture of old and new will produce an equally satisfactory environment. Each case on its merits.

Renewal Techniques

19

Two invariable rules if effective planning is to be possible are that:

a. The unit of redevelopment should be large enough for the purpose.

b. Phasing should be contrived so that each phase produces a civilized environment.

20

It may be found that to get large-scale urban renewal undertaken by private enterprise, particularly in the 'twilight' areas that outstandingly need it, planning authorities will be wise to restrict the release of new building land in step with such renewal.

21

These problems can only be solved by teamwork in which the local authority, the user, the professions and the construction industry work closely together, as they already do in many large-scale building operations. But we are agreed that when all the necessary survey has been done, when all needs are known, and methods decided, there is no substitute, as in the past, for the imagination of the individual designer.

22

While the designer must think concurrently on several related levels – the social level, the technical level, the economic level, the permissive level and the aesthetic level – the paramount consideration must always be the environment of those who actually live in the town and use the new buildings. If this is lost sight of, sectional interests ranging from developers' profits to motorists' convenience will at once predominate.

23

The repeal of the financial provisions of the 1947 Act and the introduction of a free market in land have led to sharp increases in land values and to speculation. Pressure for piecemeal renewal of profitable areas and sprawl on the fringes are very powerful; and the temptation to relax planning standards and controls will need to be strongly resisted. But negative controls will sooner or later break down unless accompanied by positive measures to provide other outlets, and by public control of urban land, backed by adequate long-term finance.

24

We are convinced that the basic obstacle to urban renewal is not lack of national resources but lack of machinery to enable a wide enough time and space scale to be used. In terms of time, we strongly support the proposal that a government corporation be set up to buy land designated for redevelopment, hold it until ripe, and sell it to public or private developers at the appropriate time. In terms of space, we consider it essential that the profits to be made (whether by public or private agencies) in the process of creating new central and suburban commercial centres be ploughed back into the renewal of the unprofitable 'twilight' areas. In other words, no single redevelopment area should be treated as an economic island.

New Towns within Cities

25

Just as in economic terms we need to strike a city-wide (and even nation-wide) balance of profit and loss, so in terms of zoning we advocate a much more even distribution of land uses over the urban area as a whole, the reintroduction of living quarters into the centre and the dispersal of large offices and some local industry into what are now the dormitory suburbs. In the seven conurbations where 2/5ths of our people live we have described this creation of new compact suburban centres as New Towns within Cities, but the principle is often valid on a smaller scale in the five-figure cities.

26

The siting of suburban centres should be the result of a careful analysis of the structure, communications and social trends of each city. In general, they should go where local employment will obviate long journeys to work, where road and rail facilities are underloaded or easily improved, where an incentive to redevelopment is required, or where new residential development lacks a social core. They must in all cases be as far out from the original centre as is necessary to avoid any risk of coalescence.

A National Urban Renewal Agency

27

To attempt the task of urban renewal, the nation must use to the full its present organizations; and some new types may also be wanted. Agencies of different kinds, whether for small individual *ad hoc* schemes, or for large comprehensive ones, are likely to have to operate side by side. They will include local authorities, public boards, trusts, property companies, and no doubt special urban renewal agencies on the lines of the New Town Corporations.

28

However, it will be the nation's competence in investigation and the quality of its research which will largely affect the results of the vast quantity of work flowing from the organizations undertaking urban renewal. There are already some specialized investigation and research agencies, for instance the Ministry of Housing and Local Government, the Building Research Station, the Roads Research Laboratory, the Roads Campaign Council and certain university architectural and planning departments. The next step should be to establish an independent National Urban Renewal Research and Development Agency, whose function would be:

    a. To coordinate existing research.

    b. To promote new lines of investigation.

    c. To comment on research results.

In these ways a serious attempt would be made to prevent the wastage of skill by duplication of efforts, and to link up the contributions of specialists. NURRDA would also be in a strong position to make comparative analyses of land usage in the different regions.

29

While analysis and rationalization of information will have long-term value, immediate interest in this work will be stimulated if it is related to visible results on the ground. The complementary step should therefore be the promotion by NURRDA of a number of pilot and demonstration projects, designed to show what can be done, how much it will cost and what works in practice. Each such project should demonstrate some particular aspect of urban renewal, whether rehabilitation, conservation, or renewal in central areas, the rebuilding of blighted inner rings or the creation of new suburban communities. Freedom should be allowed to experiment in any branch of urban renewal process: finance, law, building regulations, planning, design, construction, phasing; but in every case firm completion dates are essential. It would be NURRDA's task to correlate these projects so that they cover the nation geographically and cover the whole range of urban renewal problems, and to publish reports on their progress and findings on their conclusions.

Local Self-Help

30

Finally we believe that local self-help is as necessary as government leadership, and we suggest that this should initially take the form of a Reconstruction Committee of the local authority, with some co-opted members and some such terms of reference as these:

    To make the necessary survey and advise the Council on a phased reconstruction programme, and in particular:

    a. To investigate the local financial, social and administrative implications of large-scale urban renewal.

    b. To consider how best to divide the work between public and private enterprise.

    c. To propose a sequence of comprehensive development areas and a detailed budget and time table.

    d. To prepare the Council's case for the definition of each successive area as a CDA.

31

In a little more than a century the quality of our urban life has tragically deteriorated. This deterioration is now gathering momentum, and will, we believe, disintegrate our cities unless immediate action is taken.

Summary

The following proposals have been made in this report:

a. More work is needed on density standards, in particular to arrive at an overall town density appropriate to social conditions in the next generation (paras. 7–10).

b. Surveys of existing land use should be refined so as to cover multiple use and point more clearly to waste of land (para. 9).

c. A national policy of decentralization is still essential (para. 12).

d. Compact 'New Towns within Cities' should be created within outer suburban areas (para. 13).

e. A radical reappraisal of urban transport techniques (para. 13).

f. Research on the needs of the pedestrian (para. 14).

g. High density at public transport stations (para. 15).

h. Research on the traffic and other planning problems of medium-sized towns (paras. 16–17).

i. Units of redevelopment should be as large as possible (para. 18).

j. New land for housing should only be released in step with redevelopment (para. 20).

k. The role of the individual designer must still be paramount (paras. 21–22).

l. No single unit of redevelopment should be treated as an economic island (para. 24).

m. Land uses should be more mixed (paras. 25–26).

n. A National Urban Renewal Research and Development Agency (paras. 27–28).

o. Pilot projects (para. 29).

p. Reconstruction Committees (para. 30).

Notes

Chapter 1: Consensus (*pages 15–71*)

1. The portmanteau word denotes MacNeice, Spender, Auden and Day Lewis.

2. See 'Where is your Vorticist' by Wyndham Lewis himself (*Architectural Review*, November 1934) in which Lewis amusingly apologizes for the austerity of Vorticism and urges the 'humanization' of the purist modern interior.

3. *The Scope of Total Architecture* (articles and lectures 1937–52), New York, 1955.

4. Forty-five years later, when a Thirties Society was formed to defend the architecture of that era, it was the MARS men who were under a cloud. It was considered that 'certain older architects would have to be excluded because they had never repented of their early work and because they still think of themselves as good architects. Such an exclusion would have to apply also to some of the campaigning writers of the thirties like Summerson and Richards who helped to create the climate of opinion in which modernism flourished.'

5. See Appendix A.

6. *Architectural Review*, January 1938.

7. 'It is one of the sad handicaps of the modern movement in architecture that the ordinary person . . . has probably never once seen an example . . . This is a handicap that time can cure, but it leads us to another more serious one. Alongside the real growth and expansion of modern architectural practice have developed the bogus modernism with which we are all familiar, one that assumes the transitory or accidental characteristics of the real thing and exploits its fashion value, without possessing either its rational justification or its artistic integrity. The existence of this 'modernistic' practice . . . presents a greater danger . . . than . . . any diehard practice of, for instance, Renaissance revivalism.' J. M. Richards in the *Architectural Review*, May 1937.

8. Seven of them, after the war, came together to form a practice, the Architects' Cooperative Partnership, which was originally to be a true cooperative, without employees. They were Anthony Cox, Kenneth Capon, Peter Cocke, Michael Cooke-Yarborough, Michael Grice and Leo de Syllas.

9. Edward Carter, RIBA Librarian, speaking in 1939 at a student conference at the Hull School of Architecture, of which Leslie Martin was then Head.

10. The key figures were William Beveridge, the Liberal official, and John Reith, the powerful but frustrated idealist. In his brief tenure of the Ministry of Works ('Seventeen months to get myself institutionalized'), Reith transformed this antique office into a true Ministry of Reconstruction, commissioned the historic Uthwatt and Scott Reports on compensation and land use, and laid down the guidelines for national and regional planning. Political jealousies ensued, and Churchill in a gesture that was both brutal and foolish dismissed him (21 February 1942).

11. The Special Areas Act of 1935 had been only marginally effective.

12. Lionel Brett in the *Observer*, May 1951; see Appendix B.

13. 'An Age of Embarrassment' by Edward Shils, *Encounter*, October 1978.

14. However, they had been pioneered by the Reema precast concrete system in England.

15. The best account of which is Reyner Banham's monograph of 1966.

16. Rudolf Wittkower's *Architectural Principles in the Age of Humanism* and his pupil Colin Rowe's lectures were also powerful influences.

17. Through the ingenuity of Max Rayne, he and the Church Commissioners shared a £5·8 million profit on this development.

18. The responsible trio was J. Austin-Smith (Chairman), Gordon Ricketts (RIBA Secretary) and Joan Milne.

19. See Appendix C.

20. See *Politics and Land Use Planning* by Stephen Elkin, 1974.

21. Thus Philip Johnson, writing in the *Observer* in May 1979: 'You come over here and you find the best modern architecture in the world.' And the Swiss magazine *Bauen und Wohnen*, in the same year, asks: 'How can a country, which is so inept in its handling of business affairs and which has such a negative attitude, produce so many creative, original and dynamic architectural ideas?'

Chapter 2: Collapse (*pages 72–88*)

1. Vividly recorded in Gillian Tindall's evocation of Kentish Town, *The Fields Beneath*, 1978.

2. This fragmentation of the preservation movement has been a waste of scarce resources, though each of the three societies has a certain individuality, the SPAB scholarly, the Georgians aristocratic, the Victorians intellectual and aggressive – no argument against amalgamation, particularly since the first Chairman of the Victorians had for 31 years been Chairman of the SPAB and had the special dislike of Victorian architecture that was natural to a man born in 1881.

3. By the author, in an address entitled 'Preservation after Buchanan'.

4. Young and Wilmot in *Family and Kinship in East London*, 1957, quote a Mr Wilkins: 'I suppose the buildings in Bethnal Green aren't all that good, but we don't look on this as a pile of stones. It isn't the buildings that matter. We like the people here.'

5. Beatle music versus hard rock.

6. Thus Raymond Mortimer called the Royal College of Physicians 'an outrage against Regent's Park'.

7. It has been a novel feature of the seventies that the reactionary vanguard has been provided by the two professions whose attachment to the neutrality of events could have been expected to override their desire to impose a moral pattern upon them.

8. J. Jacobs, *The Death and Life of Great American Cities*, 1961; C. Alexander, *A City is not a Tree*, 1964; R. Venturi, *Complexity and Contradiction in Architecture*, 1966; O. Newman, *Defensible Space*, 1973.

9. This was by no means a purely British débâcle. France built 2·5 million subsidized flats between 1950 and 1970. By 1979 0·5 million were described as 'beyond rehabilitation'. The official HLMS declared in that year that 'no country in the world has made such an expensive error on such a grand scale'.

10. Oliver Marriott, *The Property Boom*, 1967.

11. RIBA President 1971–3.

12. In a Japanese periodical, 1977. 'Thus we see the fragility of the Unbuilt English scene. For we are a country of cynics and sometimes lack a quality that I might call consistency or I might call stamina: which prevents our sustenance of a solid school or architectural style.'

13. See page 19.

14. *Crisis in Architecture*, 1974.

15. D. Watkin, *Morality and Architecture*, 1978.

Chapter 3: London (*pages 89–171*)

Part B: The City Region 1940–1970 (*pages 95–139*)

1. Matthew's first Development Group, led by Colin Lucas and Rosemary Sternstedt, included Whitfield Lewis and Michael Powell and was soon joined by Cleeve Barr, Oliver Cox, William Howell, John Killick and John Amis, among others.

2. Revisiting Lansbury in 1978, Richard Edmonds, a leading LCC figure in the fifties, declared wistfully: 'It was a period in the Council's effort when we were all working together.'

3. Described by Nicholas Taylor as 'a wolf in sheep's clothing' (RIBA June 1973).

4. The LCC never submitted to Government pressure to reduce space standards below those of the 1944 Dudley Report, and were to be vindicated when Parker Morris returned to higher standards in 1961.

5. Hard by conviction, it should perhaps be said, not by nature. The leading Hard men were Colin Lucas, Colin St John Wilson, W. G. Howell and Philip Bottomley.

6. Reviewing the Arts Centre in the *Architectural Review*, Charles Jencks remarks that its designers, several of whom were members of 'Archigram', were influenced by the Smithsons' unsuccessful entry for the Sheffield University competition. They considered it 'a waste of time to invent new forms', preferring to let things happen: the building was 'probably intended to be conventionally ugly'.

7. Seifert's Centre Point was an early exception, and was unlet for over a decade partly for this reason.

8. This included East Anglia.

9. 'The Rise and Fall of the High Block' in *Estates Gazette*, October 1978.

10. All in, the council houses at Branch Hill cost £109,000 each.

Part C: The Retreat (1970–1980) (*pages 139–71*)

1. The story is fully told in the *Architectural Review*, April 1962.

2. In fact the move did not take place till October 1974.

3. The Covent Garden Community Association, curmudgeonly to the last, wrote formally to the Council of Europe in June 1980 urging it *not* to make an award to the GLC for restoration of the Central Market building, as it was a waste of money.

4. 'Inner Cities and Social Priorities', Royal Society of Arts, August 1977.

5. In his *Rubbish Theory*, 1979, Michael Thompson points out that 'in many ways "gentrification" is an unfortunate term; for those young couples – actors, graphic designers, architects, art-school teachers, and television executives – who formed the vanguard of the frontier middle class were, we can now see with the benefit of hindsight, forceful and successful social climbers who competed (on very unequal terms) with the indigenous inhabitants of those run-down areas who, alas, had no access to durability. Something no gentleman would do (or need to do!).

'Those much satirized trendies, crashing through social barriers with the same insensitive arrogance that they knocked through the dividing walls of their terraced Georgian houses, believed themselves to be the harbingers of that egalitarian millennium where we would all end up like David Frost – classless and close-cropped. Even in the mid seventies the diligent anthropologist could still occasionally experience the thrill of hearing the classic remarks: "We're knocking through, you know" and "Yes we were the first people to come and live here".' In a hilarious chapter entitled 'Rat-infested Slum or Glorious Heritage', Thompson goes on to define the attitude of the indigenous working class; '... that, in buying and doing up a rubbish house, the frontiersman was throwing good money after bad: "They're all coming down, them houses" was their endless refrain. These are the Ron-and-Cliffs: proud, competitive, working class, frequently self-employed, villainous, anti-union, racially prejudiced, Conservative-voting inhabitants of rubbish or near-rubbish houses.' The third component of the twilight areas, known to the Ron-and-Cliffs as 'Darkies and Bubbles' (rhyming slang: Bubble and squeak = Greek), 'don't seem to know about the rules at all. The Greek Cypriots, in particular, are much addicted to metal-frame windows and to brick façades painted pink with all the mortar laboriously picked out in pale blue. As the transfers to durability gain momentum, so Conservation Areas are designated and legislation is now contemplated forcibly to prevent the Bubble from going to this enormous trouble to knock thousands of pounds off the market value of his house.'

6. *London: Urban Pattern, Problems and Politics*, Donnison and Eversley (eds.), 1973.

7. David Eversley, an urban economist, was not put in charge on the retirement of the town planner Bernard Collins until after the GLDP was completed in 1969.

8. *Motorways in London* by Michael Thomas, 1969; *Towns against Traffic* by Stephen Plowden, 1973.

9. Speaking at a seminar in 1980, Sheila Roberts, Policy Committee Chairman, claimed that London had less road space per head than any other Western industrial city.

10. *Daily Telegraph*, 17 December 1977.

11. There was no such project.

12. NAM – the New Architecture Movement – was the creation of Brian Anson's militant Architects' Revolutionary Council. SAG – the Salaried Architects' Group – was a RIBA move to retain the more radical salaried elements within the fold.

13. Letter in *The Times*, 13 November 1978, from F. Vermorel.

14. Lambeth in 1979 had 24 conservation areas and 682 listed buildings.

15. In fact in 1980 refurbishment has begun and there is now a waiting-list for tenancies. But the Government's cuts, rabidly resisted by Lambeth, threaten its completion.

16. In August 1980 an all-party parliamentary committee forecast an annual output of only 30,000 council houses and 100,000 privately built houses within two years. This, it said, would create a shortage of nearly half a million houses by 1985. Meanwhile the existing stock was said to be deteriorating at a rate of 50,000 houses a year.

17. 'Sakyamani cried out in pity for a yogi by the river who had wasted twenty years of his human existence in learning how to walk on water, when the ferryman might have taken him across for a small coin.' Peter Matthiessen, *The Snow Leopard*, 1978.

18. Though much is taken, much abides: and though
     We are not now that strength which in old days
     Moved earth and heaven: that which we are, we are.
                              Tennyson, 'Ulysses'

19. Examples are:
Gollins, Melvin and Ward: P & O Commercial Union Buildings, Leadenhall Street.
Llewelyn-Davies, Weeks, Forestier-Walker and Bor: Stock Exchange.
William Whitfield: Institute of Chartered Accountants, Great Swan Alley.
Yorke, Rosenberg and Mardall: Old Broad Street.
Richard Sheppard, Robson and Partners: Milestone House, Cannon Street; 12-13 Lime Street.
Richard Rogers: Lloyds, Leadenhall Street.
Of the 'regulars' in addition to Seifert, Fitzroy Robinson has been outstanding: Rothschild's, St Swithin Lane and Billiter Street.

20. Virginia Woolf, *Mrs Dalloway*, 1925.

Chapter 4: Newcastle-upon-Tyne (*pages 172–93*)

1. For example 'A vital link in the A1 is now being built on the eastern fringe of central Newcastle.' *Newcastle upon Tyne: Planning Progress and Policy 1973.*

2. ibid. The writer was Diana Rowntree, architect and critic, then briefly on Galley's staff.

3. ibid. 'First of all, members of the Revitalization Agency canvass the owners, by visiting every house at times to suit the residents, explaining what opportunities exist, what grants and help are available, and discussing each individual's situation. A questionnaire is then posted to every house, asking the residents to express their opinions on the area, its condition and prospects and their attitude to it. When the replies have been read and analysed, the Council takes the decision whether to declare

a General Improvement Area. A public meeting is then held announcing the intention and the opening of show houses in the near future. At this meeting a notional scheme is exhibited.

'When the show houses are opened, members of the public can meet their area planning officer there and talk to him about the scheme and their particular problems. The area officers then organize the formation of street groups, with volunteer street leaders. These leaders canvass every house to discover each householder's wishes in detail on such matters as parking, closures of streets to traffic, planting and outdoor works. Further street meetings are held at which the team of all civic departments involved (Health, Police, Engineer, Housing, Planning) may be present to answer questions and learn the residents' reactions first-hand. The area planning officer will meanwhile have produced a scheme which resolves the conflicts and meets the majority demand. He will present this final scheme at a meeting for the residents' approval.'

4. John Gray, Director of Housing, February 1979.

5. Peter Malpass, 'The Politics of Participation', in the *Architects' Journal*, 16 May 1979.

6. *Choices for the Future*, 1978, and *Public Response*, 1980.

7. The cost was estimated to reach £280 million by 1980 and the Tyne and Wear Passenger Transport Executive has applied for EEC assistance towards the shortfall.

8. Three local firms of architects were employed, coordinated by Faulkner-Brown, Hendy, Watkinson and Stonor.

9. John Ardagh. His book, *A Tale of Five Cities*, compares Newcastle illuminatingly with Stuttgart, Toulouse, Bologna and Ljubljana.

Chapter 5: Sheffield (*pages 194–216*)

1. Mary Walton, *Sheffield: Its Story and Its Achievements*, 1948.

2. So constituted in 1624.

3. Quoted in *Victorian Cities*, Asa Briggs, 1963.

4. Quoted by Walton, op. cit.

5. Francis Gladstone in *The Politics of Planning*, 1976.

6. Martin Richardson, *Architects' Journal*, June 1965.

7. 'In our zeal to erase the evils arising out of a lack of proper water-supply, sanitation and ventilation, we had torn down streets of houses which, despite their sanitary shortcomings, harboured a social structure of friendliness and mutual aid. We had thrown the baby out with the bath-water.' Jack Lynn in the *RIBA Journal*, December 1962.

8. Published in *Building Environment*, February 1966.

9. The Gloucester Street Scheme in the short-lived 5M System was designed by the Ministry's Development Group.

Chapter 6: Liverpool (*pages 217–45*)

1. In that one year 50,000 slaves were carried across the Atlantic in Liverpool ships.

2. An inaugural ode read to the Society for the Encouragement of Designing Drawing and Painting in 1773.

3. Benjamin Robert Haydon, *Life*, 2nd ed., 1853.

4. This was within the city limits. The 25-kilometre commuter radius now contains 3 million, and the population working in the centre is larger than Birmingham's or Glasgow's.

5. The difference was due to the poor prospects after 1945 for speculative building which contributed only 8,214 houses, compared with 26,415 after 1918.

6. George Chandler, *Liverpool*, 1957.

7. This was done against the advice of Ronald Bradbury, who wished to combine the role with his own. He became Director of Housing on the change-over.

8. 'City Planning Policy Report: Analysis and Preliminary Conclusions', 1964.

9. Birmingham, Leeds, Manchester, Newcastle and Sheffield (E.S.P. Evans, *City in Transition*, 1977).

10. Walter Bor was now a member of the Minister's Planning Advisory Group (PAG) which reported in 1965.

11. The others were Birmingham (Small Heath) and Lambeth (see p. 161).

12. *Architects' Journal*, 5 July 1978.

13. In *Alternative England and Wales*, 1975.

14. Lisa Peattie and Andrew Hake, quoted by Colin Ward in *New Society*, 22 March 1979.

15. She was to succeed Frederick Pooley in London in 1980.

Chapter 7: Milton Keynes (*pages* 246–71)

1. He was not, for example, an advocate of what later became known as Garden City densities. Mumford calculates that his diagrams work out at 70 to 100 p.p.a.

2. The Cherry Tree at Welwyn Garden City was a licensed restaurant owned by the Welwyn Garden City Company.

3. See, for an explanation of this adjective, Reyner Banham's *Megastructures*, 1970.

4. In 1963 Professor Peter Hall in *London 2000* calculated that in addition to 1·5m people housed by town expansion schemes, 17 New Towns the size of Hook would be required in the London region alone.

5. In a lecture on science and architecture at Harvard in 1975, Richard Llewelyn-Davies attributes to the 1920s and 1930s, 'the age of atomic physics', the image of the nucleus surrounded by electrons which dominated the thinking of Abercrombie and the earlier New Town planners (and incidentally the planning of York University). The Milton Keynes grid, on the other hand, he claims to be based on Heisenberg's principle of indeterminacy, with its acceptance of the unpredictable. In practice there seems to have been little to choose between the flexibilities of the two systems.

6. The main change (and improvement) was the elimination of the east–west motor-way and the consequently more even loading of the central network.

7. The Corporation, in a reaction against the star system, now appointed a trio of equals – Stuart Mosscrop to manage the central area, Nigel Lane the north and Frank Henshaw the south. Later Mosscrop became responsible for the south as well as the centre, while Henshaw became Roche's deputy.

8. Space Left Over In Planning.

9. See page 79.

Chapter 8: At Low Tide (*pages* 272–87)

1. Jacquetta Hawkes, *A Land*, 1949.

2. It was known as Stinks by classics masters at Eton.

3. Asa Briggs, *Victorian Cities*, 1963.

4. In Newcastle in 1978, of a total population of 300,000, only 7,400 (1 in 40) people lived in high (non-walk-up) flats. In Sheffield, the figure is 18,000 out of 554,000 (1 in 30). In Liverpool, it is 6,500 out of 570,000 (1 in 87).

5. The 15-storey flats in the centre of Leicester, built in 1979 for single-person 'working-class' households by a housing society and over-subscribed eight times, are surely a portent.

6. Thus Alvar Aalto: 'What matters in architecture is Time. Repetition and use make things acceptable.'

7. Perhaps the most interesting of these arcadian work-places are James Stirling's Olivetti headquarters near Haslemere, Powell and Moya's London and Manchester Insurance Company at Winslade Manor near Exeter, and Darbourne and Darke's IBM Headquarters at Hursley Park near Winchester.

8. Of all British cities, the one hardest hit is the little silver-grey granite city of Aberdeen, whose delicate Gothic silhouette has been ruined by two tower blocks erected in the city's heart by the authority responsible for its protection.

9. Armstrong and Wilson in *Vandalism*, edited by Colin Ward, 1973.

10. The word is here used in the sense given to it by Karl Popper in his critique of the claim that in any period history has a theme with which it is necessary for us to ally ourselves if our work is to have any value. In his *Morality and Architecture* (1977) David Watkin applies Popper's critique to purist advocates of modernism.

11. Colin Rowe and Fred Koetter, *Collage City*, 1978.

Acknowledgements

The author and publishers are grateful to Methuen Children's Books Ltd for permission to quote from 'Noise, By Pooh' by A. A. Milne and to the Executors of the Estate of C. Day Lewis, Jonathan Cape Ltd and the Hogarth Press for C. Day Lewis's 'Where Are All the War Poets?' from *Collected Poems*, 1954.

In the following list of photographic acknowledgements, these abbreviations are used: *AR* = *Architectural Review*; GLC = Greater London Council; MKDC = Milton Keynes Development Corporation. NCC = Newcastle City Council. The photographs which have been omitted from this list were taken by the author.

1. Unwin, *Town Planning in Practice*, 1908; 2. Erith and Terry; 3. *AR*; 4. *AR*; 5. *AR*; 7. GLC Photograph Library; 8. *AR*; 9. *AR*; 10. *AR*; 11. *AR*; 12. *AR*; 13. *Architects' Journal*; 14. *AR*; 15. *Traffic in Towns* (The Buchanan Report), 1963 (Controller of Her Majesty's Stationery Office); 16. *Traffic in Towns* (The Buchanan Report), 1963 (Controller of Her Majesty's Stationery Office); 17. *AR*; 20. Brecht-Einzig Ltd; photo: Richard Einzig; 21. Maurice Lee; 22. Feilden and Mawson; 23. Peter Joslin; 24 Abercrombie, *County of London Plan*, 1943; 25. Louis Hellman; 26. Charles Jencks; 27. *AR*; 28. *London Replanned*, 1942; 29. Abercrombie, *County of London Plan*. 1943; 30. *AR*; 31. Corporation of London; 33. Aerofilms and Aeropictorial Ltd; 34. GLC; 37. Martyn Beckett; 40. Corporation of London; 41. Brecht-Einzig Ltd; photo: Richard Einzig; 44. GLC; 45. GLC; 46. GLC; 47. GLC; 48. John Walters; 50. Neave Brown; photo: Martin Charles; 52. Bews and Hodge; photo: Alf Bews; 54. RIBA; 56. Lambeth Borough Council; photo: Sam Lambert; 59. Lambeth Borough Council; photo: Sam Lambert; 62. Martyn Beckett; 64. Martyn Beckett; 66. Arena; 67. NCC; 68. NCC; 69. NCC; 70. Mayo Ltd; 71. NCC; 72. NCC; 73. NCC; 75. Newcastle City Centre; 76. Newcastle City Centre; 77. Civic Trust Library; photo: Colin Westwood; 79. Sheffield City Council; 83. Sheffield City Council; 84. Sheffield City Council; 87. Taylor Richardson Associates; 90. Anthony Gascoigne; 91. Quentin Hughes; 94. Quentin Hughes; 95. Graeme Shankland; redrawn by Julian Bishop; 96. Liverpool City Council; 98. Liverpool City Council; 99. Anthony Gascoigne; 100. Anthony Gascoigne; 101. Anthony Gascoigne; 103. MKDC; 104. MKDC; 105. MKDC; 106. MKDC; 107. MKDC; 109. MKDC; photo: John Walker; 110. MKDC; 111. MKDC; photo: Ivor Leonard; 112. Henk Snoek; 115. John Donat; 116. Arup Associates; photo: Peter Cook; 117. Arup Associates; photo: Crispin Boyle; The Strip Cartoon on pp. 298–9, Louis Hellman.

Index

(Page numbers printed in *italic* refer to illustrations)